Africa and the Indian Ocean World from Early Times to Circa 1900

The history of Africa's historical relationship with the rest of the Indian Ocean world (IOW) is one of a vibrant exchange that included commodities, people, flora and fauna, ideas, technologies and disease. This connection with the rest of the IOW, a macro-region running from eastern Africa, through the Middle East, South and Southeast Asia to East Asia, was also one heavily influenced by environmental factors. In presenting this rich and varied history, Gwyn Campbell argues that human-environment interaction, more than great men, state formation, or imperial expansion, was the central dynamic in the history of the IOW. Environmental factors, notably the monsoon system of winds and currents, helped lay the basis for the emergence of a sophisticated and durable IOW "global economy" around 1,500 years before the so-called European "Voyages of Discovery". Through his focus on human-environment inter-action as the dynamic factor underpinning historical developments, Campbell radically challenges Eurocentric paradigms, and lays the foundations for a new interpretation of IOW history.

GWYN CAMPBELL is founding Director of the Indian Ocean World Centre at McGill University. He served as an academic consultant for the South African Government in the run-up to the formation of an Indian Ocean regional association in 1997 and has published widely on Africa and the wider Indian Ocean world, including *David Griffiths and the Missionary 'History of Madagascar'* (2012) and *An Economic History of Imperial Madagascar, 1750–1895* (Cambridge University Press, 2005).

T0384619

New Approaches to African History

Series Editor
Martin Klein, *University of Toronto*

Editorial Advisors
William Beinart, *University of Oxford*
Mamadou Diouf, *Columbia University*
William Freund, *University of KwaZulu-Natal*
Sandra E. Greene, *Cornell University*
Ray Kea, *University of California, Riverside*
David Newbury, *Smith College*

New Approaches to African History is designed to introduce students to current findings and new ideas in African history. Although each book treats a particular case and is able to stand alone, the format allows the studies to be used as modules in general courses on African history and world history. The cases represent a wide range of topics. Each volume summarizes the state of knowledge on a particular subject for a student who is new to the field. However, the aim is not simply to present views of the literature; it is also to introduce debates on historiographical or substantive issues and may argue for a particular point of view. The aim of the series is to stimulate debate and to challenge students and general readers. The series is not committed to any particular school of thought.

Other Books in the Series

1. *Africa since 1940: The Past of the Present* by Frederick Cooper
2. *Muslim Societies in African History* by David Robinson
3. *Reversing Sail: A History of the African Diaspora* by Michael A. Gomez
4. *The African City: A History* by Bill Freund
5. *Warfare in Independent Africa* by William Reno
6. *Warfare in African History* by Richard J. Reid
7. *Foreign Intervention in Africa: From the Cold War to the War on Terror* by Elizabeth Schmidt
8. *Slavery and Slaving in African History* by Sean Stilwell
9. *Democracy in Africa: Successes, Failures, and the Struggle for Political Reform* by Nic Cheeseman
10. *Women in Twentieth-Century Africa* by Iris Berger
11. *A History of African Popular Culture* by Karin Barber
12. *Human Rights in Africa* by Bonny Ibhawoh
13. *Africa since 1940, Second Edition* by Frederick Cooper
14. *Africa and the Indian Ocean World from Early Times to Circa 1900* by Gwyn Campbell

Africa and the Indian Ocean World from Early Times to Circa 1900

Gwyn Campbell
McGill University, Montréal

CAMBRIDGE
UNIVERSITY PRESS

CAMBRIDGE
UNIVERSITY PRESS

University Printing House, Cambridge CB2 8BS, United Kingdom

One Liberty Plaza, 20th Floor, New York, NY 10006, USA

477 Williamstown Road, Port Melbourne, VIC 3207, Australia

314–321, 3rd Floor, Plot 3, Splendor Forum, Jasola District Centre, New Delhi – 110025, India

79 Anson Road, #06-04/06, Singapore 079906

Cambridge University Press is part of the University of Cambridge.

It furthers the University's mission by disseminating knowledge in the pursuit of education, learning, and research at the highest international levels of excellence.

www.cambridge.org
Information on this title: www.cambridge.org/9780521810357
DOI: 10.1017/9781139028769

First published 2019

Printed in the United Kingdom by TJ International Ltd. Padstow Cornwall

A catalogue record for this publication is available from the British Library.

Library of Congress Cataloging-in-Publication Data
Names: Campbell, Gwyn, 1952– author.
Title: Africa and the Indian Ocean world from early times to circa 1900 / Gwyn Campbell.
Other titles: New approaches to African history.
Description: New York: Cambridge University Press, 2019. |
Series: New approaches to African history |
Includes bibliographical references and index.
Identifiers: LCCN 2019000702 | ISBN 9780521810357 (hardback) |
ISBN 9780521008068 (paperback)
Subjects: LCSH: Indian Coast (Africa)–Foreign economic relations–Indian Ocean Region. | Indian Ocean Region–Foreign economic relations–Indian Coast (Africa) | Indian Coast (Africa)–Economic conditions–History. | Indian Ocean Region–Economic conditions–History. | Human beings–Effect of environment on–Indian Ocean Region–History. | Human beings–Effect of climate on–Indian Ocean Region–History. | Human ecology–Indian Ocean Region. | Trade routes–Indian Ocean Region.
Classification: LCC HF1611.Z4S6442 2019 | DDC 337.60165–dc23
LC record available at https://lccn.loc.gov/2019000702

ISBN 978-0-521-81035-7 Hardback
ISBN 978-0-521-00806-8 Paperback

Er cof annwyl am fy chwaer, Ruth Myfanwy,
a fy mrawd, David John

Contents

Figures

Maps

Tables

Acknowledgements

I wish to acknowledge the Social Sciences and Humanities Research Council of Canada (SSHRC), Alexander von Humboldt Foundation, Max Planck Institute for Social Anthropology in Halle, and Institute for Social Anthropology and Centre for Interdisciplinary Area Studies at the Martin Luther University in Halle, all of which supported research for this book.

Also a number of people whose work and ideas have helped me to shape this volume, including Abdul Sheriff, William Clarence-Smith, Alessandro Stanziani, Edward Alpers, Joseph Miller, Michael Pearson, Anthony Reid, Geoff Wade, Tansen Sen, Angela Schottenhammer, Alexander Adelaar, Waruno Mahdi, Pierre-Yves Manguin, the graduate students of the Indian Ocean World Centre, McGill University, and especially Martin Klein for his insight and patience.

Finally to my wife, Marianne Ackerman, whose encouragement has been critical, and to Rhiannon, Rhys and Lludd for their forbearance and support.

1

Introduction

This volume explores the relationship between Africa and the wider Indian Ocean world (IOW) from early times to 1900 through perspectives that challenge conventional approaches to the history of the non-western world. It takes into full account, for the first time for such a macro-region and timespan, the impact of environmental and climatic forces on peoples and economies, and their role in shaping historical change, notably in the creation and development of an IOW "global economy". It also differs from most conventional works in its emphasis on the dynamic contribution of Africans to the wider IOW economy even after Europeans entered the IOW. This introductory chapter identifies and defines the regions of Africa that formed part of the IOW, explores the major environmental factors that influenced the evolution of the IOW global economy, examines the notion and significance of human-environment interaction for Africa and the wider IOW, and summarises the main issues to be discussed in later chapters.

The discipline of history as currently taught in Western academic institutions first developed in Western Europe in the nineteenth and early twentieth centuries. It reflected concerns of the educated elite of the time and region, notably the rise of Western civilisation, European expansion and global dominance, the emergence of nation states, and the role in those processes of great men – chiefly monarchs, military, and political leaders. These themes reflect quintessentially Eurocentric perspectives, as do the temporal and spatial paradigms adopted – and that continue to be routinely used in historical analysis. Periodisation

FIGURE 1.1 Al-Idirisi's World Map, 1154 (with the south at the top)

Note: No copyright – source: http://en.wikipedia.org/wiki/File:1154_world_map_by_Moroccan_cartographer_al-Idrisi_for_king_Roger_of_Sicily.jpg (accessed 05/12/10).

based on concepts such as the "ancient", "medieval", "early modern", and "modern" eras reflects attempts to better understand the temporal evolution of European history. However, such periodisation does not necessarily accommodate the temporal shifts in the histories of the extra-European world to which it is also customarily applied. Similarly, despite the welcome rise over recent decades of more comparative and "global" studies, most histories of the non-western world rely on European spatial paradigms that focus on states, empires, and colonial regional demarcations such as the East Indies, and colonial political entities such as Kenya – the borders of which had little historical meaning prior to its creation as a British colony in 1920.

Moreover, throughout the IOW, such artificially imposed borders have remained porous, as is demonstrated by continued large clandestine cross-border flows of money, people, and commodities such as arms, drugs, and ivory.

Studies of the Indian Ocean world began in the mid-1980s with the publication of a number of path-breaking works, by K.N. Chaudhuri, Janet Abu-Lughod and others, challenging conventional Eurocentric interpretations of Asia. These scholars revealed extensive long-distance commercial networks linking the major Asian civilisations that long predated European intrusion into the region, and which remained preeminent up to the mid-eighteenth century. André Gunder Franck argued that indigenous powers continued to economically and politically dominate the region into the nineteenth century. Moreover, European predominance was, in historic terms, of short duration, being challenged again from the 1980s by the rise first of the Southeast Asian "tigers", and subsequently by India and, above all, China. Such Asianists firmly established the Indian Ocean world alongside the Atlantic world as a founding pillar of the newly emerging discipline of global history. Their studies nevertheless have two major limitations. First, in placing Asia at the centre of their historical perspectives, they largely exclude the role of Africa and Africans. Thus Chaudhuri considered the IOW to have been created by four "Asian" civilisations: Irano-Arabic, Hindu, Indonesian, and Chinese, but excluded Africa because "indigenous African communities appear to have been structured by a historical logic separate and independent from the rest of the Indian Ocean".[1] Indeed, he largely buttresses the conventional Eurocentric view that the history of Africa was forged by external forces, first Muslim and subsequently European. Other Asianists have attempted to integrate Africa into their perspectives of IOW history, but for them it has remained either peripheral, or – as for Thomas Metcalf – a field of Indian economic or even imperial endeavour.[2]

In reaction, Africanists have over recent decades stressed early indigenous African initiatives and economic development that included

[1] K.N. Chaudhuri, *Asia Before Europe. Economy and Civilisation of the Indian Ocean from the Rise of Islam to 1750* (Cambridge: Cambridge University Press, 1992), 36.
[2] Thomas R. Metcalf, *Imperial Connections. India in the Indian Ocean Arena, 1860–1920* (Berkeley: University of California Press, 2007).

involvement in the wider IOW. However, their discussion of Africa's relations with the IOW has largely been confined to the colonially defined region of "East Africa", and has concentrated on mercantile elites and rulers, notably the Swahili. Their seminal contribution to the debate over Africa's relations with the wider IOW is in repudiating the traditional view that the Swahili were the result of Muslim immigration and influence from the Middle East, and asserting the currently dominant view that the Swahili were representatives of an authentic African civilisation which engaged fully in trans-IOW exchange (see Chapter 6).

However, while revisionist historians of both Asia and East Africa have underscored the vitality of early indigenous economic and cultural life, they have largely focussed on themes at the centre of Eurocentric historiography, notably the rise and demise of states and civilisations, and the role of male elites. Moreover, while some emphasise indigenous initiatives prior to the European "Voyages of Discovery", their major preoccupation is the post-1500 "early modern" European arrival and impact in the IOW, first of the Portuguese, and subsequently of the Dutch, English, and French. Thus one of the central Asianist debates is the timing and magnitude of the so-called "Great Divergence", when the gap between Asian and European economies widened to the point at which Europeans developed an insuperable economic and political advantage.[3] In their turn, with some notable exceptions such as Thomas Vernet,[4] Africanists have also assumed that from around 1500, European intervention ended the golden epoch of Swahili civilisation, extinguishing African entrepreneurship and involvement in the wider IOW. With the European arrival in the Indian Ocean, and their dominance of the East African littoral, the peoples of the East African interior, while sometimes undergoing considerable migration, and forging various short-lived political entities, were largely cut off from the coast and external economic and other relations. The focus of historical attention has largely been on the slave export

---

[3] See e.g. Kenneth Pomeranz, *The Great Divergence: China, Europe and the Making of the Modern World Economy* (Princeton, NJ: Princeton University Press, 2000); Prasannan Parthasarathi, *Why Europe Grew Rich and Asia Did Not. Global Economic Divergence, 1600–1850* (Cambridge: Cambridge University Press, 2011).

[4] Thomas Vernet, "East African Travelers and Traders in the Indian Ocean: Swahili Ships, Swahili Mobilities ca. 1500–1800" in Michael Pearson (ed.), *Trade, Circulation, and Flow in the Indian Ocean World* (Houndmills, UK: Palgrave Macmillan, 2015), 167–202.

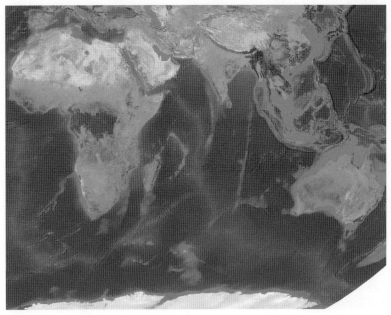

MAP 1.1 The Indian Ocean World
Note: Crop of Earth Map in Robinson Projection, by xingmin07 / Getty Images.

trade which, it is argued, was driven by external demand and agents and, in combination with European colonial exploitation, laid the basis for the economic underdevelopment of Africa.[5]

Indian Ocean World and Indian Ocean Africa

In a volume exploring the historical relationship between Africa and the wider IOW, it is necessary to explain the terms Indian Ocean world (IOW) and Indian Ocean Africa (IOA) that are employed throughout.

Indian Ocean World

This volume is not a history of Africa and the Indian Ocean. It is a history of Africa's historical relationship with the IOW. The IOW here

---

[5] See e.g. Ralph Austen, *African Economic History* (London: James Currey, 1987), 56–76.

has two geographical components: maritime and terrestrial. It includes the oceans (Indian Ocean, Indonesian, and China Seas) affected by the monsoon winds and currents (see section on human-environment interaction below), as well as their maritime offshoots such as, in the western IOW, the Persian Gulf and Red Sea, and the southern hemisphere maritime spaces dominated by trade winds that fed into the monsoon system to its north. It also includes the islands in those seas, as it does the continental littorals and hinterlands to which the IOW oceanic zones were significantly connected through trade, migration, and the interchange of ideas and technology. Thus, the IOW also comprises a wide terrestrial belt that runs from the deep interior of Africa through the Middle East, South Asia, and Southeast Asia to East Asia.

Indian Ocean Africa

Of central concern in this volume is Africa. In African historical studies, spatial paradigms have largely derived from colonial divisions whereby sub-Saharan Africa was divided geographically into West, Central, East, and southern regions, and linguistically into Anglophone, Francophone, and Lusophone zones; or focus on histories of modern-day states. Such essentially political divisions significantly underestimate communalities of environment, and forces of human-environment interaction that played a vital role in shaping historical developments over the *longue durée*.

This study of the relationship between Africa and the wider IOW over the longue durée aims to focus less on conventional historical spatial divisions than on those regions of Africa with major commercial outlets to the Indian Ocean and its Red Sea tributary. In this context, areas of Africa located east of a line running approximately from the Cape to Cairo are considered to comprise a distinct region, here termed Indian Ocean Africa (IOA), that formed a significant and intrinsic part of the IOW. These include the territories of present-day Egypt and South Africa, and extend eastwards to Madagascar and neighbouring island groups. Such a spatial configuration runs counter to conventional academic approaches that often exclude Egypt and the western Indian Ocean islands of Madagascar, the Comoros, Mascarenes, and Seychelles, from African Studies.

The IOA coastline runs some 18,800 km, between about 30°N and 35°S, and includes Red Sea shores of present-day Egypt, Sudan, Eritrea, Djibouti, Ethiopia, and Somalia, the Indian Ocean littorals of

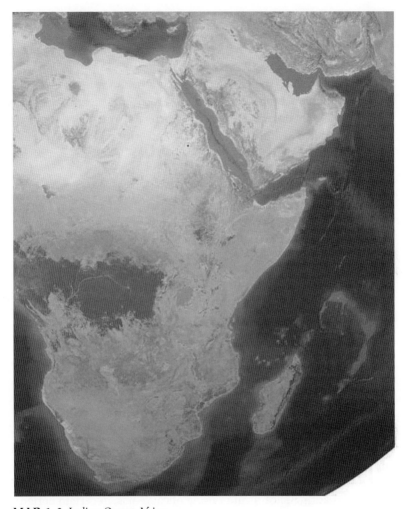

MAP 1.2 Indian Ocean Africa

Note: Crop of high resolution 3D render of Planet Earth, by janrysavy / Getty Images.

Somalia, Kenya, Tanzania, Mozambique, and South Africa, and those of the western Indian Ocean islands.

In general, the IOA coastline is characterised by a narrow coastal plain, arid in the north, but subject to increasing rainfall below about 2°S, mid-way along the modern-day Swahili coast. In Madagascar, the littoral is humid in the north and east, and arid in the south and southwest.

The IOA interior comprises the hinterlands of the above regions, including present-day South Sudan, Uganda, Rwanda, Burundi, Malawi, Zimbabwe, Eswatini, and Lesotho, and parts of Botswana, Zambia, and the Democratic Republic of the Congo – in all covering an area of some 9.5 million km². In northern IOA, the coastal plain gives way to vast sterile deserts in the Horn of Africa, Sudan, and Egypt where only the Nile, the world's longest river (6,695 km), offers the possibility of cultivation. In Ethiopia, eastern Madagascar, and South Africa, the coastal fringe is backed by highlands. In East Africa, south of 2°S and in western Madagascar, the coastal plain is wider, rising in the interior to high plateaus. The plateau in Madagascar rises to from 1,300 to 1,700 metres above sea level and runs on a north-south axis almost the entire 1,592 km length of island. The plateau in the continental interior of IOA is generally between 1,000 and 1,500 metres above sea level, but in places is punctuated by mountains that rise much higher. This highland mass, which stretches from Ethiopia to South Africa, is dissected by the Rift Valley, a geological fault line almost 10,000 km in length, that runs from Lebanon down the 2,000 km-long Red Sea and on via the Great Lakes to the Mozambique Channel.

Human-Environment Interaction

Of central importance to this volume is the concept of human-environment interaction, signifying the complex interaction of human and environmental forces in which human activity occurred. In the period under review, human destruction of forests, burning of wood and coal, smelting of ores, and raising of cattle has, in certain periods, significantly affected the environment, while natural factors have also greatly affected human activity.

Most historians of the IOW underestimate the impact of environmental forces beyond a largely static notion of the monsoon system that facilitated trans-oceanic sail in the northern sphere of the Indian Ocean and in the South China Sea. A range of other, often associated, environmental factors also had significant impact on IOW history, including the El Niño–Southern Oscillation (ENSO), the Indian Ocean Dipole (IOD), the Intertropical Convergence Zone (ITCZ), volcanism, and cyclones. As these phenomena play such an important role in the IOW, they require a brief explanation.

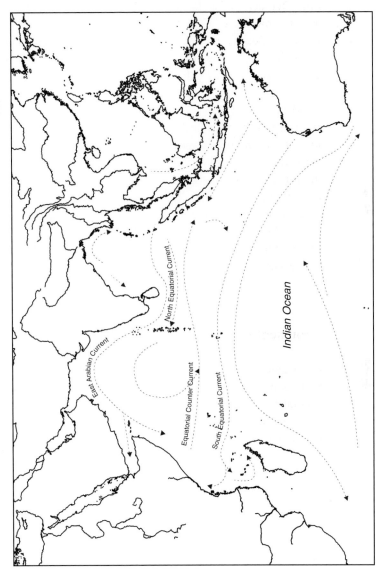

Winter Sea Surface Currents

Indian Ocean

East Arabian Current

North Equatorial Current

Equatorial Counter Current

South Equatorial Current

MAP 1.3 Indian Ocean Surface Currents

Note: Produced by Carl Hughes, IOWC.

9

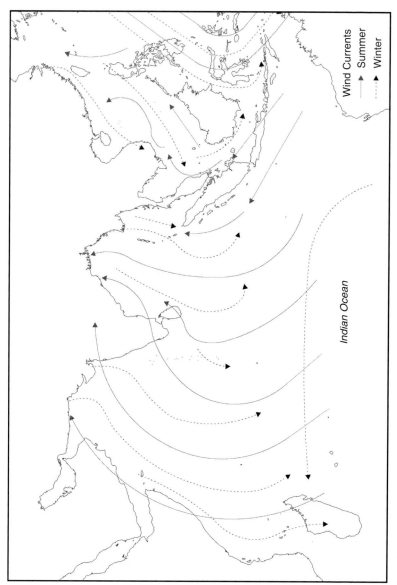

MAP 1.4 Indian Ocean World: Monsoon-driven Currents

Note: Produced by Carl Hughes, IOWC.

The IOW, its seascapes, islands, continental littorals, and interior landscapes, formed a significant and coherent historical space primarily because of the monsoon system of winds and currents which is unique to the Indian, Indonesian, and Chinese seas and their hinterlands. The monsoons mark the IOW apart from the Atlantic and Pacific worlds, for unlike the latter, IOW seas are capped by a huge continental mass: Asia is the world's largest continent, some 44 million km² in area or about one-third of the globe's surface. As the Asian landmass heats up in the boreal or northern hemisphere summer, warm air rises off its surface creating a vacuum which, through a process of convection, sucks in moist air from neighbouring oceans to the south. In winter, the reverse process occurs, and air is expelled from the continent over the seas to its south, creating the northeast monsoon.

This regular biannual alternation of winds and currents, which governs the IOW littorals and oceans to about 12°S of the equator, fundamentally influenced primary patterns of production and trade, and therefore of human history, across most of the IOW. The southwest monsoon directly affects South and Southeast Asia and, through heavy precipitation over, and runoff from, the Tibetan Plateau and Himalayas, is responsible for the annual rise in water levels in China's Yellow and Yangtze Rivers. Similarly in the western IOW, the meeting of the Indian Ocean monsoon and ITCZ is primarily responsible for heavy summer rains over Ethiopia. These in turn provoke an increase in the flow of water down the Blue Nile that in Egypt was responsible for annual flooding of the Nile. By dictating precipitation patterns over this vast macro-region, the southwest monsoon fundamentally shaped agricultural production in which probably over 90 per cent of its indigenous population was engaged. It brought heavy seasonal rains. Monsoon rains that were essential to wet crop, primarily rice, cultivation across South Asia, Southeast Asia, and China; grains, notably teff in highland Ethiopia; and in Egypt they caused seasonal Nile floods essential to the growing of wheat and barley. Consequently, communities in these regions were highly vulnerable to any changes in the monsoon system which, when it failed, could trigger drought, crop failure, famine, disease, high mortality, and migration – which in turn could provoke widespread socio-economic and political instability. In Asia, beyond the reach of the monsoons, lies a belt in which dry crops, such as wheat and barley, are grown, and beyond that semi-arid grasslands that are inhabited by pastoralists. The monsoons are thus

largely responsible for basic division in Asia between the wetter littoral and drier hinterland agricultural zones. Moreover, the monsoons
deeply influence overland communication, for overland travel and
trade, hindered by the heavy monsoon rains, are largely restricted to
the dry season.

Further, the biannual change of monsoons, winds, and currents
facilitated the development of direct trans-oceanic sail, and hence
of regular and comparatively rapid maritime commercial exchange
across the maritime zones stretching from eastern Africa and Arabia
in the West to China in the East. This IOW seascape comprises the
Indian Ocean, the world's third largest ocean (some 73.5 million
km² in area), the South China Sea (2.3 million km²), East China Sea
(1.25 million km²), Indonesian Sea (400,000 km²), and their natural
extensions, notably the Persian Gulf (240,000 km²) and Red Sea
(440,300 km²). A major distinguishing feature of the Indian Ocean is
that its main access points were easily controlled. Entry from the east
was chiefly via the 965-km-long Straits of Malacca between the Malay
Peninsula and Sumatra, which narrows sharply at its southern end (to
4.6 km in the Singapore Strait) where sail is hindered by innumerable
small islands, reefs, and sand ridges. Entry from the west was initially
restricted to the Red Sea and Persian Gulf. The Red Sea (320 km at
its widest), dividing northeast Africa from the Arabian Peninsula, is
a major sea lane connecting Asia to Europe. It is separated from the
Mediterranean by the by Suez Isthmus (160 km wide at its narrowest),
and from the Indian Ocean by the 16.7-km wide Straits of Ras Bab-
el-Mandeb. It, too, is characterised by small islands and reefs that
rendered sail hazardous. The Persian Gulf offered a much safer
opening to the Indian Ocean via the 178-km-long Hormuz passage
(54 km wide at its narrowest). A third access point, the passage around
the Cape of Good Hope, largely unused until the early sixteenth century, was characterised by dangerous winds and currents that often
imperilled maritime traffic.

The chief sea lane connecting the core IOW civilisations of China,
India, and Mesopotamia ran along the northern rim of the IOW maritime space via the Straits of Malacca in the east, the southern tip of Sri
Lanka, and the Persian Gulf. Historically, the IOW seascape through
which this sea lane passed was conceived as constituting three bodies
of water: the South China Sea, and the eastern and western Indian
Oceans – termed in Arabic "Bahr Harkand" (the "Eastern Ocean")
and "Bahr al-Zandj" (the "Erythraean Sea") respectively. Each of

these was separated from its neighbour by peninsula-island chains running roughly north-south. The Malay Peninsula and Indonesian Archipelago running south-east through Sumatra and Java to the Timor Sea formed a land-island chain, separating the Indian Ocean and South China Sea, which extended as far as Australia and Papua New Guinea to the southeast. The eastern and western Indian Ocean zones were separated by a north-south land-island chain comprising the Indian peninsula (some 1,600 km in length), Sri Lanka, and the Maldive Islands (extending 800 km to just south of the equator). This peninsula-island land bridge possibly accounts for pre-sixth century CE Hindu, Arabic, and Greek references to Sri Lanka as a huge island. In the *Periplus* (mid-first century CE), western Sri Lanka (the northern Maldives lie some 640 km to the west of Sri Lanka) is considered to approach the East African coast. Some early authorities even considered that Sri Lanka extended southwards to a continent capping the southern periphery of the IOW. Indeed, in Ptolemy's second-century and Idrisi's twelfth-century maps, the coastline of southeast Africa curves eastwards to join the Indonesian Archipelago.

As the monsoons regulated much of both agriculture and trade in the IOW, there was from the outset remarkable synchronism between land-based production and commercial systems, and trans-oceanic trade. Moreover, as other IOW wind systems such as the southern hemisphere trades, and the equatorial currents, could be used to link into the monsoon zone, the impact of the monsoon network of exchange extended to regions such as the inner Persian Gulf, and southeast Africa that lay beyond the reach of the monsoons. Sail was further assisted by the fact that the Asian continent largely blocks the monsoon seas from cold polar waters. In addition, much of the monsoon maritime zone lies in the tropics and so is unaffected by the heavy mists that often characterised the seas in temperate regions. In the IOW, the lack of mists assisted astral navigation.

Taken together, these natural factors laid the foundations for the rise and development of a highly productive agricultural sector, and of a sophisticated and durable network of long-distance exchange connecting Africa, the Middle East, South Asia, Southeast Asia, and East Asia. There were, of course, linkages with other major regions, such as the Mediterranean, Atlantic, and Pacific worlds. However, the unique environmental endowments of the IOW and their influence in moulding the material life of its peoples forms clear justification for also treating the IOW as a "world".

Of major immediate influence on the monsoons, and thus on the IOW climatic regime, are the El Niño Southern Oscillation (ENSO) phenomenon, which has a global impact, and the Indian Ocean Dipole (IOD), which have frequencies of two to seven years and two to five years, respectively. ENSO is characterised by warming (El Niño) and, in the subsequent year, cooling (La Niña) of the eastern equatorial Pacific. In the Indian Ocean, a positive ENSO (El Niño) event warms surface temperatures. This process peaks from March to May when it is characterised in the southwest Indian Ocean by an increase in precipitation and tropical cyclones. Persistent warming of the southwest Indian Ocean anchors convection south of the equator, which delays the onset of the south-west monsoon in May. The IOD also involves an oscillation between warming and cooling of Indian Ocean sea surface temperatures (SSTs). For example, in its warmer or positive phase, higher sea temperatures in the western Indian Ocean accelerate evaporation rates, creating moist air, which brings increased rain to Mozambique and other parts of eastern and southern coastal Africa. A corresponding cooling of the eastern Indian Ocean can bring drought to Indonesia and Australia. The IOD can sometimes be triggered by ENSO. When El Niño and IOD combine, East Africa experiences unusually wet and warm conditions in the austral summer. By contrast, La Niña is associated with unusually dry conditions. However, the influence of ENSO in central East Africa can be tempered by airstreams driven from the Atlantic, which may produce the opposite conditions. Moreover, the climatic impact of ENSO in southern Africa is generally the opposite of that experienced in East Africa.

The Intertropical Convergence Zone (ITCZ) also has a marked impact on IOA. Africa's basic climatic zones are to some degree decided by latitude. The extreme northern and southern tips of IOA (north coast of Egypt and the Cape) are characterised by Mediterranean-type dry summers and wetter winters. They border subtropical deserts, the Sahara in the north and the Namib coastal desert in the southwest. Between them lies a wide tropical zone governed by the seasonal migration of the ITCZ, which results in northern and southern belts of monsoonal climate characterised by summer rains and winter drought. In Ethiopia, the southwest monsoons from June to September overlap with the northward migration of the ITCZ, bringing heavy rainfall essential to local agriculture and, through runoff, boosted Blue Nile flows of water that were of paramount importance to Nile Valley cultivation.

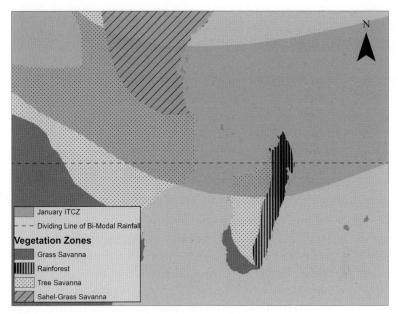

MAP 1.5 East Africa and Madagascar: January ITCZ
Note: Produced by Carl Hughes, IOWC.

This pattern was not duplicated over the rest of continental IOA where the monsoons bring little rain, due chiefly to a semi-permanent low pressure system centred over the Lake Victoria region which deflects the main monsoon winds. East Africa experiences most rainfall in the transition periods when the monsoons change and the low pressure bubble is temporarily displaced by movements in the ITCZ. During southern hemisphere summer, when the ITCZ usually moves south to span the region between 5°S and 10°S, atmospheric convection and thus precipitation in the southwest Indian Ocean increases. However, there is high annual variability in ITCZ movements. Hence, large areas of East Africa frequently experience less than the 750 mm minimum of rainfall needed to cultivate maize and other crops. The notable exception is the East African equatorial zone characterised by a double rainfall maximum – the "long rains" from March to May, and "short rains" from October to December.

Other factors that had a significant impact on IOW history include cyclones and volcanism. Cyclones were prevalent in a number of IOW regions, including the Philippines, Bay of Bengal, and the western Indian Ocean where, chiefly from January to March, they affected notably the Mascarene Islands (Mauritius and Réunion) and

Madagascar. Madagascar's position in the Indian Ocean, with its wide range of altitudes, makes it particularly susceptible to a high variability in temperature, precipitation, and cyclonic activity. Generally, however, northern Madagascar appears to show an ENSO pattern similar to that of East Africa, and most of the west, southwest, and centre of the island a pattern akin to that of southern Africa. During the austral summer, the ITCZ moves as far south as 20°S, bringing heavy rain to northern Madagascar. When it moves north during the boreal summer and fall, the southeast trade winds strengthen and shift north, feeding the ITCZ. This, coupled with the southwest Indian Ocean SST, determines the amount of regional precipitation in Madagascar. High regional SSTs and strong winds promote maximum ITCZ convection, drawing in air and moisture, creating an annual average of ten tropical cyclones, concentrated in the austral summer. These cyclones, travelling westwards, often first affect Mauritius and Réunion before hitting northeast Madagascar. Most precipitation over Madagascar thus falls during summer (November–April), winter rainfall being restricted to the island's eastern and southern coasts. Easterly trade winds carry moisture to the east coast for much of the year, while mid-latitude winter storms can bring lower temperatures and rain to southern Madagascar which, nevertheless, receives on average less than 800 mm each year compared to 3,500 mm for northeast Madagascar. The island's rugged topography causes most westward moving rain to fall on the eastern escarpment. The central uplands and most western regions receive rainfall during summer, mostly through convective activity and thunderstorms linked to the ITCZ then lying across northern Madagascar.

Volcanic activity has also greatly affected the environment and human activity in the IOW. It is centred on the western side of the "Ring of Fire", running from New Zealand through New Guinea, the Indonesian Archipelago, and Philippines to Japan, before curving eastward in a giant arc to embrace the entire western littoral of the Americas. Over 80 per cent of the world's largest earthquakes occur along this arc. The second most active region, the Alpide belt, runs from Java through the Himalayas to southern Europe. IOA possesses some active volcanoes, notably along the East African Rift zone, and on Réunion. Volcanoes can emit vast amounts of gas, primarily carbon dioxide, water vapour, sulphur dioxide, and fine solid rock particles. Large sulphur-rich eruptions create a so-called "dust veil" effect in which stratospheric aerosol clouds obscure the sun, and result in a fall in surface temperatures of up to 2°C or more for two or three years. Giant sulphur-rich eruptions, or a concentrated succession of sulphur-rich volcanic eruptions, could induce protracted global cooling, widespread crop failure, and the onset of lengthy arid periods characterised by socio-economic and political disturbances.

Human-Environment Interaction and Periodisation

The above environmental elements did not respect man-made political boundaries, and could have inter-regional, trans-IOW, even global impacts on the material and cultural lives of human beings – sometimes decisively so. This is not an argument for environmental determinism. It is today only too apparent, in a period of escalating climate change, due largely to unchecked fossil fuel emission and deforestation, that humans can have major impacts on the environment. Indeed, recent research indicates that, chiefly through the use of, for example, fire, deforestation, cultivation, cattle-raising, and metalworking, humans contributed significantly to climate change well before the BCE/CE changeover.[6] What is argued here is that, in order to gain a deeper insight into the processes of historical change, it is necessary to challenge the traditional pre-eminence given to human beings as agents of historical change, and instead place human-environment interaction at the centre of historical narrative. Human-environment interaction involves a complex interplay of factors. Some of the major environmental elements have already been alluded to above. Human contributions include production, trade, migration, imperialism, conflict, and enslavement. Human-environmental interaction has never been static. Certain combinations of environmental and human factors may come close to reproducing the same patterns, with similar consequences, but their interplay has always been dynamic, changing according to time and place.

A focus on human-environment interaction as the key historical dynamic immediately challenges conventional Eurocentric periodisation. The first major influence on the Holocene (the latest geological epoch) environment and human activity in the IOW came at the end of the last great Ice Age, some 11,700 years ago when

---

[6] See e.g. Guoyu Ren, "Changes in Forest Cover in China During the Holocene" *Vegetation History and Archaeobotany* 16. 2–3 (2007): 119–26.

global warming enabled humans to disperse from the tropics, and from areas characterised by favourable micro-climates, such as the Mediterranean basin, to exploit the resources of vast territories of the northern hemisphere revealed by retreating ice shields. Production, population, and exchange increased. The onset of a significantly drier climate from around 6000 BCE led to an expansion of deserts, and migration of humans to locations with adequate water resources for their needs. In order to minimise the impact of periods of drought, people sought to control and conserve supplies of water, and utilise them efficiently. This in turn accelerated the process of domestication of plants and animals, known as the Neolithic Revolution, which reached an advanced stage by around 2000 BCE. The same processes profoundly affected the social, religious, and political makeup of human societies. For example, the heavy labour input required to construct and maintain structures of large-scale irrigated agricultural production in the "wet" zones of Asia demanded a system of government able to geographically and ideologically control its subject population. This entailed the development of coercive labour regimes, and of belief systems that reinforced hierarchy and inter-generational social rigidity, including those associated with caste structures. In all, by about 2000 BCE, sedentary communities of subject peasants were producing sufficiently regular food surpluses to support specialist craftsmen and a religio-political elite. A number of powerful hierarchical polities emerged that engaged in both warfare, in order to expand the lands under their domain, and long-distance exchange. One result of increased trade was the emergence of the so-called Silk Road connecting Mesopotamia and China through Central Asia. This route became fully functional from around 500 BCE. At about the same time, the monsoon system strengthened and, with advances in astral navigation and boat-building, enabled humans to engage in direct trans-oceanic sail in the Indian, Indonesian, and China Seas from about 300 to 200 BCE.

The dynamics and linkages of trans-IOW overland and maritime commerce laid the foundations of an IOW global economy – a regular, sophisticated, and durable structure of long-distance exchange that preceded that of the Atlantic world by over 1,500 years. The centres of production and trade were China, South Asia, and the Middle East, core regions of the Neolithic Revolution. The indications are that the IOW "global economy" experienced three major upswings and two major downturns. The periods of prosperity occurred between about

300 BCE and 300 CE, from the ninth to thirteenth centuries, and from
the mid-nineteenth century to the present day. These eras experienced
generally greater and more consistent rainfall, agricultural and craft
production, demographic growth, expansion of human settlement,
and deforestation. They also witnessed a rise in trade, greater central-
isation of power, and military expansion. The traditional Eurocentric
view is that the religions of the East, notably Islam, Hinduism, and
Confucianism, stifled factors promoting economic development, such
as entrepreneurship and the profit motive. However, courts, religious
institutions, and associated elite households, the chief recipients of
domestically produced wealth, constituted important markets. The
courts generated demand for "military" commodities – armaments,
military animals (e.g. elephants, horses, mules), and loyal soldiers
and guards (often slaves) – required to promote and secure political
power. Elite institutions and households fostered demand for luxuries – precious metals and stones, aromatics, medicines, aphrodisiacs
and other stimulants, exotic animals and animal products, fine fabrics
and other craft products, and slaves – chiefly as items of conspicuous
consumption to reflect their elevated status. However, IOW trade
also involved low-value, high-bulk goods such as grains and rock.
Moreover, it was much more than a commercial network in the conventional sense of the term, for it also comprised an exchange – sometimes purposeful, often involuntary – of scientific, philosophical, and
religious ideas and structures, and of plants, animals, technologies,
and peoples.

The intervening periods, from about 300 CE to 800 CE, and 1250
to 1830, were characterised by economic downturns or stagnation.
These were generally characterised by extended intervals of drought,
increased volcanism, reduced agricultural and craft production, epidemic disease, lower demographic growth or even population decline,
desertion of peripheral agricultural areas, and migration. Such periods
also witnessed reduced commercial exchange, considerable social and
political turmoil, greater impoverishment, and enslavement.

The period from the 1830s to the present day is distinct. First,
it marked the transition from the Little Ice Age (LIA) to the
current period of rapid global warming and climate change, during
which periods of considerable human-environment adversity were
experienced. Second, the long nineteenth century witnessed the creation of a truly international economy, one characterised by acceler-
ating technological change that, for the first time in history, created the

possibility for humans to break free of the Malthusian nightmare. In Europe, it resulted in agricultural, industrial, and financial revolutions that permitted unheralded and sustained demographic growth. It also led to the creation of a truly international economy that, by the close of the nineteenth century, had drawn all regions of the world into its orbit. In the IOW, this resulted in a major expansion in the cultivation of tropical and semi-tropical cash crops, exploitation of forest products, collection of animal products, and overland and maritime transport. As capital was limited in the IOW, much economic expansion in the macro-region was dependent upon labour inputs, which in turn promoted unparalleled human migration. However, enhanced transport and migration also facilitated the dispersal of disease. Further, unrestrained deforestation and exploitation of natural resources resulted in major damage to the environment, which in turn affected the climate. This process has continued in the modern era of globalisation and, if the ensuing impact in terms of global warming is not effectively countered, threatens the survival of future generations.

Issues

This volume holds that human-environment interaction, more than great men, state formation, or imperial expansion, is the central dynamic in IOW history. Within this context, a number of salient issues emerge in the historical relationship of Africa with the wider IOW: historical developments in IOA and the wider IOW from the end of the Great Ice Age; Africa's role in the emergence of an IOW global economy; its role in the major economic cycles of the IOW economy; the rise of the Swahili and Great Zimbabwe civilisations; and the human settlement of Madagascar. Other themes of particular interest include the role of Islam, a faith born in the Middle East that spread throughout the IOW, including IOA. Of particular concern here is the impact of Islam on the IOW global economy, and in IOA. Another theme of central concern is the impact of the European intrusion into the IOW and IOA from 1500 to the early 1800s (the "Early Modern"). This is of particular interest because the bulk of research on pre-1800 IOW history has focussed on the history of European exploration, and political, military, and economic expansion and domination. This volume challenges this approach, arguing that it is important to re-evaluate the role and impact of Europeans within the context of human-environment interaction and the contours of a long-established IOW global economy.

Again, most research on nineteenth-century IOW history has focussed on two issues: European imperial expansion and colonial conquest, and the East African slave trade. This volume will examine the reaction in IOA to Western economic and political forces active in the nineteenth century as the modern international economy developed. This forms the context for case studies of indigenous reactions to such forces in Egypt, Madagascar, and Ethiopia. In the first two cases, the indigenous regimes adopted centralised programmes of economic modernisation and imperial expansion aimed at keeping Western forces at bay, and of making them major players on the international scene. Both regimes ultimately failed to realise their goals. By contrast Ethiopia, while forging a regional empire, did not seriously attempt to modernise its economy before the twentieth century. It nevertheless avoided being colonised by European powers in the "Scramble for Africa" – a theme more widely developed in the penultimate chapter. The final theme is slavery. This is of particular interest in light of the enormous public and academic interest in slavery and the common perception that its history involved predominantly a transatlantic traffic in Black African slaves to New World plantations owned by Europeans. This volume explores first the origins and structure of IOW slavery. Second, it reassesses the history of the IOA slave trade through a re-examination of the contribution of East African slaves to the 869–883 CE Zanj Revolt in Iraq, and of highland Malagasy slaves to the Swahili slave network of the western Indian Ocean from 1500 to 1750. Finally, the role of IOA in the history of IOW slavery during the long nineteenth century is examined in the context of the burgeoning international economy, abolitionist forces, and European colonisation.

2

—

Africa in the Making of an IOW Global Economy

Almost 12,000 years ago, global warming signalled the end of the last great Ice Age and the start of the current interglacial era known as the Holocene. Prior to that, human settlement was concentrated in small hunter/gatherer/fisher communities scattered throughout the tropical and semi-tropical regions, and to their north in geographical pockets such as the Mediterranean basin, which benefitted from more hospitable conditions. The melting of much of the Arctic pack-ice established the conditions in the northern hemisphere for cultivation of previously inhospitable areas, enhanced food production, population growth and dispersal, higher artisanal output, and greater trade.

Moreover, from around 6000 BCE a prolonged dry period helped provoke a "Neolithic Revolution". Beginning in the Tigris-Euphrates valleys of Mesopotamia, it was characterised by sophisticated water storage and irrigation, and domestication of wild food crops, notably wheat, barley, peas, and lentils, and of animals, notably sheep and goats. By about 5000 BCE, these domestication techniques were also apparent in Central Asia, the Nile Valley, and Greece; and by about 3500 BCE in the Indus Valley. Similar revolutions occurred around the same time in Mesoamerica, involving the domestication of squash, beans and later maize, and in China involving the domestication by around 6000 BCE of millet, pigs, and poultry, and by 5000 BCE of swidden rice. The Neolithic Revolution greatly increased agricultural production, which in turn promoted demographic expansion: the world's population is estimated to have increased from about 14 to 27 million between 3000 and 2000 BCE, to 50 million by 1000 BCE, to reach 100 million by 500 BCE.

Early Economic Development in IOA

In regions of the world where the climate remained relatively stable, such as Australia and the equatorial lowlands, hunter-gatherer societies experienced less pressure to adopt radically innovative techniques. However, Africa was greatly affected by early Holocene climatic changes. At the end of the Ice Age, the Sahara – a hitherto inhospitable tract – experienced a sudden and protracted period of heavy rainfall,

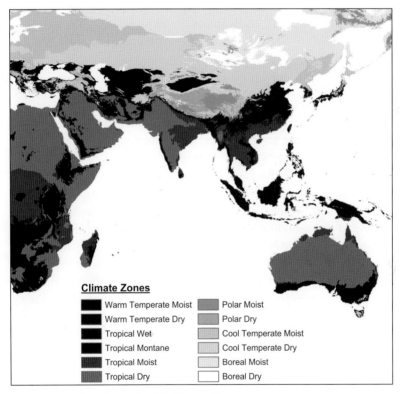

MAP 2.1 Indian Ocean World: Climate Zones

Note: Climatic Zone, "European Soil Data Centre (ESDAC)," European Commission, 10 June 2010. https://esdac.jrc.ec.europa.eu/projects/renewable-energy-directive#. Adapted by Henry Coomes, IOWC.

TABLE 2.1 *Domesticated Animal Introductions to Africa*

Species	Probable area of domestication	Time of domestication	Time of introduction to Africa	Probable region of introduction
Cattle	Mesopotamia	ca 8800–8200 BCE	ca 7000 BCE	Nile Valley
Goat	Mesopotamia	ca 9000–8000 BCE	ca 5000–4000 BCE	Mediterranean N. Africa; Red Sea Africa
Sheep	Mesopotamia	ca 8500 BCE	ca 5000–4000 BCE	Nile Valley; Horn of Africa
Chicken	S. Asia, SW China and SE Asia	ca 4000–3000 BCE	ca 2000 BCE	Nile Valley
Camel	SE Arabia and E. Iran	ca 3000 BCE	from ca 1500 BCE	Nile Valley

followed from around 7000 to 5200 BCE by less intense but regular precipitation. The rains transformed the desert, encouraged growth of wild flora, and induced wild animals and people to migrate into the region. In the southern Sudanese Sahara, for example, lush vegetation, forests, large rivers, and permanent fresh-water lakes developed, attracting elephants, rhinoceroses, hippopotamuses, and crocodiles. However, from around 5200 BCE, irregular precipitation and progressive desiccation led humans and animals to concentrate in shrinking habitable pockets of the Sahara. When the rains largely ended around 3400 BCE and the desert began to expand, they migrated to the Nile Valley and other areas with viable water sources.

The conventional view is that the Sahara subsequently formed a desert barrier isolating Africa from the outside world, so that the continent largely failed to experience and benefit from the Neolithic Revolution. Indeed, some scholars maintain that Africa failed to benefit from technological innovation until the arrival of Europeans in the modern colonial era. Africa possesses abundant wild life, including for example roughly 50 per cent of the world's wild hoofed animals, but only the guinea fowl and probably the cat, donkey, and indigenous cattle were domesticated. Other major animal contributions to African economies, including camels, sheep, goats, and major cattle species, were adopted from sources outside the continent.

However, it is increasingly evident that domestication was less a "revolutionary" affair, experienced in specific core locations, than a long process, involving many false starts, dispersed over large areas. Moreover, human ingenuity was as manifest in adopting and adapting new species and technologies as in developing them, and Africans were as implicated as people in other regions of the Old World. Africa possessed three indigenous domesticated plant complexes, the Saharan, Forest-margin, and Ethiopian. All three probably developed from originally sub-Saharan wild species, although debate as to origins continues as plants are difficult to trace in the archaeological record, which in turn obliges scholars to rely chiefly on historical linguistic reconstruction.

In northern IOA, domestication started early. Auroch, a type of humpless cattle, were domesticated on the Egyptian-Sudanese borderlands possibly as early as 7500 BCE, certainly by 4000 BCE. By 6100 BCE sorghum, and between 4850 and 3350 BCE pearl millet, were also being cultivated in the Sahara. From 5200 to 4500 BCE, greatly increased aridity provoked significant human migration out of the Sahara, many migrants moving to the Nile Valley where sophisticated water-control techniques were adopted, enabling settled farming communities to develop along the river. The Delta region, which benefitted from a moderate climate and plentiful water resources, attracted the highest concentration of settlers. Between July and November, due to enhanced precipitation on the Ethiopian plateau and an increase in the flow of water down the Blue Nile, the Nile rose on average about six metres, causing flooding in Upper Egypt from the end of May (peaking in early September) and in Lower Egypt, around present-day Cairo, from early July (peaking in late September). Subsequently, the river level fell, to mid-way point by mid-November and to its nadir in mid-May. Cultivators erected earthen banks to trap the flood waters, which permitted field irrigation for up to four months after the floods ended. Prolonged periods of drought in about 4200 BCE, 3800 BCE, and 3000 BCE caused annual Nile floods to fall by about one metre, which accelerated the search for better ways to capture, conserve, and control the Nile waters.

At the same time, domestication of plants and animals increased, assisted by Egypt's access to domestication techniques elsewhere: it held a strategic location at the crossroads between North Africa and the Near East, Mediterranean and Red Sea, with access south via the Nile Valley to tropical zones of Africa. The appearance in the Nile Valley of Saharan-style pottery around 4500 BCE suggests the arrival of Saharan food-production techniques involving wild sorghum and pearl millet. Nile communities also adopted winter rainfall crops of Asian origin, notably Emmer wheat and barley. Sedentary agriculture dispersed upriver to the confluence of the White Nile and Blue Nile (the location of present-day Khartoum) where by about 3000 BCE wheat, barley, peas, and lentils were being cultivated. By that time, the watermelon, of probably Kalahari and semi-tropical southern African origin, which was a source of both food and water, was also being grown in Egypt. It subsequently spread to the Near and Middle East, Russia, and Asia Minor – probably prior to the BCE/CE changeover, China by the mid-tenth century and southern Europe by the thirteenth century. By the first centuries CE, Egyptians were cultivating cotton (*Gossypium herbaceum*) for the manufacture of cloth. In addition, the Roman scholar Pliny (23–79 CE) refers to a shrub in Upper Egypt that produced a "white and soft" "wool", possibly a reference to tree cotton (*Gossypium arboretum*) which yielded a soft, silky texture, used in India as luxury padding for cushions and pillows.

The goat, a valuable source of milk, fibre, manure, meat, and leather, was domesticated in Egypt by about 4000 BCE. The donkey was domesticated from the Nubian wild ass around 3000 BCE in response to the need for a pack animal in an increasingly arid environment, and was quickly adopted in the Near and Middle East where it became an important draft animal before the camel. For example, by about 2000 BCE, donkeys were used in large trading caravans to carry cloth and metals between Ashur, on the Upper Tigris, and Central Asia Minor. Around 2000 BCE, the chicken was introduced into Egypt. The plough, initially wooden and possibly of Egyptian origin, was drawn first by humans and from around 2000 BCE by oxen. Its usage spread up the Nile to the Nilotic Sudan and Ethiopia, but not elsewhere in Africa. Further, Egypt and the Sudan adopted Middle Eastern wheels for irrigation and pottery.

Nile Valley irrigation works and settlements were smaller and more dispersed than those of Mesopotamia, but appropriation of agricultural surpluses permitted a similar type of warrior religio-political elite to emerge, and Egypt became a unified state (1st Dynasty) by about 3000 BCE, at approximately the same time that secular rulers became dominant in Mesopotamia.

Ethiopia also experienced a Neolithic Revolution influenced by its specific environment: fertile volcanic soils (shallow laterite soils characterised much of the rest of Africa); plentiful rainfall primarily due to its elevation, proximity to the Indian Ocean monsoon system, and seasonal migration of the ITCZ; and connection (Sabaean Way) via the Red Sea to the Middle East.

MAP 2.2 Northern Indian Ocean Africa and the Sahara
Note: Crop of World Globe, by alexsl / Getty Images.

Cultivation techniques, possibly adopted from Egypt and south-west Asia, led from around 3000 BCE to the rapid domestication of indigenous durra sorghum, finger millet or eleusine, teff, nug, garden cress, coffee, fenugreek, castor, enset ("Abyssinian banana"), and saf-flower. Around 3000 BCE, Ethiopians also domesticated the donkey from the Somalian wild ass. By 1000 BCE, the donkey was being cross-bred with horses to produce mules that proved hardier than donkeys or horses and recovered quicker from arduous exertion.

The Sabaean Way was, from the start, a prime avenue of exchange, via Ethiopia, between IOA and the wider IOW. A number of Asian crops and animals entered Ethiopia and spread south, including barley in the first half of the first millennium BCE, cucumber, hemp, mango, and zebu cattle. Sesame, valued as a grain and for seed oil, was probably first domesticated in South Asia by 1400 BCE and sub-sequently spread to northeast Africa. The counter flow of plants was

FIGURE 2.1 Abyssinian Ass and Female Indian Onager

Note: From a colour lithograph by Vincent, Brookes, Day & Son after a picture by Sheldon Williams. Published in Samuel Sidney, *The Book of the Horse: (Thorough-bred, Half-bred, Cart-bred) Saddle and Harness, British and Foreign* (London: Cassell, [1881]), 175.

noteworthy. During the second millennium BCE, sorghum, which alongside sugar cane and beet was a major sugar-producing crop, reached India where it ultimately became the second most important food grain after rice, and its stalks were used as cattle fodder. Sorghum reached Indonesia about 1000 BCE and China around the BCE/CE changeover. By ca 1000 BCE, pearl millet reached India, where it was particularly valued in the drier areas of Gujarat, Maharashtra, and Uttar Pradesh. Significantly, these drought-resistant African crops opened up new Asian lands for settlement. By contrast, finger millet, which also reached India around 1000 CE, and which requires mild weather and considerable rainfall, became a staple in the very south of the South Asian Peninsula and in the Himalayan foothills. Other minor food crops, such as the cowpea and fra-fra potato, both of West African origin, spread via northeast Africa to India, as did some spices and condiments, and probably the primitive form of cotton which was possibly first valued for its oil. However, the only African crop cultivated in Arabia by the BCE/CE changeover was sorghum, except for teff which was adopted in Yemen.

Enhanced agricultural production and trade laid the basis for the emergence of the Ethio-Sabaean state in the mid-first millennium BCE. The adoption of the plough from 500 BCE, most likely from southern Arabia, in combination with the use of draft oxen and cattle manure, and favourable climatic conditions, increased agricultural productivity. This resulted in high population densities in grain- and enset-growing regions of Ethiopia. By contrast, population densities were low in regions of hoe-based yams and taro cultivation where cattle were of minor importance.

From early times, Egypt, the Sudan, and Ethiopia were in contact with East Central Africa where, from about 2500 BCE, considerable change occurred. Increasingly arid conditions in their homelands induced Nilotic herders of cattle, sheep, and goats, and southern Cushitic cultivators of sorghum, bulrush millet, and finger millet to migrate south to the interlacustrine (Great Lakes) region of East Africa where the confluence of Rift Valley grass- and forest-lands, and of fertile and volcanic soils, provided a hospitable environment for, respectively, their animals, and cultivation techniques. Although the interlacustrine region also experienced drier conditions from around 6000 BCE, it did not become as arid as regions further to the north. Indeed, through reducing the size of the local savannah tsetse zone, and of lakes, greater aridity created a healthier environment for cattle, and exposed fertile lakefront soil for cultivation. There, Nilotic and southern Cushitic groups also encountered Khoisan hunter-gatherers, who probably once inhabited all of eastern Africa as far north as the Sudan and Ethiopia. Relatively close relationships developed between the three groups, opening the way for greater division of labour, specialisation, and trade. In years of low rainfall, and thus poor grass, the pastoralists depended more on supplies from farmers and hunter-gatherers. Sometimes, they abandoned pastoralism for a settled agricultural existence. By 1000 BCE, this interaction led to the development of what Christopher Ehret terms a pastoral Neolithic community.

About the same time, the ancestors of the present-day "Eastern Bantu" speakers arrived in the region. They originated from the equatorial grasslands of Central West Africa, probably the Cross

River (Oyono) Valley region of eastern Nigeria and western Cameroon. Initial theories that their migration east was impelled by possession of Iron Age technology and adoption of Southeast Asian food plants such as the banana and coconut have largely been rejected. The currently dominant view is that the expansion of the Sahara caused the West African tropical rainforest to retreat southwards, and many West Africans to make major shifts of life-style, from hunting, fishing, and foraging to farming and animal husbandry. It also triggered human migration. The Bantu-speaking migration eastwards probably started after 3000 BCE. The conventional view is that they followed the northern edge of the Central African tropical rainforest. The forest-savannah border was the environment most suited to their techniques of cultivating the West African yam (*Dioscorea spp*), legumes, peppers, and gourds, and also permitted them to hunt (with dogs), fish, and gather wild edible fruits and plants.

However, recent research by historical linguists and human geneticists suggests that the Bantu-speakers followed coastlines, then rivers through the rainforest to East Africa. Their migration was slowed by the abrupt onset around 2000 BCE of a severe 200-year long drought that affected the entire western IOW. However, this drought also possibly created the opening of a grassland corridor in the forest by between 1000 and 500 BCE that facilitated movement through it. Certainly, around 1000 BCE pioneer Bantu-speaking groups reached the Great Rift Valley where they adopted and adapted local Nilotic and Cushitic agricultural techniques, including cattle-raising, and cultivation of finger millet and possibly sorghum. A pattern of land use evolved whereby specialist pastoralists, such as the present-day nomadic Ngisonyoka of northern Kenya, dominated higher rainfall (up to 600 mm) areas, and Cushitic and Bantu-speaking agriculturalists occupied drier lands that nevertheless received adequate rainfall, or were sufficiently well irrigated, for the cultivation of crops. The different groups inevitably developed trading relations, exchanging the products of their specialist activities.

The Neolithic interlacustrine culture was transformed by two new factors: iron and the Southeast Asian plant complex. In Africa, humans moved straight from the Stone to Iron Age, skipping the intermediate Bronze Age that characterised Europe. Bantu-speakers either acquired iron-making technology from migrants from Sudan or developed it independently. There is considerable debate about when they started producing iron goods, proposed dates ranging from 800 CE onwards. Certainly by the fourth century BCE, Bantu-speakers in southwest Uganda were producing medium-grade carbon steel in preheated forced-draft furnaces – a technique achieved in Europe only with the Siemens process in the mid-nineteenth century. Iron tools, notably the hoe, cutlass, knife, and axe, enabled Bantu-speakers to exploit the Great Lakes region more intensively than their Cushitic and Khoisan neighbours. They used the hoe rather than plough because savannah and forest soils (but not highland volcanic soil) were generally shallow and vulnerable to leaching. Iron hoes were more effective than wooden ones in breaking soil, and iron axes more effective in cutting trees than quartz or stone axes. Bantu-speakers probably used iron tools to clear dense rainforest in the Lake Victoria region where, by around 500 BCE, they were growing grain (notably sorghum) and root crops, and herding cattle.

Of arguably greater significance than iron was the introduc-tion into eastern Africa of the Southeast Asian complex of crops and animals, notably the banana, sweet potato, East Asian yam, taro, sugarcane, rice, chicken and possibly pig. The westward diffusion of Asian plants probably occurred up the well-watered Zambezi Valley. Of particular importance was the banana. The cultivated banana can only be propagated through the interven-tion of humans, by planting parts of its underground stem. It was domesticated in highland Papua New Guinea around 4950 to 4440 BCE, then diffused to Southeast and South Asia, where it was crossed with local inedible wild species. The banana subsequently reached Africa where, because of its sugar, vitamin, and potas-sium content, its cultivation may have supported unprecedentedly dense populations and, by extension, sophisticated polities. It is a staple or co-staple in parts of the interlacustrine region, in a con-tinuous band running west from Lake Victoria through the Congo rainforest to the Guinea coast, and in some parts of coastal West Africa. It is also economically important in adjacent zones, and in northeastern Madagascar. Recent disputed claims that the banana was cultivated in Uganda by 3000 BCE and the Cameroons by 500 BCE, could indicate that Southeast Asian plants were introduced into Africa over a much longer period and in a more geographically haphazard fashion than originally thought. The conventional view is that Bantu-speakers in East Africa also adopted the Southeast Asian yam, which they considered superior to their own West African variety. If, as some think, American crops also reached Indonesia prior to the arrival of Europeans, maize, beans, and squash might have augmented the impact in Africa of Southeast Asian crop complex.

As they migrated, Bantu-speakers assimilated, pushed out, or in some cases were assimilated by other groups: For example, an estimated 5 per cent of Bantu-speakers in Mozambique, rising to 25 per cent and 50 per cent respectively amongst the Xhosa and Zulu, are of Khoi origin, while the Khoi "Hadza" of Tanzania, and "Vasikela! Kung", "Sekele! Kung", and "Khwe" – all originally from Angola – assimilated Bantu-speakers who subsequently adopted the Khoi language. By the BCE/CE changeover other Khoi had migrated south to northern Botswana, possibly as far as the Cape region, diffusing sheep and goat herding techniques that they had adopted a thousand years earlier from Nilotic speakers.

Trans-IOW Trade

The Neolithic Revolution promoted regular agricultural surpluses which, together with improved storage facilities, encouraged the emergence of specialist non-agriculturalists, including artisans and soldiers, and gave Neolithic farming communities dominance over smaller, peripatetic, hunter-gatherer groups. Enhanced agricultural and craft production, and growth in elite demand for luxuries, also laid the basis for regular long-distance inter-regional trade. Most attention has focussed on exchange between the centralised polities of the Middle East, South Asia, and China. Of early IOW routes, the most celebrated was the "Silk Road", a term adopted in the nineteenth century for a complex of fluctuating trans-Asia routes that carried a wide variety of commodities. Parts of the system functioned from 3000 BCE, and by the fifth century BCE goods flowed across the entire region. From Nishapur, in northeast Iran, commercial trails ran to China's Mongolian border; to northern India, then eastwards along the Ganges to the Bay of Bengal, and southwards along the Indus to the Arabian Sea; to Mesopotamia and on to the Persian Gulf or up the Euphrates and Tigris valleys to, respectively, Greece and Syria (and on to Egypt); and north via the Caspian Sea to Russia. At the pace

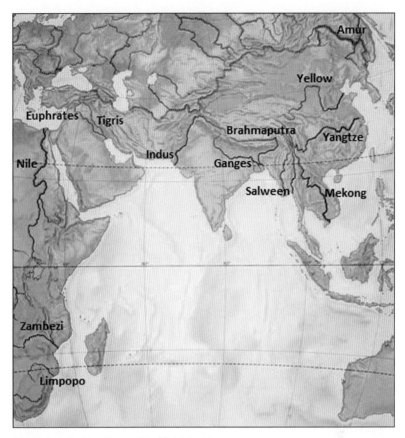

MAP 2.3 Indian Ocean World: Main Rivers

Note: Produced by author, from map in IOWC Archives.

of 30 km a day, it would have taken just over four months to travel from China's Mongolian border to Nishapur. A separate route, taking approximately 30 days, connected China with Burma and Bengal via the Brahmaputra valley.

Coastal maritime routes complemented trans-IOW overland exchange. For example, from at least 3000 BCE, coastal and inter-island traffic linked Harappa and Mohenjodaro in the Indus Valley, Dilmun (a region around Bahrain Island) in the Persian Gulf, and Sumer in lower Iraq. By about 500 BCE, local maritime networks connected the entire northern rim of the IOW, from the Red Sea to China, through five interlinked but largely discrete trading zones: from

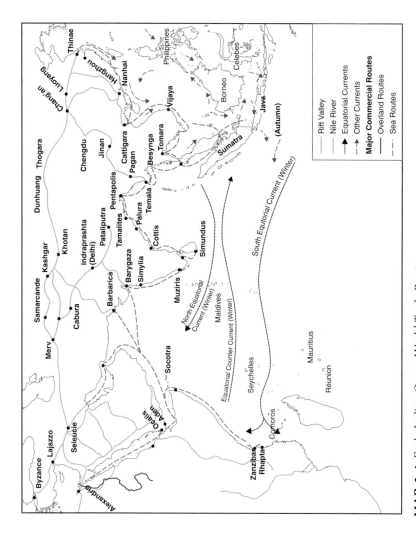

MAP 2.4 Early Indian Ocean World Trade Routes

Note: Produced by Carl Hughes, IOWC.

Egypt to northwest India; thence to South India (Malabar and Sri Lanka); South India to eastern India (Coromandel and Bengal); South and eastern India to the Malay Peninsula and Indonesia; and thence to China. Sea-going vessels could carry a larger cargo faster and with less human supervision than land transport, and required fewer stops. However, boats were initially small, hugged the coasts, and encountered many hazards especially shoals and pirates. Even on clear runs, early maritime transport was a lengthy process. For example, it took five days to tranship goods across, and six weeks to sail around, the Malay Peninsula. Indeed, maritime commerce failed at first compete with overland transport, even declining from around 2000 BCE. Nevertheless, land and maritime trade routes were largely complementary, and when one was threatened, merchants generally transferred merchandise onto the other. For instance, from around 2000 BCE, following the Aryan invasion of the Indus Valley and growth in piracy, merchants operating in the Arabian Sea switched from coastal to overland routes, while Red Sea trade transferred to the overland "Incense Road" linking Cana, situated between Aden and Mukalla in Oman, to Petra, located south of modern-day Amman. Domestication of the camel sometime between 2000 and 1500 BCE further encouraged long-distance overland trade, notably across more arid regions such as the Arabian Peninsula and the Sahara. By the mid-first millennium BCE, camels were being utilised as pack animals across the IOW, from China to the Sudan.

On overland routes, merchants used rivers where navigable, and tracks when necessary, as when crossing mountains. If indications for the mid-first millennium CE can be backdated, Silk Road caravans typically comprised from 250 to 500 young adult traders, of mixed ethnicity, who travelled together for security against attack from bandits and other armed groups. Caravans often comprised horses as mounts for merchants and guard-hunters, and 1,000 camels or more, together with other animals. Camels carrying goods of a maximum average weight of 230 kg could travel at 4.8 km an hour, although on long journeys they generally carried loads of 130 to 180 kg and averaged 30 to 50 km a day over reasonably passable surfaces. Camels were of little utility on very rough or steep terrain for which primarily donkeys or mules were used. Mules had greater endurance and a quicker recovery time than donkeys, but being sterile were a limited-term investment. Sturdy pack mules could carry loads of 100 to 160 kg up to 80.5 km a day on the coast, 55 km in highland terrain and around 32 km in the jungle. Occasionally, oxen were also employed to carry merchandise.

Both land and maritime trade networks possessed staging posts with fresh water and food supplies, accommodation, and provisions for storage, maintenance, and repair. Larger settlements offered credit and religious facilities, and entertainment. Such posts developed at key locations along overland routes, chiefly where good water sources were located, and at major "break-in-transport" points where commodities were moved onto other forms of transport, notably between freight animals, human porters, and boats. Where significant overland and coastal sailing routes met, ports developed. However, most IOW political and religious elites, in contrast to those of the Mediterranean, were based in inland centres. Moreover, many early IOW ports operated seasonally, according to the monsoon rhythm, and thus needed no permanent bureaucratic or military presence. Also, as many early IOW craft, coastal and trans-oceanic, had shallow drafts, they did not require safe havens or deep water and could often simply be hauled ashore. The first ports in the IOW were thus generally situated less in protected coastal harbours than at landing places close to river mouths, which also provided convenient fording points and access to hinterland routes.

Indian Ocean Africa's Relations with the Wider IOW

Two main routes connected IOA and the overland Asian trade network. The first linked Syria and Egypt, via the Suez Isthmus, and the second the Persian Gulf and Ethiopia, either direct across the desert or coastwise, to the Hadhramaut, in Yemen, and from there across the Red Sea. Commercial routes also connected Egypt and Ethiopia with the tropical zones to their south. From around 3400 BCE, due to the expanding Sahara, the Nile became the main avenue of communication between northern and sub-Saharan Africa, notably during the annual floods when boats could sail upriver on north to north-westerly winds (coming from the Mediterranean), and navigate downriver on currents travelling at about 4 knots (7.4 km) an hour. Vessels could travel the 900 km between Thebes and the region of present-day Cairo in a fortnight. Nile Valley cultivators exchanged agricultural goods for the cattle products of neighbouring desert nomads, and from at least 3000 BCE imported gold from Nubia, a region in present-day northern Sudan south of the Nile's first cataract, some 1,000 km upriver from Alexandria.

Indeed, by about 2500 BCE, Egypt dominated a regional trading network extending from Syria to Nubia. By at least 1320 BCE, Egyptian hegemony had expanded from Syria into the Euphrates Valley, and under Thutmose III (r. 1479–25) the southern limit of their empire extended to the fourth cataract. By about 1800 BCE, "equatorial" products such as ivory, ebony, leopard skins, ostrich feathers, precious stones, and slaves flowed into Egypt in exchange chiefly for trinkets and weapons. Cataracts hindered movement along the upper reaches of the Nile, but around the BCE/CE changeover, Ethiopians introduced collapsible boats which facilitated passage over the cataracts. It was traditionally thought that on the White Nile further south, the Sudd (from the Arabic *sadda*, "to obstruct"), the world's largest fresh-water swamp, prevented passage to the Equatorial Africa or the Great Lakes region until crossed by an Egyptian military expedition in 1840. However, communications across the Sudd had existed for millennia. The Sudd shrinks sharply (currently from 92,000 km² to 10,000 km²) in the dry season, which facilitates passage across it. It could also be circumvented by either ascending the Blue Nile or passing overland through the Ethiopian highlands and following the well-established Rift Valley route to the Great Lakes. Certainly by about 5000 BCE, pastoralism had spread from the eastern Sudan to the Lake Turkana region, and by ca 200 BCE Egyptians knew of the Nile's course as far as the confluence of the White and Blue Niles, and were aware that its source lay in two lakes to the south.

Egypt was hit from around 2200 BCE by the onset of severe drought, the Nile floods failing from 2180 to 2135, and in 2005 and 1992 BCE, and by devastating floods between 1840 and 1765 BCE. Crop failure and disease followed. For example, severe flooding in about 1715 BCE disturbed the natural habitat of the Nile rat which in consequence fled to urban areas where its appearance coincided with the world's first "virgin soil" epidemic of a virulent rat-spread disease – probably tularemia. This series of natural disasters, combined with harvest failure and epidemics, precipitated socio-political disorder, economic stagnation, and a decline in population that lasted until about 700 BCE.

At the same time, from 1000 BCE, as aridity increased and lakes dried up, the tsetse-fly zones of Tropical Africa, where *nagana* (animal trypanosomiasis or sleeping disease) prevailed, retreated south, facilitating the growth of donkey- and mule-carried trade between northern IOA and central East Africa. Such exchange was further boosted by the use of the dromedary (single-humped) camel which was introduced into Egypt around 500 BCE and had become common from around 1500 CE. However, in regions where the tsetse-fly continued to prevail, pack animals were of limited use, necessitating the use of human porters.

Maritime exchange between Africa and the wider IOW initially flowed chiefly through northern IOA via the Red Sea – which was characterised by north to north-westerly winds in the northern sector, and southerly winter and northerly summer winds in the southern sector. By about 3100 BCE, Egyptians had replaced reed rowing boats with wooden sailing vessels and started regularly plying the 2,000 km-long Red Sea to trade with the wider IOW. By about 2200 BCE, Arabian and Sumerian merchants were visiting the ports of Red Sea Africa. However, the subsequent onset of severe drought, due to a failure of the monsoon rains, provoked an economic crisis throughout the western IOW which contributed to the collapse of the Indus Valley civilisation, economic decline in Egypt, and a growth of piracy.

Maritime trade in the western IOW revived from the tenth century BCE due primarily to the end of a long period of aridity in the Middle East lasting from the twelfth to tenth centuries, and to the onset of a moister, more favourable climate. In consequence, the region experienced greater prosperity, notably Assyria, a kingdom based in present-day northern Iraq. In the eighth century BCE, Sabaean merchants (from Saba in present-day Saudi Arabia), who were major beneficiaries of revitalised western IOW exchange, established a colony at Axum, on the Ethiopian coast. There they introduced irrigated agriculture. Naukratis, located in the Nile Delta, emerged as a major international entrepôt. The spread of coinage from the seventh century BCE further facilitated Egyptian trade, as did the promotion by Egyptian fleets, using Syrian timber and Phoenician personnel, of Red Sea and East African trade during the late seventh to early sixth centuries BCE. The prosperity of Egypt attracted the attention of Persian kings: Cambyses (r. 529–522 BCE) captured Egypt in 525, although he failed to take Ethiopia, while Darius (r. 521–485 BCE) conquered Socotra and Egypt. In Egypt, Darius constructed or renovated a canal linking the Nile near Zaqāzīq to Suez and the Red Sea – which his navy dominated. Indeed, he was deified by Egyptians due in part to the prosperity experienced under his rule.

Regular long-distance maritime trade developed early between northern IOA and the wider IOW for both high-value luxury and lower-value bulk items. Luxury IOA products found a ready market in the Middle East and India. By 5000 BCE, Yemen imported obsidian artefacts from the Ethiopian highlands. By the third millennium BCE, Egypt exported Nubian gold to the Near East and probably India, papyrus to Mediterranean countries and Southwest Asia, and wheat and barley to the Near East. By at least 3100 BCE, cowry shells, probably of Maldivian origin, reached Egypt where they were highly valued by the local elite. They were possibly obtained at Punt, a seasonal (January to September) market generally identified as Opone (present-day Ras Hafun) in Somalia just south of Cape Guadarfui. From about 2200 BCE, Egyptian vessels systematically called at Punt for exotic "African" commodities including spices, myrrh, animals, and aromatic woods, the gums and resins from which, mixed with spices, formed the basis for incense which was greatly valued in Egypt for religious (sacrifice, ablation, purification, sanctification) purposes, and to counter catarrh. Ancient Egyptians treated catarrh with East African aloe, of which there currently exist some 200 taxa, at least 20 of which have medicinal uses. They also used hashish and "Punt" frankincense, which contained tetrahydrocannabinol, as painkillers. At Punt they traded with merchants from the Persian Gulf, and from Gujarat where excavations at the site of the important Harappan port of Lothal have revealed model African mummies dating to between 3000 and 2500 BCE.

By 1991 BCE, staple Egyptian exports from equatorial African regions to the wider IOW included ivory, ebony, leopard skins, ostrich feathers, precious stones, and slaves, as well as locally manufactured trinkets and weapons. Ethiopia and the Horn exported myrrh, ebony wood, ivory, gold, baboons, monkeys, greyhounds, leopard skins, slaves and, from at least 900 BCE, Somalian frankincense. By 1200 BCE, Egyptian fleets sailed every three years to "Ophir" for gold, silver, jewels, ivory, apes, and peacocks. Some scholars speculate that Ophir was a location in East Africa, but as the round-trip took three years, and local commodities included peacocks, the majority view is that it was located in a gold-producing region of southwest India, or in a third country that traded with India. Certainly, by then, imports into Egypt also included Indian pepper.

Claims to a very early maritime connection between the present-day Swahili coast of East Africa and the wider IOW have a long but disputed heritage. Under king Necho (r. ca 610–595 BCE), an Egyptian fleet sailed first down the East African coast to survey its commercial potential, then almost certainly circumnavigated Africa, a voyage of some 23,000 km. Herodotus, writing 150 years later, noted of the epic three-year voyage:

> he [Necho] dispatched Phoenicians in galleys, giving them instructions to sail eventually through the Pillars of Heracles into northern waters and so to return to Egypt. So the Phoenicians embarked and sailed out of the Erythraean Sea into the Southern Ocean. And when it came to autumn, they would disembark and sow their seed, to provide for each occasion when they might be coasting along Africa; and there they waited for the harvest-time, and then they would reap their grain and sail on. And so, when two years had passed, in the third year they doubled the headland of the Pillars of Heracles and returned to Egypt. Now the only aspect of this story, as they tell it to me, that to me seems hardly credible – though others may understand it – is the statement that, as they sailed round Africa, they had the sun rising on their right hand. This is how Africa first came to be known.[1]

Egyptians were particularly interested in locating sources of gold and aromatic woods, but their fleet probably found little of interest along the East African coast which, between the Horn and the equator, lacked easy anchorage and provisions, and was sparsely populated.

Nevertheless, some scholars assert that by then East Africa had well-established maritime connections with the wider IOW. The most notable advocate of this viewpoint, Felix Chami, asserts that by 3000 BCE non-Bantu-speaking Sub-Saharan Africans had settled the present-day Swahili coast and offshore islands of Zanzibar and Kilwa, and from possibly 2400 BCE started to sail the high seas of the Indian Ocean. Shell beads from the coast dating to around 2000 BCE have been found deep in the East African interior and, about the same epoch, copal was possibly shipped from Mozambique to

---

[1] Quoted in J. Innes Miller, *The Spice Trade of the Roman Empire 29 B.C. to A.D. 641* (Oxford: Clarendon Press, 1969), 266–7.

Iraq. Again, recent assertions of a human presence on the north, northwest and southwest coasts of Madagascar, dating to around 2400 BCE, 2343 to 1461 BCE, and 805 to 204 BCE respectively, may indicate sail from East Africa to Madagascar – in the earlier cases by Stone Age people.

Chami further claims that, from 1000 BCE, Bantu-speakers also started to settle the East African coast where their iron-working and inland water techniques, including baskets, dugouts, and possibly "sewn boats", facilitated a rapid transition to a maritime lifestyle. Constructing outrigger canoes and proto-types of the modern-day dhow, they reached offshore islands and engaged in trans-oceanic sail. He asserts that by at least 600 BCE Bantu-speakers had forged trade relations with India from where they adopted the chicken, rice, cotton, and possibly the coconut. East African staple exports included ivory, rhinoceros horn, copal, and probably a few slaves. However, very early connections between East Africa, Madagascar, and the wider IOW are contentious (see Chapter 6).

In sum, the early trans-IOW and IOA-IOW trading network was dominated by overland routes, supplemented by coastal shipping. However, the balance between overland and sea-based routes fundamentally altered when humans started to utilise the monsoon winds – the subject of the next chapter.

3

—

Indian Ocean Africa in the First Great Upswing in the Indian Ocean World Global Economy, ca 300 BCE to ca 300 CE

Conventional Eurocentric history asserts that the Greeks were the first to discover the workings of the IOW monsoons in the second to first century BCE, and that from about 41 CE the Romans created the first deep-sea trade network in the western Indian Ocean. However, it is now clear that peoples indigenous to the IOW established a monsoon-based trans-oceanic commercial system much earlier, one that largely complimented the overland silk road and led to the rise of a durable and sophisticated system of maritime and land-based exchange across the entire macro-region from Africa to China that led to the rise of an Indian Ocean world "global economy".

Most historians assume the monsoon system of winds and currents to have been a constant unchanging factor in IOW history. However, the system has changed over time. Even when it attained the stability noted by the time of the BCE/CE changeover, ENSO and other climatic factors caused considerable annual variation in its performance. The monsoon system was strong from around 9000 to 3500 BCE, then weakened due to changes in the earth's orbit around the sun. Subsequently, from about 2600 to 1700 BCE, the northeast monsoon grew stronger, and from around 500 to 300 BCE the entire monsoon system strengthened. Indeed, the period from about 300 BCE to 300 CE was characterised by particularly benign climatic factors. For the western IOW, the indications are that solar activity was stable between 200 BCE and 100 CE, volcanic activity exceptionally low from 150 BCE to 40 CE, and temperature and rainfall patterns favourable until the late third century CE. It is in this context that the rise of monsoon sailing from around 300 BCE, the development of regular direct trans-oceanic voyages, and the emergence of an IOW global economy should be examined.

A more vigorous and regular alternation of monsoon winds and currents, combined with enhanced IOW trade, spurred developments in astral navigation and shipbuilding. It led, for example, to the construction of sturdy flexible craft capable of handling robust winds and rough seas characteristic of the southwest monsoon. Whereas Eurocentric historiography has emphasised the weakness of some IOW shipbuilding techniques in which planks were sewn rather than, as in the European tradition, nailed together, sewn ships proved more flexible, and hence more capable of handling monsoon conditions, than did nailed ships. In addition, the use of teak and other appropriate timber gave IOW ships a longer life than the oak ships of Europeans. In about the year 1771, after many IOW shipbuilders had replaced sewn with nailed planks, English East India Company (EIC) employee, James Forbes commented of India:

> The southern mountains are woody, and abound with teak trees, often called the oak of Hindostan, from their great value in shipbuilding. Teak timber is more durable than oak, from its oleaginous quality preserving the wood and the iron necessarily used in naval architecture, for a considerable time longer than the British oak, which contains a corrosive quality, tending to consume the iron-work. I saw a ship at Surat which had been built near eighty years; and which, from veneration to its age and long services, was only employed in an annual voyage to the Red Sea, to convey the Mohamedan pilgrims to Juddah [Jeddah] on their way to Mecca; and then, returning with them to Surat, after the hodge [hajj], or religious ceremonies were finished, the vessel was oiled, and covered up on shore until the following season.[1]

Direct two-way trade across the Bay of Bengal developed as early as 300 BCE. Buddhist *Jātaka* folk tales from India indicate that by then, improvements in the rigging and size (possibly of up to 75 tons) of ships, enabled Indian and Southeast Asian merchants to sail on the monsoons directly between South India (Chola and Sri Lanka) and the Malay Peninsula. From about 120 BCE, direct mercantile traffic also developed between Egypt and western India. However, mastery of the monsoons probably first occurred in the eastern IOW where

---

[1] James Forbes, *Oriental Memoirs: A Narrative of Seventeen Years Residence in India*, vol. I (London: Richard Bentley, 1834), 146.

Austronesians had a long-established reputation as expert boat-
builders and navigators. The Indonesian Archipelago, comprising over
13,000 islands stretching from approximately 8°N to 11°S, constituted
an environment particularly favourable to the early development of
a maritime culture, one spurred from 12,000 to 5000 BCE when sea
levels rose, flooding the Sunda Shelf and forcing affected peoples to
disperse. Between about 1500 BCE and 1500 CE, Austronesians sailed
to and colonised previously uninhabited islands over halfway across
the circumference of the globe, east across the Pacific to Easter Island
and west across the Indian Ocean to Madagascar (21,263 km apart).
They introduced their boat-building techniques to China and, Waruno
Mahdi argues, South Asia. By 300 CE, they possessed 400 to 500 ton
ocean-going vessels, 50 metres long, with four sails, built in a lashed-
lug rather than western IOW sewn-boat tradition, and which could
carry up to 700 people long distances in rough seas. It may have been
these boats that were described in a Chinese account dating from the
end of the third century CE:

> The men from foreign lands call their boats "*p'o*." The large ones are
> over 200 feet [61 m] long and are twenty to thirty feet [6–9 m] high
> [above the water-level] ... they can hold 600 to 700 men, and a cargo of
> over 10,000 ho [about 88 cubic metres].
>
> The men from beyond our frontiers use four sails for their ships,
> varying with the size of the ships. These sails are connected with each
> other from bow to stern. There is a kind of *lu t'ou* tree whose leaves are
> like lattice [windows]. These leaves are more than 10 feet [3 m] long,
> and are woven into sails. The four sails do not face directly forwards,
> but are made to move together to one side or the other with the direc-
> tion of the breeze ... when they [the ships] sail, they do not avoid strong
> winds and violent waves, and therefore can travel very swiftly.[2]

The Southeast Asian islands experienced intensified commercial
exchange between about 300 BCE and 300 CE, while local mariners,
particularly active in the clove trade, sailed to markets as far east as
China and as far west as India, possibly also to the Red Sea and East
Africa.

As noted, the IOW maritime trade network comprised two compli-
mentary systems, one coastal, characterised by small boats and distances,

---

[2] The *Nan Chou I Wu Chi*, quoted in Wang Gungwu, "The Nanhai Trade: A Study of
the Early History of Chinese Trade in the South China Sea" *Journal of the Malayan
Branch of the Royal Asiatic Society* 31.2 (182) (1958): 38.

and the second monsoon-based and trans-oceanic, that involved larger vessels sailing greater distances. However, few vessels sailed the entire maritime length of the IOW. This was because, although it was theoretically possible to cross the Indian Ocean on one monsoon, cargoes were rarely single-destination consignments, associated procedures such as docking, off- and on-loading, storage, taxation, exchange, and provisioning were lengthy, crews (25–40 strong on Arab oceanic vessels) needed respite, and ships frequently required repairs due to rough seas and storms. As the Buddhist monk Fa Xian (337–422) commented of the voyage from Sri Lanka to Java in ca 399 CE:

> [Fa Xian] took passage in a large merchant ship which had about 200 people on board, and at the back of which was secured a smaller vessel lest the big one be shipwrecked, for sea voyages were dangerous. They sailed east on favourable monsoon winds, but after three days encountered a violent storm. The ship sprang a leak and when water started to come in the merchants wanted to enter the small one. However, the people in the smaller vessel feared that this would mean too many people, so cut the rope. Afraid that the ship would fill with water and that they would die, the merchants threw all unnecessary cargo overboard … The storm endured for thirteen days when they reached the shores of an island. There, after the high tide had receded, the hole was discovered, the leak repaired, and they set sail again.
>
> The sea is frequented by pirates, an encounter with whom is perilous. The great ocean extends without limit, and the only way to navigate is through observing the movement of the sun, moon and stars. Should it rain or the sky be obscured, the ship is carried along without these means of orientation. In the dark of the night one sees huge waves wrestling each other, throwing up white foam, as giant turtles, crocodiles and other oceanic monsters [swirl around]. The merchants were very frightened for they did not know where they were heading. The sea was deep and bottomless, and there was no place where they could drop anchor. Only when the sky cleared could they again recognise the direction, and set the ship on the correct course. Even then, if reefs had been encountered, all would have been lost. So they sailed for a little more than ninety days, until they reached a country called Yepo-ti [Java].[3]

Therefore, a pattern developed whereby most vessels remained within one of the three main IOW maritime zones: the Arabian Sea, Bay

---

[3] Fa Xian, original text adapted from Alfred J. Andrea, James H. Overfield, *The Human Record. Sources of Global History* (Boston: Houghton Mifflin, 2001), vol. I, 164–5.

of Bengal, and the China and Indonesian Seas. Two routes developed. The first and major one connected points along the northern rim of the Indian Ocean, from the Bab-el-Mandeb Straits (entrance to the Red Sea) to the Strait of Hormuz (entrance to the Persian Gulf), the Indus Delta, Gujarat, the Malabar Coast, and Sri Lanka. From South India and Sri Lanka, vessels for the Indonesian Archipelago sailed either directly to northwest Sumatra or via the Nicobar Islands and Kedah (on the Malay Peninsula); those continuing to China sailed via the Gulf of Thailand. A secondary "southern" route connecting China and the western Indian Ocean ran via the eastern Indonesian islands and the Sunda Straits to the Maldives or Sri Lanka, and on to the Persian Gulf, Red Sea, and East Africa.

Major transhipment centres arose on the frontiers of these three great maritime zones. One was in the Straits of Malacca through which from the late fourth or early fifth century most east-west traffic, formerly transhipped across the Isthmus of Kra, started to flow. This reflected the greater transhipment costs of the overland route due notably to a high rate of breakage of glass and ceramic commodities, and a decline in piracy in the Straits of Malacca. Other transhipment centres developed on Sumatra, in South India, Sri Lanka, and at the entrances to the Persian Gulf and Red Sea.

With a favourable wind, voyages generally took 70 to 84 days between the Egyptian Red Sea port of Berenice and Malabar in India, 21 to 56 days between South India and the Straits of Malacca, and 20 to 50 days between Malacca or western Indonesia and Guangzhou (formerly Canton) in China. Gradual improvements in shipbuilding and navigation boosted speeds so that by the early 1800s junks from Guangzhou covered the 2,900 km to Java in about 15 days. Transhipment, and the need to await favourable winds, entailed considerable delays for goods and agents travelling across two or more of the IOW maritime zones. Thus merchants sailing from India to China reached the tip of the Malay Peninsula in August, then waited four months for the appropriate winds to carry them to China. A return trip from India or Egypt to China commonly took two and three years respectively.

Over time, these inter-maritime zone and other transhipment centres, linking oceanic spaces to one another, and main maritime to overland trade routes, developed into major entrepôts. Many such entrepôts were situated at river mouths, entrances to a gulf, or on a strait, most on a defensible site – frequently an island. Entrepôts constituted break-in-transport points, major markets, and distribution centres. Examples from the BCE/CE changeover in the western IOW include Barygaza (Broach) in the Gulf of Cambay, in northwest India, Barbaricum (close to present-day Karachi) at the mouth of the river Indus, and Ormuz at the entrance to the Persian Gulf. In IOA, major entrepôts developed at Alexandria in the Nile Delta, Adulis located in present-day Eritrea where the Rift Valley meets the Red Sea, Opone (Ras Hafun – possibly present-day Olok), just west of Cape Guardafui in Somalia, and Rhapta on the East African coast. Those that arose on the India to Maldives axis included Muziris (Pattanam), on the Kerala coast of South India which was the chief outlet for black pepper; and on Sri Lanka, a reputed source of cinnamon, pearls, and gems, and around which all ocean-going ships sailed because the Palk Strait separating Sri Lanka from southern India was dangerous, characterised by reefs and half submerged islands. Similar break-in-transport points developed along the Malay Peninsula to Java axis, notably on the Malacca and Sunda straits, for trade flowing between the Indian Ocean on the one hand, and the Indonesian and South China Seas on the other. However, the geographical locations of IOW entrepôts sometimes changed as a result of shifting natural and human forces, such as the silting up of a river or estuary.

Coastal entrepôts are conventionally portrayed as externally orientated enclaves, isolated from their largely agricultural and autarkic hinterlands. However, major entrepôts generally also facilitated exchange between maritime and terrestrial trade networks. Further, their occupants necessarily developed relations with local people who provided them with food, fuel, labour, and sometimes water. Such centres inevitably attracted the attention of regional political authorities who generally sought to protect, encourage, and tax, but rarely to participate directly in maritime commerce. For instance, the Egyptian state under Augustus (63 BCE–14 CE) taxed Red Sea merchant shipping at 25 per cent of the declared value of the commodities they carried, but in return offered protection from pirates. Some authorities employed ambassadors to forge treaties with foreign powers, and to gather commercial information. Thus in the period from 273 to 238 BCE the Indian emperor, Asoka (r. 268–232 BCE), sent envoys to Egypt and the eastern Mediterranean, while in ca 166 CE, a Roman-Egyptian embassy presented African ivory, rhinoceros horn, and tortoiseshell to the Chinese court. Political authorities that provided insufficient protection, exacted exorbitant taxes, or imposed trade monopolies risked losing the merchants, and associated tax revenue, to rival trade centres.

Commodities and Personnel

Most historians of IOW trade have focussed on luxury commodities and elite consumers. For example, trans Bay of Bengal trade included the exchange of Indian bronze bowls, glass and carnelian beads, textiles and possibly Buddhist icons for spices, gold, tin, and semi-precious stone ornaments; while IOW commodities in demand in first-century CE Mediterranean markets included pearls, emeralds, crystals, rubies, muslins, dyes, spices, and ivory that were exchanged chiefly for gold, much in coin form (*denarii*). However, low-value bulk cargoes, comprising for example rice, wheat, base metals, timber, stone, salt, coarse cloth, earthenware, and cowries, were also significant in IOW exchange. Such goods were often used as ballast, a vital component of sailing ships, and as such could, if necessary, be sold at a loss, generally with little impact on longer-term profits.

Trans-IOW maritime trade could generate very large profits but required substantial investment, the returns on which often took two or more years to be realised, while risks were high due to natural hazards, pirates, and disease. In core IOW economies, gold and silver and sometimes cowries served as currencies, while in more peripheral markets, beads, salt, cloth, and occasionally animals and slaves acted as commodity monies.

Maritime trade encouraged the early development of specialist groups, from merchants, bankers, and moneyed investors to boat-builders, provisioners, captains, pilots, and crew. They originated chiefly from coastal societies with a long tradition of shipbuilding, navigation, and oceanic trade, that forged discrete, tightly knit communal ties, bound by trust and rules of conduct often cemented by common religious adherence. An example was the Sabaeans of the Yemen and Hadhramaut. By around 113 BCE, according to Agartharchides, a second-century BCE Greek historian and geographer, the Sabaeans dominated the western IOW trade in spices and, like other maritime mercantile communities, had established trading colonies at key locations such as Sri Lanka. While the skills of some maritime peoples appeared almost hereditary, mastery of monsoon sail necessitated for pilots and captains long years of apprenticeship learning about winds

TABLE 3.1 *Luxury Items in Early Indian Ocean World Maritime Trade*

Provenance	Items	Provenance	Items
China	Silks, cassia, ginger, jade, and iron		
India (Gujarat, Bengal)	Quality cottons; silks (from 3rd century CE)	Southeast Asia	Rhinoceros horn, spices, tortoiseshell, gold, tin
South Asia	Pearls, gems, carnelian and glass beads	Persian Gulf	Pearls, jewels, dates, gold and slaves
Eastern Africa	Spices, resins, ivory, rhinoceros horn, tortoiseshell	Egypt (and its tropical hinterland)	Rhinoceros horn, tortoiseshell, ivory, glassware
West Asia, Middle East	Tree resins, textiles, coral, pearls, amber	Near East	Glassware

and currents, astral navigation and how to interpret landmarks and oceanic signs such as marine life and sea colour. A first-century CE Indian reference to a ship's pilot (as opposed to a captain) stated:

> Knowing the course of the celestial luminaries, he was never at a loss with respect to the regions of the ship, being perfectly acquainted with the different prognostics, the permanent, the occasional and the miraculous ones, he was skilled in the establishment of a given time as proper or improper, by means of manifold marks, observing the fishes, the colour of the water, the species of the ground, birds, rocks etc. he knew how to ascertain rightly the parts of the sea, further he was vigilant, not subject to drowsiness and sleep, capable of enduring the fatigue of cold, heat, rain and the like, careful and patient. So being skilled in the art of taking a ship out and bringing her home, he exercised the profession of one who conducts the merchants by sea to their destination.[4]

Ship commanders also learned how to care for their crew. For example, to ensure the health of sailors on long trips, Egyptian captains took with them "green" ginger leaves which, rich in catechins (a natural

---

[4] Extract from the Jatakamāla of Aryā Sūra, quoted in G.R. Tibbetts, *Arab Navigation in the Indian Ocean before the Coming of the Portuguese* (London: Royal Asiatic Society of Great Britain and Ireland, 1971), 1–2.

phenol and antioxidant), helped to settle intestinal troubles and stomach upsets.

Indian Ocean Africa and the Monsoon Trade Network

IOA, like Southeast Asia, is conventionally considered to have been peripheral to the main IOW production centres of China, India, and Mesopotamia to which it supplied manual labour (slaves) and unrefined tropical products in return for cheap manufactures such as coarse cloth, plain beads, and iron bars. According to some scholars, this constituted an inequitable exchange, a "proto-colonial" basis for the "underdevelopment" of Africa. However, there is increasing evidence that by the BCE/CE changeover, IOA constituted a core rather than peripheral IOW sector.

Egypt

In Egypt, Nile river floods, which reflected Indian Ocean monsoon precipitation, were comparatively good from 450 BCE to 200 CE. This, and the adoption between 550 and 330 BCE of the Persian *qanāt* system whereby underground passages channelled aquifer water to irrigate desert lands, laid the basis for enhanced agricultural production, notably of wheat and barley. Indeed, Egypt's economic vibrancy precipitated a series of foreign conquests: the Persians from 525 to 402 BCE and 343 to 332 BCE, Greeks from 332 to 330 BCE, and Romans from 30 BCE to 646 CE. Egypt's reputation as the regional breadbasket was particularly high during good Nile flood years, especially from 30 BCE to 155 CE when the Roman-Egyptian regime shipped grain from the Delta to points throughout the Roman Empire and beyond. The colonial administrators forged close ties with the Egyptian elite upon whose cooperation they relied and, initially at least, promoted Egyptian production and trade.

   Alexandria, founded by Alexander the Great in 331 BCE on the site of Rhakotis, at the crossroads between the Mediterranean, Red Sea, and Nile Valley, quickly developed into a major industrial centre and IOW port famous for its 120–137 metre high lighthouse (Pharos). It produced internationally reputed linens, silks, and glassware (noted in China by at least the third century CE), processed local, Arabian, and

Somali incenses for the domestic and Mediterranean markets, and was the world's sole paper (papyrus) manufacturer until the BCE/CE changeover when skin parchments started to be used. It also exported low-value products including mats, clothing, and rope. Egypt and its hinterland was also a source of precious metals: In the first 200 years of their rule, the Romans transferred such amounts of Egyptian gold and silver to Rome that property prices there rose sharply and interest rates fell. Moreover, Egypt possessed its own closed monetary system, a widespread village-level banking network, and a vibrant credit market wherein money was advanced on various forms of collateral ranging from future harvests to the pledge of labour or use of land. It was also probably the only region of the Roman Empire where cheques were used in the modern sense of orders addressed by payers to their bankers but given to the payee. The output of a mint established in Alexandria, notably high from 42 to 66 CE, helped finance Roman imports of IOW spices, silk, and precious stones.

Alexandria rapidly became a major port and entrepôt. The Ptolemies (r. 323 to 30 BCE) improved the canal system linking the Mediterranean and Red seas, built dockyards at Alexandria and Clysma, and established naval patrols to protect Red Sea settlements and maritime trade. Egyptian vessels shipped fine cloth, craftwork, and jewellery to the Horn of Africa, and to India, a populous market and source of peppers. Over time, however, Arab merchants came to dominate Red Sea traffic. Their craft, using the Persian innovation of fore-and-aft rigging, and planks joined by coconut fibre, were able to sail closer to the wind than Egyptian vessels characterised by Phoenician-style square-rigged vessels and nailed timbers. By the BCE/CE changeover, Ethiopian and Somali traders were also prominent in the Red and Arabian seas.

Eurocentric histories consider that Roman demand for IOW luxuries stimulated the first regular direct monsoon-driven crossings between the Red Sea and India. Certainly, during the first century CE, some Roman merchants took the six-month voyage from Alexandria to Malabar, and considerable Mediterranean merchandise reached Arikamedu near Pondicherry, in southeast India. However, this traffic could more accurately be described as Egyptian because the vessels sailed from Egypt where IOW trade was conducted mostly by locally based Greeks, Syrians, Jews, and Arabs. As Latinist Eric Warmington noted: "True Romans visited Egypt not often, Arabia

and the Euphrates seldom, the Caspian and India never."[5] Some of
these agents belonged to consortiums, indicating that Egypt's maritime commerce involved modest as well as wealthy merchants.

Indian, Arab, and Persian merchants sailed on the more manage-
able northeast monsoon directly to Red Sea and northeast Africa
before vessels started to regularly use the stronger, and riskier, southwest monsoon to make direct crossings in the reverse direction. Thus
initially, Egyptian and Arab ships followed the Arabian coast north
to Cape Fartaque (15° 45′ N) before crossing to northwest India.
However, by 120 to 110 BCE, Egyptian boats were sailing from the
Red Sea to Malabar on the southwest (summer) monsoon, either directly, or via Socotra which by the third century BCE was a significant Indian entrepôt for trade with the western IOW. The Red Sea
section took about 30 days, and the crossing to Malabar 40 days –
much quicker than the coastal route favoured by Arabs. After sub-
duing certain Arabian rulers, notably in Yemen in 25 BCE and Aden in
1 BCE, and concluding treaties with other Red Sea powers, Egyptians
were no longer obliged to make landfalls en-route and started sailing
directly from Egypt to India. However, because of contrary winds in
the northern reaches of the Red Sea, most returning vessels docked
at Berenice, a more southerly Red Sea port, from where goods were
transported overland to Egyptian markets.

By the first century CE, some 120 merchant ships sailed each
year from the Egyptian port of Myos Hormos, on the Red Sea, to
Somalia and India, although insistence by Malabar authorities that
foreign merchants travel on only one vessel encouraged the sending
of one large ship a year of from 200 to 300 tons, and up to seven
sails, that could carry 700 passengers. To facilitate their IOW trade,
Alexandrian merchants established resident agents in major ports on
the Red Sea coasts, on Socotra, and in South India and Bengal. Chola,
the most prosperous Tamil kingdom, famed for its muslins, attracted
an important settlement of Egyptian traders and artisans. Its three
most important ports possessed lighthouses, perhaps in emulation
of Alexandria, and traded in large ships with entrepôts elsewhere in
India, Sri Lanka, and the Malay Peninsula. Valuable African produce,
such as the ivory laid in the tomb of king Zhao Mo of Nanyue in

[5] Eric Herbert Warmington, *The Commerce between the Roman Empire and India* (New
Delhi: Munshiram Manoharlai Publishers, 1995 – reprint of 1928 edition), 38.

Guangzhou in 122 BCE, was shipped to China through such trading centres.

In their turn, foreign merchants visited Alexandria. They included Ethiopians, "Trogodytes" (possibly Ethiopians or Somalis), Jews, Greeks, Italians, Sicilians, Syrians, Arabs, Persians, and merchants from Eastern Europe, Central Asia (Scythia), Afghanistan, Tajikistan (Bactria), and India. The scope of this commerce is reflected in the fact that, by the second century BCE, camphor from Baros in northwestern Sumatra was being used in Egypt to preserve mummies. Celebrating IOW commercial prosperity, and Alexandria's role in it, Dio Chrysostom (40–ca 115 CE) addressed the city as follows:

> You also receive goods from the whole Mediterranean sea because of the beauty of your harbours, the greatness of your fleet and by the abundance and selling of the goods of every place; and you have also the power over the outer seas, both the Red Sea and the Indian ... so that the trade ... of ... virtually the whole world comes to you.[6]

Axum

Despite being a highland power, Axum (in present-day Eritrea, and Tigray in Ethiopia) established a major maritime commercial empire in the first 500 years CE. Located close to the headwaters of the Blue Nile, Axum controlled busy caravan routes between the Red Sea and the southern and western Ethiopian plateau, East Africa, Upper Egypt, and Sudan. By the mid-first century CE, it had largely diverted trade flowing north from Sudan, away from Egypt and to the Axum-dominated Red Sea ports of Ptolemais Theron and Adulis.

Axum's exports included ivory (elephants existed in the forested highlands of Ethiopia into the 1800s), gold, hippopotamus hide, rhinoceros horn (rhinos also roamed the Ethiopian highlands), musk, incense, apes, and slaves from the African interior; emeralds from Red Sea Hills; turtle shell from the Dahlak Islands near Adulis that were in high demand in Muza (a Yemeni port) and Barygaza (in the Gulf of Cambay) for the manufacture of small boxes, plaques, and disks; obsidian from Red Sea islands generally; and probably civet (again from the Ethiopian highlands) and civet musk. Imports included

---

[6] Quoted in Gary K. Young, *Rome's Eastern Trade. International Commerce and Imperial Policy, 31 BC–AD 305* (London: Routledge, 2001), 52.

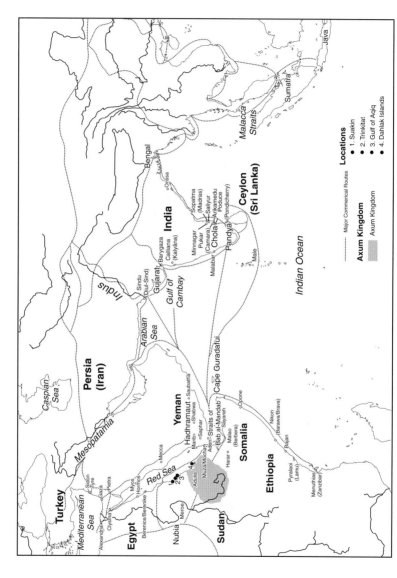

MAP 3.1 The Axumite Commercial Empire

Turkish, Italian, and Egyptian wine; Egyptian olive oil; Egyptian and Indian clothes and cloth; Indian iron and steel; and – of diverse origin – precious metal objects, iron, glass and brass ornaments, brass money, soft copper sheets used to manufacture cooking utensils and bracelets, copper drinking cups, axes, adzes, and swords. Of these, salt, ironware, linen, and cattle were the chief items distributed into the African interior.

Axum expanded militarily to dominate Ethiopia, portions of the southwestern Red Sea coast, and northwestern Arabia. From the end of the first century CE it minted its own coinage (Axumite coins have been found in Egypt, Palestine, Arabia, and India), and its commercial fleet, using Adulis crew and traditional IOW sewn boats, maintained a vigorous trade with Somalia, Socotra, Egypt, the Near and Middle East, India, and (through intermediaries) East Asia. By about the third century, Axum's merchants and courtiers had adopted Greek as a lingua franca, and in 303 CE its court converted to Christianity – a reflection of its important commercial relations with Christian communities in Egypt and the Levant.

The Horn of Africa

The Horn of Africa was geographically inhospitable, possessing an arid hinterland, and a coastline with few protected anchorages and little fresh water – a critical factor for traders as the dry season and trading season coincided, both starting in December. This helps to explain the importance to the Horn of neighbouring Aden and Socotra. At Aden, a major IOW emporium on the Arabian Peninsula, 170 km east of Bab-el-Mandeb (the Indian Ocean entrance to the Red Sea), Himyarites (Sabaeans) had in the first millennium BCE carved out of volcanic rock an intricate system of cisterns, dams, and channels to ensure adequate supplies of water. Socotra, an island 240 km east of Cape Guardafui and 955 km from Aden, on the main sea lanes connecting East Africa, the Red Sea, and the Persian Gulf, possessed sheltered anchorages, fresh water, and provisions. By the BCE/CE changeover Socotra was a major entrepôt, a renowned market for both East African and local products. The latter included dragon's blood (a deep-red resin used as stimulant, medicine, and dye), frankincense (used widely as an incense, also much valued by Egyptians as the chief ingredient of *kohl* which was used to make black eyeliner),

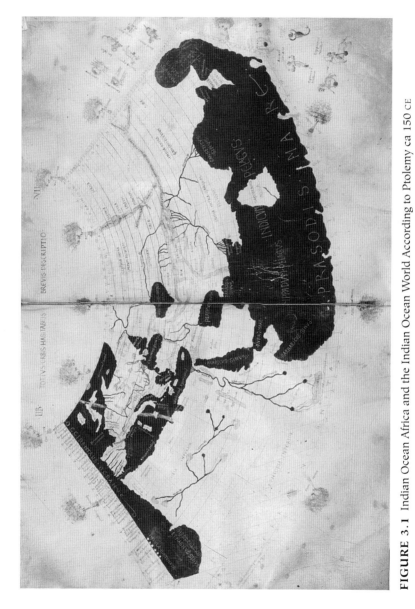

FIGURE 3.1 Indian Ocean Africa and the Indian Ocean World According to Ptolemy ca 150 CE

Note: Ptolemy's *Geography* (Harleian MS 7182, ff 58–59).

aloe (used in herbal medicine), and high-quality hawksbill turtle shell (valued in jewellery). The island was home to a cosmopolitan mercantile community of Indians, Arabs, Greco-Egyptians, Axumites, other Africans, and probably Persians. Greek, used possibly as early as 330 BCE, was by the sixth century the local lingua franca.

By the BCE/CE changeover, the Horn of Africa possessed a number of important seasonal markets. The Somali coast southeast of the Straits of Bab-el-Mandeb was characterised by a series of independent ports, possessing adequate mooring, which sold spices, myrrh and fragrant gums, tortoiseshell, ivory, and occasionally slaves, to foreign ships. Merchant vessels called there from South Yemen, probably with locally produced grain and IOW products: from Egypt they carried glassware, unripe olives, clothing, wine, wheat, barley, and tin; and from northwest India, notably Barygaza, wheat, Indian millet, rice, ghee, sesame oil, cotton cloth, girdles, and cane sugar. Additional imports, from non-specified sources, included drinking cups, iron, coinage, gold, silver, and precious stones. Immediately south of the Horn lay the more significant markets of Opone, Malao (Berbera), and "Nikon" (probably Barawa/Brava) – the latter two being favoured due to reasonably protected anchorage and fresh-water sources.

These ports, dominated by "Arab-African" merchants, were renowned sources of spices, especially cinnamon, which Indian, Arab, and African merchants exported to IOW markets, notably Egypt, Axum, Arabia, Persia, India, and Southeast Asia, as well as to the Mediterranean. Other exports included tortoise and turtle shell which was shipped to China for the manufacture of ornaments, and to Egypt, in part for re-export to Mediterranean markets, as well as ivory, and "better-quality" slaves destined chiefly for the Egyptian market. There was a return flow of cups, wine, maize, coloured glass, jewellery, gold, silver, rice, ghee, sesame oil, belts, sugar cane, precious stones, iron, Egyptian clothes and cloths, including fine linens, Persian pottery, and possibly copper.

There is considerable debate about the Horn as a source of spices. Greek language sources, notably the *Periplus* (ca 50–60 CE)[7] and Ptolemy's *Geography* (ca 150 CE),[8] which derived their information

---

[7] Anon, *The Periplus Maris Erythraei*, trans. & commentary Lionel Casson (Princeton: Princeton University Press, 1989).

[8] See J. Lennart Berggren and Alexander Jones, *Ptolemy's Geography by Ptolemy* (Princeton: Princeton University Press, 2001).

chiefly from merchants in Alexandria involved in IOW trade, emphasise the Horn of Africa, termed the "Cape of Spices", as the world's premier source of cassia and/or cinnamon, while Cosmas (mid-sixth century)[9] specified that cinnamon originated from the Somali interior. However, there is much confusion in the literature over the terms "cinnamon", which is not mentioned in the *Periplus*, and "cassia". Both are of the same generic origin (belonging to the genus *Cinnamomum*) and were used for similar purposes. The Greek texts might have been referring to plants indigenous to the countries at the eastern end of the Red Sea. Certainly Somalia produced myrrh and frankincense. However, cinnamon and cassia could not have grown in northeast Africa or Arabia. Derived respectively from *Cinnamon zeylanicum Nees* and *Cinnamomum cassia Blume,* they were members of the laurel family and required a constant supply of moisture – something signally absent in that region. Indeed, a passage from another early source, Pliny the Elder (23–79 CE), appears to indicate an overseas origin for cinnamon:

> Cinnamomum, or cinnamum, which is the same thing, grows in the country of the Æthiopians, who are united by intermarriages with the Troglodytæ. These last, after buying it of their neighbours, carry it over vast tracts of sea, upon rafts, which are neither steered by rudder, nor drawn or impelled by oars or sails. Nor yet are they aided by any of the resources of art, man alone, and his daring boldness, standing in place of all these; in addition to which, they choose the winter season, about the time of the equinox, for their voyage, for then a south easterly wind is blowing; these winds guide them in a straight course from gulf to gulf, and after they have doubled the promontory of Arabia, the northeast wind carries them to a port of the Gebanitæ, known by the name of Ocilia. Hence it is that they steer for this port in preference; and they say that it is almost five years before the merchants are able to effect their return, while many perish on the voyage. In return for their wares, they bring back articles of glass and copper, cloths, buckles, bracelets, and necklaces.[10]

Some scholars contend that this passage refers to a maritime trade in spices directly from the Indonesian Spice Islands. This is a plausible hypothesis given that cloves, which until the late eighteenth

[9] *The Christian Topography of Cosmas, an Egyptian Monk,* trans. J.W. McCrindle (London: Hakluyt Society, 1897).
[10] Pliny, *Natural History,* ed. & trans. John Bostock and H.T. Riley (London: Henry Bohn, 1855), 138.

century were produced only in the Molucca Islands, in eastern Indonesia, were being shipped to India and China by about the fourth and third century BCE respectively, and the Mediterranean via Egypt by the first century CE. However, most scholars consider that it probably refers to trade with South Asia, the source of black pepper (Malabar) and cinnamon (Sri Lanka), and a staging post for maritime trade with the eastern IOW. Thus, the conventional interpretation of Egypt's ignorance of the true origins of cinnamon and cassia is that these spices were initially shipped from Southeast Asia and southern China to India. From India they were transported to Somalia in Arabian or Indian ships, the captains of which kept the true source of the spices secret in order to maintain their hold on a highly lucrative traffic. Nevertheless, the *Periplus* was written as a commercial guide by someone with a detailed knowledge of western Indian Ocean trade, while none of the early texts, including that of Procopius (sixth century),[11] note India as a source of spices. This adds to speculation that the spice trade may have been conducted by Indonesian traders.

Moreover, reports in Europe of cinnamon and other spices originating from northeast Africa persisted into the eighteenth century, well after their true origins had become clear. Thus in 1790, the Scottish explorer James Bruce (1730–1794) noted Somalia as "the Regio Cinnamonifera where a considerable quantity of that wild cinnamon grows, which the Italian druggists call canella";[12] and as late as 1849, Irish geographer William Cooley (ca 1795–1883) informed the Royal Geographical Society that cinnamon was native to northern Somaliland.[13]

By contrast, frankincense and myrrh were sourced on both sides of the Red Sea. Most Arabian frankincense probably came from Dhofar, in present-day Oman, between the coastal plain and the lower slopes of the Qara Mountains. In Somaliland, two species of frankincense, *Carterii* and *Frereana*, grew in an area topographically similar to Oman that ran from the coast, some 13 km east of Malao

---

[11] H.B. Dewing (ed.), *Procopius* 7 vols. (Cambridge, MA: Harvard University Press, 1914–40).

[12] James Bruce, *Travels to Discover the Source of the Nile in the Years 1768–1773* (London: Robinson, 1790), vol. 1, 444.

[13] Jon R. Godsall, "Richard Burton's Somali Expedition, 1854–55: Its Wider Historical Context and Planning" *Journal of the Royal Asiatic Society of Great Britain and Ireland* 11. 2 (2001): 155.

(Berbera), to a vast interior plateau. The adult myrrh tree, which stood at a height of between 2 and 4.5 metres, and was harvested in the dry season, grew on the African side of the Red Sea at Ras Khanzira, east of Berbera, and in a region running from the coast between Adulis and Heis inland as far as the Nogal Valley. However, the main area of commercial exploitation and export of frankincense and myrrh was the hinterland of Mocha, in Yemen. The major processing centres were Alexandria for Mediterranean markets; and for Persian Gulf and Indian markets, Gherra (possibly near present-day al'-Uqair on the east coast of the Persian Gulf), Omana (possibly Sohar or Muscat in Oman), and Barbaricum, (a port at the mouth of the Indus), and possibly Barygaza and Muziris (Cranganore/Kodungallur). The trade in incense brought enormous wealth to South Arabia and, presumably, to the Somali ports and traders dealing in it.

Azania

Claims to a very early IOW maritime connection with East Africa have been discussed in the previous chapter. Certainly by the BCE/CE changeover, the southern sector of IOA also benefitted from relatively benign environmental factors and Azania – the term used in the *Periplus* and by Ptolemy for the modern-day Swahili coast of East Africa (called "Zanj" by later Arab geographers) – formed an integral part of the IOW economy. Merchants from Mocha, a South Arabian entrepôt, played a particularly important role in its external trade, although other Arab, Egyptian, Mediterranean, and perhaps Indian and Axumite trading vessels also traded with Azania. While the Azanian littoral was more hospitable than that of Somalia, only certain offshore archipelagos possessed perennial fresh-water sources and coral-reef protected anchorages. Some of the earliest trading posts thus appeared on these islands, notably Bajun (off southeast Somalia), Pyralaoi (probably Lamu, off northeast Kenya), and Menuthias/Menouthias (off the coast of present-day northeast Tanzania). However, some foreign traders visited regions further south, possibly the Comoros, Madagascar, or even the Natal coast.

On the return voyage to the Red Sea, Persian Gulf or India on the southwest monsoon (June–October), the optimum departure point for ocean-going vessels sailing from Azania was from ports north of Zanzibar. Hence sizeable markets south of that point required resident

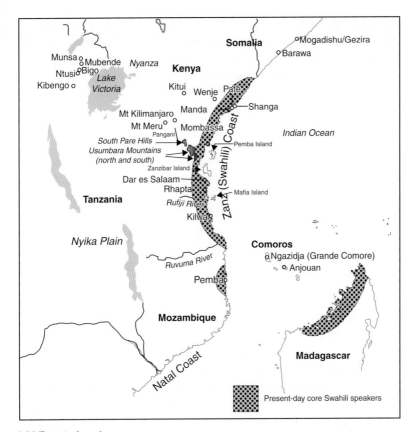

MAP 3.2 Azania

Note: Produced by Carl Hughes, IOWC.

agents to store both imported goods and export staples, collected from neighbouring and more southerly regions. The largest such location was Rhapta, the southernmost stop for Egyptian merchants, which by the first century CE was home to many foreign ship captains and traders, mostly Arabs, who had taken local wives and spoke the local language.

By the second century, Rhapta had developed into what the *Periplus* calls a "metropolis", a term applied elsewhere only to Meroe and Axum in IOA, Saphar and Saubatha in Yemen, and Minnagar in India. Rhapta's location is the subject of considerable conjecture. The *Periplus* indicates that it was situated near a coastal promontory and major river somewhere in the vicinity of Menuthias – generally considered to be modern-day Pemba. Scholars have placed Rhapta variously opposite Manda and Pate, at Mnyuzi 48 km up the Pangani River, in the Rufiji estuary opposite Mafia, and near present-day Dar es Salaam – which a recent study combining GIS techniques with the information in the *Periplus* and Ptolemy's *Geography* indicates to be its most probable location.[14]

Menuthias and Rhapta exported considerable quantities of tortoise shell, considered the most valuable after the Indian variety. In addition, Rhapta exported large quantities of ivory, classed second in quality to that of Adulis. In IOW markets, African ivory was generally considered superior (larger, whiter, straighter, and more malleable) to Asian ivory. Rhapta was, alongside Adulis, the sole IOA source of rhinoceros horn, exported chiefly to China. It also produced small quantities of nautilus shell. Further, it is likely that the relative efficiency of sea over land transport permitted East Africa, unlike early West Africa, to export non-luxury commodities such as mangrove poles that, dense, heavy, and termite-resistant, were in high demand in Arabia and the Persian Gulf for house construction; and iron ore or semi-processed iron, and Mozambique copal, for the Indian and Iraqi markets respectively.

Imports into Azania included lances (from Muza), axes, knives, small awls, glass objects including beads and, in some localities, wine and grain. Michael Pearson asserts that Muza merchants imported wheat and ghee,[15] and Pra Shirodkar that maize, rice, ghee, sesame, cotton, sugar, and iron goods, were shipped to Azania directly from India,[16] although Sunil Gupta contends that literary and archaeological evidence around the BCE/CE changeover for Indian exports to Africa points to only northern IOA markets.[17] From excavations at Unguja Ukuu, on Zanzibar, Chami claims to have discovered pre-Islamic Roman and Egyptian imports, and from Rufiji Delta sites, Middle Eastern pottery, glass fragments, darkish beads, and "Roman" (possibly Egyptian) beads.[18] However, Marilee Wood considers that,

---

[14] See Carl Hughes and Ruben Post, "A GIS Approach to Finding the Metropolis of Rhapta" in Gwyn Campbell (ed.), *Early Exchange between Africa and the Wider Indian Ocean World* (New York: Palgrave, 2016), 135–156.

[15] M.N. Pearson, "The Indian Ocean and the Red Sea" in Nehemia Levtzion and Randall L. Pouwels (eds), *The History of Islam in Africa* (Athens: Ohio University Press, 2000), 37.

[16] P.P. Shirodkar, "Slavery in Coastal India" *Purabhilekh-Puratatva* 3.1 (1985): 28.

[17] Sunil Gupta, "Contact between East Africa and India in the first Millennium CE" in Campbell (ed.), *Early Exchange*.

[18] See reference to Chami in Select Bibliography at end of chapter.

while Roman captains may have shipped beads from India and Sri Lanka to Azania in the early centuries CE, Unguja Ukuu and similar imported beads are of an eighth- to ninth-century CE Middle Eastern origin.[19]

Coastal-Hinterland Trade

Most scholars now reject the traditional view that IOA ports formed outward-oriented enclaves, commercially integrated into the IOW maritime network but largely isolated from the deep interior. Certainly, there existed considerable geographical barriers to coastal-interior linkages, notably deserts and mountainous plateaux to the north and northeast, and the wide arid Nyika plain to the hinterland of the central Swahili coastal belt. A further hindrance was the tsetse-fly zone of equatorial East Africa, where the prevalence of trypano-somiasis necessitated the use of human porters rather than freight animals. This restricted the volume and value of exports, in contrast to West Africa where from the third millennium BCE camels sustained a growing trans-Saharan trade with North Africa, the Mediterranean world, and the Middle East. Nevertheless, coastal-interior linkages existed in both northern and southern sectors of IOA. As noted in the previous chapter, by at least the time of Eratosthenes (276–194 BCE), who lived in Alexandria, Egyptians had an accurate idea of the Nile's course as far as the confluence of the White and Blue Niles, and were aware that its source lay in two lakes to the south. Nero (r. 54–68 CE) ordered an expedition that explored the Nile as far as the Sudd, and Ptolemy's (ca 150 CE) report of a trader's visit to a land inhabited by the "Agisymba" people that abounded in rhinoceroses may indicate that Egyptians had by then reached the headwaters of the Nile.

Further, by the sixth century CE, sub-Saharan "Sasu" gold was being exported through Axum's main port of Adulis, primarily to Alexandria. There is speculation that Sasu was located in the gold-rich areas of present-day Botswana or Zimbabwe from where gold was transported overland, possibly along the Rift Valley into southern Sudan or southeastern Ethiopia. As Wilfred Schoff commented:

---

[19] Marilee Wood, "Eastern Africa and the Indian Ocean World in the First Millennium CE: The Glass Bead Evidence" in Campbell (ed.), *Early Exchange*.

This rift valley of East Africa is a striking feature of its topography, and must have had a great bearing on its early trade ... It is a natural depression beginning at the lower shore of the Red Sea between Massowa and the straits, taking a south-westerly direction through Abyssinia [Ethiopia] to the British and German East African possessions [Kenya, Uganda, Tanzania], including lakes Rudolf, Nyanza [Victoria], Tanganyika and Nyassa, and running almost to the Zambesi ... it is probable that the tribes inhabiting it were in more or less regular commercial relations with the North, and that it was a more important avenue of trade than the sea-coast with its broad and un-healthy swamps.[20]

According to Schoff, "Mashonaland (northern Zimbabwe) gold, which lay at no great distance south of the [Rift] valley, might to some extent have found its way along this natural trade route by exchange from tribe to tribe."[21] Chami supports Schoff's theory, arguing that salt as well as gold travelled from interior southeast Africa to the Great Lakes region and Ethiopia, or down the Nile to Egypt.[22]

The first major imports into the hinterland of Azania were Indian Ocean seashells, and the coral grinding stones used to transform them into adornments and currency. Coastal shell beads have been discovered in the deep plateau interior of Mozambique dating to around 2000 BCE. From around 300 BCE, with the onset of regular monsoon sail, enhanced maritime trade stimulated coastal-interior linkages. The monsoon system guaranteed that, during the same season each year, merchant vessels arrived on the East African coast where they remained in a limited number of ports for four to six months until the monsoon changed. These monsoon-based trading centres created significant local, albeit seasonal, linkages. This is illustrated by Berbera, in Somalia, which during the northeast monsoon from September to April operated a seasonal market that endured into the 1800s, attracting vessels from the Red Sea, Arabia and probably the Persian Gulf and northwest India. Observers in the early nineteenth century noted that Berbera's population exploded to between 10,000 and 20,000 during the trading season.[23] Of vital importance

[20] Wilfred H. Schoff (trans.) [ca 1911], *The Periplus of the Erythraean Sea* (New Delhi: Munshiram Manoharlal, 2001), 98–9.
[21] Ibid., 98–9.
[22] Felix A. Chami, "East Africa and the Middle East relationship from the first millennium BC to about 1500 AD" *Journal des africanistes* 72.2 (2002): 21–37.
[23] C.J. Cruttenden, "Memoir on the Western or Edoor Tribes, inhabiting the Somali Coast of N-E Africa, with the Southern branches of the family of Darrood, resident

was traders' access to good water. At Berbera two wells were sunk on the beach, but their water turned brackish over time causing wealthier merchants to send for fresh water from neighbouring inlets. By the first century CE, at about the time of the construction of Aden's elaborate water system, a 14.5-km-long stone and lime aqueduct was constructed at Berbera, conveying inland spring water to a reservoir on the beach.

Visiting vessels also required maintenance. In bigger coastal centres, this created considerable local activity, including tree felling, carpentry, and rope and sail manufacture. Demand from visiting crews, almost exclusively male, also prompted the provision of linguistic and religious services. Further, as ships' merchants and crews, almost exclusively male, often remained for up to six months, they established a demand for local entertainment, including sexual services. In some regions, women hired themselves out to foreign merchants for the trading season as wives and commercial agents, their linguistic expertise, knowledge of customs, and local connections often proving invaluable to the visitors. Permanent trading posts required a far greater infrastructure, including houses and stores. They also hired locals, both unskilled, as porters, packers, and guards, and skilled, including artisans, translators, guides, supervisors, "wives", prostitutes, entertainers, and servants – to perform more than seasonal services.

Demand for certain staples, such as ivory, from the outset one of the most valued IOA exports, stimulated coastal-interior linkages even further. The tracking and killing of elephants required the expertise of hunter-gatherer groups who were itinerant and rarely found on the coast. Again, elephant herds along the littoral were unlikely to have satisfied seasonally concentrated demand, and were liable to shift location. Wild elephants are shy and travel long distances. Adult males, that possess the largest and thus most valuable tusks, often travel alone or in small groups with fellow males, unencumbered by young elephants. Thus the collection and transport of ivory necessarily involved ever-increasing links with the interior. Chami argues for early and continous coastal-interior trading links with interior Bantu-speaking groups, with Cushites who supplied cattle, and (possibly via Cushites) with Khoisan hunter-gathers who supplied ivory, rhinoceros horn, and tortoise shell – the most valued export staples.

on the banks of the Webbe Shebeyli, commonly called the River Webbe", Aden, 12 May 1848, in *Journal of the Royal Geographical Society of London* 19 (1849): 49–76.

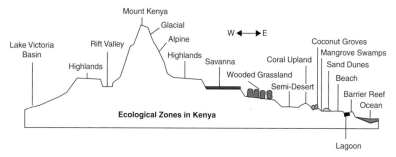

FIGURE 3.2 Ecological Zones, Kenya

Note: Adapted by Carl Hughes of the IOWC from www.cotf.edu/ete/modules/rift/
ecozonepict.html – reprinted by permission of Westview Press.

By the second century CE, visiting traders reported the existence
of two snow-covered mountains (Ptolemy referred to one as the
"Mountain of the Moon") in interior Azania that were reputedly the
source of the Nile. These were probably Kilimanjaro (5,895 m) and
Meru (4,566 m), respectively the highest mountain in Africa and
second highest in Tanzania. According to Ptolemy, a Greek merchant
named Diogenes even witnessed the mountains first hand and noted
two sizeable lakes in their vicinity. Large swamps lie just to the north
of Kilimanjaro, while trade caravans travelling west to Angola and
north to Guinea and northern IOA habitually passed Lake Victoria,
some 300 km to the northwest of the mountains.

Long-distance inter-regional trade developed early in the Great
Lakes region, where hunter-gatherers, pastoralists, and cultivators
exchanged their specialist, and mineral and craft, products. The production of basketry, pottery, cloth, leather, salt, and wood and metal
objects, and other artisanal products, required varying degrees of
often inherited specialisation; and were sold in response to demand in
local, regional, and long-distance markets – rarer, more valuable, often
low-bulk products being traded at greater distances than cheaper bulk
commodities. Some goods, including fine salt, iron bars, cloth, beads,
and seashells, served as commodity monies, as probably did gold –
alluvial and mined: Over 200 prehistoric gold mines operated between
Domboshoba and the Tati River in Botswana. Valuable products, such
as gold and salt, attracted merchants from afar, and developed linkages
that could transform them into industrial and commercial centres.
For example, fine salt, produced from around the fifth century BCE
at the Uvinza brine springs, in the Kigoma region of Tanzania, east of

Lake Tanganyika, necessitated woodcutters and porters, and proved so valuable that it dictated the trajectory of caravan routes and attracted the attention of political authorities.

Indeed, advocating the formation of a vast system of interlocking trade routes, Chami argues that Rhapta was by around 200 CE part of an Early Iron Age "industrial complex" linking the coast to the South Pare Hills and Usambara Mountains of interior northeastern Tanzania. He asserts further that by the fourth century an emerging Swahili Early Iron Age coastal culture ran from Gezira in Somalia to Chibuene in Mozambique, and across the sea to the Comoros and northwest Madagascar – a network previously associated with the Late Iron Age culture of the seventh to thirteenth centuries (see Chapter 6).

4
–

Economic Instability, ca 300 to ca 900 CE

From the late second to late eighth century CE, the IOW global economy experienced significant turbulence that had a major impact, both on the main IOW polities of China, South Asia, the Middle East, and Egypt, and on eastern Africa where Rhapta disappeared from the record. The downturn in the IOW economy is conventionally ascribed to political instability, but it is increasingly clear that environmental factors were as, if not more important. This chapter addresses these issues for the IOW in general, and IOA in particular.

The dominant view is that political factors were the chief cause of volatility in the IOW from around 300 CE. In the western IOW, military conflict between Persians and Romans, that started in 92 BCE and continued for some 700 years, exacted an increasing social, economic, and political toll. In the third century CE, the Persian Parthian Empire collapsed. In the Roman Empire, internecine strife erupted, accentuated by debasement of the currency – which led to inflation, loss of commercial confidence, and an increase in barter exchange. At the same time, the disintegration of the Han Empires (206 BCE–220 CE) heavily disrupted economic life in the eastern IOW. For much of this period northern China was wracked by political turmoil and crippled by the costs of a huge bureaucracy: Han China had an estimated 100,000 civilian officials, over three times the number of bureaucrats in the Roman Empire. Political turmoil, accentuated by economic instability, resulted in mass migration from Central China to regions south of the Yangtze, particularly marked in the fourth century. In 420, engulfed by internecine conflict, the Eastern Jin dynasty (317–420 CE) collapsed.

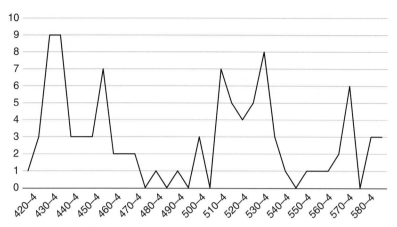

FIGURE 4.1 Maritime Tribute Missions to China, 420–584 (in five-year clusters)

Note: From Wang Gungwu, "The Nanhai Trade: A Study of the Early History of Chinese Trade in the South China Sea" *Journal of the Malayan Branch of the Royal Asiatic Society* 31.2 (182) (1958): 51.

Relatively political stability, notably in Axum, Ethiopia, and under the Sasanian (224–651) and Hindu Gupta (320–550) regimes, helped maintain some buoyancy for the IOW global economy in the fourth to fifth centuries CE. Indeed, trans-IOW maritime exchange received considerable impetus when, in response to blockages to the Silk Road, Chinese authorities diverted overland trade to sea routes and, from about 350 CE, Southeast Asian mariners established the first regular direct shipping routes between Sri Lanka and China. The Chinese economy received additional stimulation in the fifth century, when iron and agricultural production increased.

Nevertheless, by the mid-sixth century, major IOW polities started to break down. The disintegration of the Gupta Empire in the mid-sixth century is traditionally ascribed to foreign invasions and domestic rebellions. In Persia, internecine political rivalry undermined central authority and imperial power withered, while further west the political, economic and social structure of the Byzantine Empire weakened beyond repair. In China, revolt erupted in 541 and 548 leading to the breakdown of the southern regime, and to mass warfare throughout the country. After the fall of the Sui dynasty (581–618), the Tang dynasty (618–907), traditionally viewed as one of the most successful in Chinese history, faced major unrest and economic decline in the north from 755, and in Central China from the 820s. China's IOW maritime relations suffered major blows in 758 when Arab and Persian commercial agents, angered at deteriorating security and trade, sacked and abandoned Guangzhou (Canton), and in 760 when Chinese rebels allegedly massacred thousands of Arab and Persian traders in Yangzhou, an important entrepôt on the Yangtze River.

Human-Environment Interaction

Absent from conventional explanations for political and economic instability across the IOW in the early to mid-first millennium CE is the role of adverse environmental forces. For example, a cluster of volcanic eruptions from 235 to 285 CE resulted in a significant fall in temperatures, widespread crop failure, and the onset of lengthy arid periods over large sectors of the northern IOW. From 338 to 377, China experienced one of the worst droughts in 3,000 years, with another severe drought from 440 to 494. In the northern hemisphere generally, the climate became markedly cooler in the sixth century and remained so until the mid-seventh century when it became warmer and wetter. There were, however, significant regional variations. For example, a weakening in the southwest monsoon from around 250 to 800 CE, and a northwards displacement of the ITCZ in the northern hemisphere summer to about 30° N, resulted in markedly wetter summers for southern Arabia and Red Sea Africa, and a generally warmer wetter period across the western IOW in the fourth and early fifth centuries.

There is growing evidence that, even before the BCE/CE change-over, human activity had a climatic impact, notably through the use of fire and innovations in water collection, control, and distribution, animal and plant domestication, and iron production. These techniques, which lay at the heart of the Neolithic Revolution, had laid the basis for the emergence of the core centralised IOW polities in China, South Asia, and the Middle East, and for the rise of the trans-IOW trading system. During the first upsurge in the IOW global economy from ca 300 BCE to ca 300 CE, there occurred a rapid expansion in water-control systems, crop cultivation, and cattle stocks, all of which helped to sustain rapidly growing sedentary populations, and large armies. At the same time, however, vast numbers of trees were felled to create fields for cultivation, for boat and building construction, and for domestic and industrial fuel – notably for iron-smelting and brick-firing. For example, deforestation in the Ganga Valley region of present-day Punjab, Haryana, western Uttar Pradesh, and the neighbouring region of Rajasthan, accelerated from around 200 BCE due to the use of burnt bricks in house construction, and extensive cattle grazing. Some scholars estimate that by the BCE/CE changeover fully 10 per cent of land on the planet was under anthropogenic use, rising to over 60 per cent in core IOW regions, such as in the Yellow River, Brahmaputra, Indus, and Tigris-Euphrates valleys.[1]

Accelerated forest clearance increased soil erosion, notably in hilly regions, and affected precipitation patterns. The regularisation of a strong monsoon system resulted in annual seasonal flooding of wetlands, which increased methane emissions, and these rose significantly due to a rapid expansion of human and cattle populations from 300 BCE to 300 CE. More critically, the huge increase in domestic and industrial wood burning released large amounts of carbon dioxide into the atmosphere. This had significant climatic impact over the same period. By contrast, methane and CO_2 emissions decreased significantly from 200 to 700 CE – reflecting a general decline in economic activity across the IOW.

The negative climatic impact of human activity was compounded by the onset of periodically intense volcanic activity. It is estimated that between 176 and 1000 CE, seven large volcanic eruptions occurred, the three largest occurring in 535, 662 (±12 years) and 758 (±10). The 535 eruption was massive (VEI 6+), causing the "greatest atmospheric aerosol loading event of the past 2000 years," which in turn lowered temperatures globally by an estimated 3°C for a decade. In 536, the Roman historian Procopius stated that "the sun gave forth its light without brightness like the moon during this whole year, and it seemed exceedingly like the sun in eclipse"[2] while John of Ephesus, another eye-witness, noted

> the sun became dark and its darkness lasted for eighteen months. Each day it shone for about four hours, and still this light was no more than a feeble shadow. Everyone declared that the sun would never recover its full light again. The fruits did not ripen, and the wine tasted like sour grapes.[3]

[1] Jed O. Kaplan, Kristen M. Krumhardt, Erle C. Ellis, William F. Ruddiman, Carsten Lemmen and Kees Klein Goldewijk, "Holocene Carbon Emissions as a Result of Anthropogenic Land Cover Change" *The Holocene* 21.5 (2011): 775–91.

[2] Quoted in Todd Richardson, *Plague, Weather and Wool* (Bloomington, IN: Author House, 2009), 84.

[3] Quoted in Simon Winchester, *Krakatoa. The Day the World Exploded: August 27, 1883* (New York: Perennial, 2003), 115.

TABLE 4.1 *Volcanic Eruptions 176 to 1000 CE of over 14 kg km^{-2} registered in the Antarctic Ice Core*[*]

Year	Duration (years)	Volcanic Flux (f)	Year	Duration (years)	Volcanic Flux (f)
318	2.3	21.8	629	2.7	27.1
346	2.5	22.4	662	3.6	38.4
411	3.6	14.7	758	3.8	41.8
535	3.2	41.9	908	4.9	26.4

[*] Dave G. Ferris, Jihong Cole-Dai, Angelica R. Reyes, and Drew M. Budner, "South Pole Ice Core Record of Explosive Volcanic Eruptions in the First and Second Millennia A.D. and Evidence of a Large Eruption in the Tropics Around 535 A.D." *Journal of Geophysical Research* 116. D17308 (2011) DOI:10.1029/2011JD015916.

The protracted global cooling that followed these volcanic eruptions ruined harvests, causing massive food shortages. For instance, China experienced a significant cool and arid period in the sixth and seventh centuries: From ca 535 to 538 there were summer frosts and snow, drought, and widespread famine, and in 536–537, some 80 per cent of the population of northern China died of starvation.

In its turn, the Gupta Empire in India, although politically stable in the early years of the sixth century, collapsed in 550. Its capital, Pataliputra, situated at the confluence of the Ganges, Gandhaka, and Son rivers, was destroyed, possibly by a major flood that devastated the Ganges plain. A long period of weaker southwest monsoons from around 250 CE resulted in less precipitation (India experienced prolonged droughts from the early sixth century, notably in the eighth century) and a series of poor harvests, while the 535 eruption provoked mass harvest failure and famine. Recently discovered Jain inscriptions dating to around the end of the Gupta era speak in apocalyptic terms of droughts, floods, famine, and depopulation in the Ganges region. The mathematician Varāhamihira (505–587), who lived through the 535 eruption, offers a description of "dust" in his prophetic writings that is remarkably similar to the comments made by Mediterranean eyewitnesses of the volcanic dust veil of 535:

> Dust appearing prominently, blocking as it were, the entire sky at sunrise for a whole day or two continuously, augurs terrible disaster. When a thick cloud spreads over a kingdom for two nights continuously, it should be understood that the country will be the victim of foreign aggression. If dust falls continuously for three or even four nights, food

grains and liquids or juicy substances will be destroyed; and if for five nights, there will be mutiny in the armies of kings.[4]

These events led to mass migration, such as that of Jains to the south and west, and to a sharp decline in both urban life and India-IOW trade. For instance, the number of official missions from India to China fell from 68 in the sixth century, to 15 in the first half of the seventh century. Further west, widespread famine affected the Near East in 546, followed by two years of cattle disease, while from 600 to 724, the Middle East experienced unusually cold winters, as well as, in January 748, a major earthquake.

Such environmental factors were accentuated by disease. At least three widespread and devastating pandemics hit the IOW in the first millennium CE. The first ("Antonine Plague"), in the late second century, probably smallpox, originated in the Near East. The second ("Plague of Cyprian"), from 250 to 271, possibly smallpox but more probably influenza, caused enormous social and economic dislocation, and seriously undermined Roman imperial power. A series of possibly related smallpox epidemics hit China from 265 to 313. The third ("Justinian Plague"), which broke out in 541, in the wake of massive volcanic eruptions in 535 and ca 539–540, was the world's first pandemic of bubonic plague. The bubonic plague results from the bite of an infected flea. After an incubation period of 3 to 7 days, patients typically experience a sudden onset of fever, chills, headaches, body aches, weakness, vomiting, and nausea. Zachariah of Mitylene, who lived through the first Justinian outbreak, noted:

> And this plague, which is the rising of a swelling on the groins and in the arm-pits of men, began in Egypt and Ethiopia and Alexandria and Nubia and Palestine and Phoenicia and Arabia and Byzantium and Italy and Africa and Sicily and Gaul, and it penetrated to Galatia and Cappadocia and Armenia and Antioch and Arzanene and Mesopotamia and gradually to the land of the Persians and to the peoples of the North-East, and it slew. And those who were afflicted with the scourge and happened to recover and not die trembled and shook: and it was known that it was a scourge from Satan who was ordered by God to destroy men.[5]

---

[4] M. Ramakrishna Bhat, *Varāhamihira's Brhat Samhita* (Delhi: Motilal Banarsidass, 1997), Part 1. 328–9.

[5] *The Syriac Chronicle Known as that of Zachariah of Mitylene*, trans. F.J. Hamilton and E.W. Brooks (London: Methuen, 1899), 313.

The bubonic plague erupted in 11 epidemics in 8 to 12 year cycles from 541 to 654 CE, while major outbreaks continued until 747. The literary evidence indicates that it ravaged parts of the Red Sea region, Europe, and the Middle East. Ethiopia was first affected in 541, as was Egypt. The following year, the Roman Empire was hit. The plague probably caused hostilities between the Persians and Byzantines to cease from 545 to 547. It erupted amongst Ethiopians in Yemen in 548, and hit Iraq in 627–628, 638, and 689, and again in a further six epidemics in the first 75 years of the eighth century – a particularly severe outbreak occurring in 745. Famine often preceded an outbreak of plague, as in Alexandria in 618, and Syria in 638 – although in Syria in 546 famine followed the plague.

Disease had a more dramatic impact upon human demography than famine or warfare. The Antonine plague had an estimated overall mortality rate of 7 to 10 per cent, rising to 15 per cent and higher in major population centres, children being the most vulnerable. In its initial phase, bubonic plague entailed from 25 to 30 per cent mortality amongst affected populations. Epidemics, combined with warfare and famine, caused mass abandonment of farms and villages, and contributed to periodically precipitous demographic declines. It is estimated that from 541 to 700 CE the global population fell by 50 to 60 per cent, largely because of plague. Angus Maddison estimated that the populations of India and China remained stagnant in the first millennium CE at about 75 million and 59 million respectively – that of China dipping to 42 million in the 740s; and John Durand estimated that the Chinese population fell from about 71 million in 1 CE to 37 million in 705, before recovering slightly to 57 million by 1000 CE.[6]

Indian Ocean Africa

Maddison, following Colin McEvedy and Richard Jones, considered that in sharp contrast to Asian demographic trends, the population of IOA trebled from 7.3 million to 21 million in the first millennium CE, and that central East Africa (from present-day Kenya to Mozambique,

[6] Maddison Angus, *The World Economy. Historical Statistics* (Paris: OECD, 2003), 249, 256; John D. Durand, "Historical Estimates of World Population: An Evaluation" *Population and Development Review* 3.3 (1977): 261.

including the Great Lakes region) increased almost nine-fold from
4.25 million to 38 million.[7] This would, in turn, have reflected phenom-
enally favourable climatic conditions and a dramatic rise in agricultural productivity. However, reconstructions of the early demographic
history of Tropical Africa are "highly speculative and hypothetical",[8]
and the McEvedy and Jones estimates have proven misguided even for
the nineteenth century.[9] Indeed, the evidence points to IOA experiencing much the same climatic and economic instability as the rest of
the IOW during the first millennium CE.

Egypt

Egypt was of critical importance to the imperial Roman economy: Its
gold and silver paid for Roman imports from the IOW and helped
pay military salaries, as did Egyptian grain which also provisioned the
massive armies required to maintain the empire. The Vandal invasion
of North Africa in 429 CE, the capture of Carthage in 439, and subsequent establishment of a Vandal state, resulted in the loss to Rome
of major grain-producing areas of modern-day Tunisia, heightening
the value of Egypt as the granary of the empire. Egyptian fleets and
recruits also largely underpinned the imperial military and mercantile
presence in the Mediterrannean and Red Sea.

The conventional view is that Roman imperial authority and economic power declined in the early centuries CE for political and economic reasons: internecine strife and the high cost of maintaining
imperial frontiers in the face of growing foreign aggression. This was
evident in Egypt, which Stewart Oost considered "the most signal
failure" of Roman imperial rule.[10] In 66 CE, the Jews of Alexandria
rebelled, leading two years later to a brutal military response in which
50,000 of them were massacred. Another uprising occurred from
115 to 117 CE. In order to suppress a further revolt in 297, the Egyptian
regime destroyed Canopus (an ancient town situated on the eastern

---

[7] Madison, *The World Economy*, 207–64.
[8] Durand, "Historical Estimates", 279.
[9] See e.g. Gwyn Campbell, "The State and Pre-colonial Demographic History: The
Case of Nineteenth Century Madagascar" *Journal of African History* 32.3 (1991):
415–45.
[10] Stewart Irvin Oost, "The Alexandrian Seditions under Philip and Gallienus" *Classical
Philology* 56.1 (1961): 15.

limits of modern-day Alexandria) and beseiged Alexandria. Syrian forces invaded Egypt from 270 to 272 CE, and repeatedly raided its border regions in the late fourth century. Moreover, Roman authorities imposed such heavy taxation on Egyptian peasants that some fled their villages, while in the sixth century others attacked a military detachment sent to collect taxes. A further serious rebellion erupted in 610.

All this caused considerable political and economic damage. However, environmental factors arguably had a more significant impact. In 320, Alexandria was hit by an earthquake. In July 365, a tsunami that followed an 8.5+ magnitude earthquake on Crete, one of the largest ever recorded, devastated the Nile Delta, and destroyed part of Alexandria – an event commemorated annually for centuries thereafter by a festival termed the "day of horror". Prolonged low Nile levels from 111 to 124 CE, 151 to 170, 254 to 265, and again at the close of the third century, resulted in sharp falls in agricultural output which impacted heavily on the health of peasants, notably in the Delta where two-thirds of the Egyptian population was concentrated. Delta peasants were also vulnerable to two of the most socioeconomically devastating parasitic diseases – schistosomiasis, passed on by the liver fluke, and malaria. Causing debilitation and often death, these diseases depleted the manpower resources required to maintain the dykes and irrigation channels upon which the agricultural base of the Egyptian economy depended. They also weakened resistance to other diseases, such the "Antonine" epidemic of 160 CE that probably killed 50 per cent of the inhabitants of the densely populated Fayum region in the central Delta. Egypt was again hit by smallpox or flu epidemics from 251 to 271 (the "Plague of Cyprian") in which an estimated 50 per cent of Alexandria's population perished.

Nevertheless, the Egyptian economy remained remarkably buoyant for the first five centuries CE, when the Red Sea and north Arabian Sea regions experienced their wettest period on record. This reflected a northward shift in the ITCZ that brought enhanced summer monsoon rain between June and September, augmented from November to March by north-westerly storms off the Mediterranean. In the mid-first millennium, Nile floods were 30 to 40 per cent higher than at present. Excessive flooding of the Nile could reduce harvest yields, as in 545–546 and 548. Generally, however, enhanced precipitation encouraged settlement, irrigation, and cultivation of normally neglected desert land. These desert colonies may in turn have attracted the attention of desert nomads, such the Blemmyes (Beja) who raided southern parts of Egypt and the eastern desert from at least 261, causing central power to recede in Upper Egypt. In 268 to 270, nomads overran Coptos, a vital trading centre connecting the Delta and Nile to major Red Sea ports.

In the fourth and fifth centuries, Egyptian exchange was maintained with the wider IOW, albeit conducted increasingly through Axumite intermediaries. However, in the sixth century the Egyptian economy collapsed. This is generally attributed to the disintegration of the Byzantine Empire, and to Sasanian forces that in 616–617 invaded and plundered Egypt, precipitating the flight of the aristocracy, and breakdown of local administration, public works, industry, and trade. Excessive Roman impositions played a role, especially restrictions on sail on the Nile, high taxes, conscription, and attacks on the church – notably in Alexandria which had hitherto possessed great wealth and a commercial Mediterranean fleet. Such impositions prompted a bloody revolt in Upper Egypt, followed by a renewed Byzantine military onslaught that forced the Persians to retreat from Egypt in 626 and from Syria by 629–630. A decade later, in 641, Muslim Arab armies invaded Egypt and, by 670, had largely overrun Nubia. Their occupation provoked revolt, by Christian communities in the south in 737 and from 767 to 772, and by overtaxed peasants from the late 700s to the 830s.

Adverse environmental events from the sixth century prob-ably damaged the Egyptian economy more than foreign armies. Earthquakes hit Egypt in 551, 748, and one in 885 killed about 1,000 people in Cairo. However, an event in 535, probably triggered by a massive volcanic eruption that occurred that same year, provoked major subsidence in Lower Egypt, causing the collapse of many buildings in Alexandria and elsewhere. An inflow of seawater flooded rich farming settlements in the eastern Delta, created Burullus Lake in the central Delta, and caused major out-migration. Subsequently, a dust veil lasting two years precipatated a decade of abnormally low temperatures, harvest failure, and famine.

Shortly afterwards, in 541, Egypt was hit by a pandemic of bubonic plague, thought to have arrived from Ethiopia. As the plague made its appearance first in Pelusium, a major harbour in the eastern Delta, it was probably conveyed by ship from Adulis, Axum's principal port. The Asian black rat (R. rattus) had long colonised Ethiopia, but is a home-loving rodent that normally ventures little distance. Moreover, travel by boat up the Red Sea would have been too hot, at between 32°C and 41°C, for the survival of rats or fleas which generally require temperatures of from 20°C to 30°C. However, the first five centuries CE were the wettest in the region for the last 2,000 years and the indications are that the water surfaces of the Red Sea were then cooler. Moreover, a sharp ten-year reduction of temperatures followed the 535 volcanic eruption. Such conditions would have offered a window of opportunity for the infected rat and its fleas to travel by sea to Egypt where, however, arid conditions restricted their spread, and limited mortality from the plague to between 20 and 26 per cent. The plague subsequently spread both to Palestine, and to Alexandria and the rest of Egypt. The rat's predilection for grain meant a rapid diffusion of the plague via grain boats through the Delta and up the Nile Valley. Further plague epidemics erupted Egypt in 618, 622, 686, 699, 704, 719, and 775.

A southwards retreat of the ITCZ from 622 ended the unusually wet period of the early centuries CE in the Red Sea region. Subsequently, Egypt experienced a prolonged and intense period of drought until 1078, characterised by deficient Nile floods in 650 and 689, and generally low flood levels from 693 to 860. These resulted in the abandonment of previously viable desert irrigation works and villages. There were also disastrous floods, as in ca 741 when inhabitants of several cities east of Alexandria were forced to flee their homes. The combined impact of these events was catastrophic, a drastic fall in agricultural production, famine, and a decline in population – that of Lower Egypt probably fell by 50 per cent. The Egyptian economy only started to recover from the late eighth century.

Axum

Axum, centred in present-day Eritrea and northern Ethiopia, flourished until the sixth century. It controlled busy caravan routes between the Red Sea and the African hinterland, and by the mid-first century CE had diverted much trade, that hitherto had flowed through Meroe and Sudan to Egypt, to Axum-dominated Red Sea ports, the commercial fleets of which maintained vigorous trade with Somalia, Socotra, Egypt, the Near and Middle East, India, and (via India) East Asia. At its commercial height in the fifth and sixth centuries, Axum hotly contested Persian Sasanian domination in the western IOW, notably over the Indian silk and East African trades. Axumite merchants and mercenaries periodically settled in Yemen which Axum occupied from 340 to 348, established rule around Zafār, some 160 km south of present-day Sana'a, in the fifth to early sixth century, and invaded again in 525.

Axum also traded extensively with Sri Lanka, a major entrepôt for Chinese goods and probably home to a colony of Ethiopian merchants. In the early sixth century Cosmas noted of Sri Lanka:

> The Island being, as it is, in a central position, is much frequented by ships from all parts of India and from Persia and Ethiopia and it likewise sends out many of its own. And from the remotest countries, I mean Tzinista [China] and other trading places, it receives silk, aloes, cloves, sandalwood and other products, and these again are passed on to marts on this side, such as Male [Malabar coast], where pepper grows, and to Calliana [Kalyan, near present-day Mumbai], which exports copper and sesame-logs and cloth for making dresses, for it also is a great place of business. And to Sindu [Diul Sindh, at the mouth of the Indus] also where musk and castor is procured, and androstachys [possibly spikenard], and to Persia and the Homerite country [Yemen] and to Adulê [Zula on the African coast of the Red Sea]. And the island receives imports from all these marts which we have mentioned, and passes them on to the remoter ports, while, at the same time, exporting its own produce in both directions.[11]

However, Axumite power declined precipitously in the sixth century. By 570, the Sasanians had expelled Axumites from Arabia, and by 576 had established control over the major emporium of Aden, largely ending Axum's maritime influence in the Arabian and Red seas.

As with Egypt, Axum's decline needs to be set in the context of climatic change and disease. A humid phase from 500 BCE to 500 CE, particularly marked in the first five centuries CE, encouraged forest clearance, intensive cultivation, and population growth. However, from 100 BCE these factors led to progressive soil erosion. Moreover, from around the mid-sixth century Ethiopia experienced a prolonged and intense arid period, major droughts occurring around 650, 689 and 694 that correlated with ENSO events. There followed a protracted period of erratic, generally low rainfall. This and progressive desiccation of highland Eritrea and Tigray resulted from 600 to 850 in periodic famine and an increasing southwards shift of population and political power. Of equal, or possibly greater significance, were

---

[11] Cosmas, *The Christian Topography of Cosmas, an Egyptian Monk*, trans. J.W. McCrindle (Cambridge: Cambridge University Press, 2010), 365–6.

volcanic eruptions, notably that of 535, and subsequent visitations of bubonic plague which probably ravaged Adulis and possibly decimated Axum's naval force. The plague was often accompanied by severe food shortages, as from 831 to 849.

Southern IOA

There is scant literary reference to southern parts of IOA between the third and ninth centuries CE. For example, Cosmas, who indicated a vibrant maritime trade in the northwestern Indian Ocean in the early sixth century, makes no mention of Azania (East Africa). There is also little trace of the region in the archaeological record for this period which traditionally was regarded as a major hiatus – the "Times of Ignorance"[12] – in the history of East Africa, one broken at the end of the first millennium by the rise of a Swahili maritime civilisation forged by Arabs and Persians. That view has been increasingly challenged over recent decades notably by archaeologists and historical linguists. They argue that, in the early centuries CE, Bantu-speakers migrated from interior East Africa to the Indian Ocean littoral where they practised a mixed Iron Age agro-pastoral economy before, in the eighth century, adopting a maritime culture and developing Kiswahili, a language solidly Bantu in structure. This formed a basis for the emergence of the Swahili civilisation, which thus owed little to foreign influence.

Radical Afrocentrists such as Felix Chami contend that Bantu-speakers engaged in IOW maritime trade much earlier, possibly by 1000 BCE, and founded Rhapta, which formed the prototype for Swahili port cities. The *Periplus* notes that Rhapta's inhabitants were "Very big-bodied men, tillers of the soil",[13] an evident reference to Bantu-speaking agriculturalists. Chami argues that their fishing techniques (baskets, dugouts, and possibly "sewn boats"), developed initially for use on inland lakes, combined with their iron-working skills, facilitated their rapid transition to a maritime lifestyle.

---

[12] A term first coined by G.S.P. Freeman-Grenville in his article, "'The Times of Ignorance': A Review of Pre-Islamic and Early Islamic Settlement on the East African Coast" *Uganda Museum Occasional Papers* 4 (1959); see also James de Vere Allen, "Swahili Culture and the nature of East Coast Settlement" *International Journal of African Historical Studies* 14.2 (1981): 311–2.

[13] *The Periplus Maris Erythraei*, trans. Lionel Casson (Princeton: Princeton University Press, 1989), 61.

Bantu-speakers used small sewn boats in shallow coastal waters, and with iron tools fashioned larger vessels on the model of modern-day dhows to sail to offshore islands and for deep-sea voyages. Moreover the outrigger canoe, found on the Swahili coast and traditionally considered to reflect Indonesian influence, was developed locally. Some Afrocentrists even speculate that the African outrigger diffused to Indonesia rather than vice-versa.

Bantu-speakers were involved in trans-oceanic trade linking Azania with markets from the Mediterranean and Alexandria to the Persian Gulf, and by the fourth rather than eighth century had created a Swahili "Early Iron Age" culture that ran from Gezira (Somalia) to Chibuene (Mozambique), incorporating the Comoros and northwest Madagascar to the east, and the African hinterland as far inland as the South Pare Hills and Usambara Mountains of northeastern Tanzania. Bantu-speakers may have built Unguja Ukuu on Zanzibar, a large (16–17 ha) mud- and timber-structured emporium occupied from ca 500 to 900 CE. Trading extensively with India, the Middle East, and Roman world, they imported pottery, glassware, beads, alabaster, and metals in return for ivory, rhinoceros horn, tortoise shell, and slaves.

Azanian History Revisited

The East African economy was indisputably vibrant during the first great upsurge in the IOW global economy from 300 BCE to 300 CE. However, the Afrocentric vision of an exceptionally entrepreneurial Bantu-speaking people who transformed themselves effortlessly from an agricultural to a sophisticated maritime society is highly speculative. First, despite a possible sixth-century origin for Unguja Ukuu, there remains a largely unexplained gap of some 300 to 400 years between the third century when East Africa's foreign trade experienced a marked decline and Rhapta disappears from the record, and the rise of a Swahili culture and revived trade from about 800 CE.

Second, agriculturalists would have faced major difficulties making a rapid transition to a maritime existence. Oceanic life required a completely different set of skills and inherited experiences to those possessed by land-based cultivators. Inter-tidal zone communities needed skills specific to hunting and gathering in coastal rivers, lagoons, marshlands, and mangrove swamps, along shorelines and on offshore islands. Deep-sea culture necessitated the mastery of more complex competencies: the construction of boats able to withstand boisterous winds, currents, and waves, and detailed knowledge of the heavenly (e.g. stars, clouds, birds) and underwater (e.g. currents, reefs, types of bottom) elements, and of weather (e.g. monsoons, trade, shifting coastal winds, cyclones). A maritime existence also implied the ability to find and tap fresh-water supplies on sandy soils with no apparent water sources, and the capital resources to construct boats, hire crew, and invest in trade. Deep-sea fishermen required the ability to locate concentrations of fish and learn their habits, breeding cycles, enemies, food supplies, feeding habits, and migratory patterns.

Given the highly unpredictable role and influence of human and environmental factors, pre-industrial societies sought to minimise risk. A sudden change of occupational techniques or land use could court disaster, even extinction. Agriculturalists preferred tried and trusted forms of cultivation suited to their immediate environment, and adopted new techniques only if their value had been proven over time, or if the core economy collapsed due, for example, to a natural catas-trophe. Bantu-speakers had a predilection for the well-watered, fertile soils of the interior where they not only maintained their predomin-antly agricultural and iron-working economy, but carried it into vast regions of southeastern Africa ideally suited to those activities. They encountered formidable obstacles to establishing a viable existence on the East African littoral where soils were saline and water supplies often brackish. Adopting a maritime lifestyle posed almost insuperable difficulties. Moreover, the incentive was lacking as specialist fishermen communities and maritime traders already existed. Agricultural land-based, coastal, and maritime communities each possessed different systems "of commonly used materials, sources of energy, types of labor and social organizations, tools and techniques, and outputs of goods and services".[14] The rational course of action, testified throughout history, was for groups practising different material cultures to profit from division of labour, and exchange the products of one economic system for those of another. This points to the co-existence of distinct communities with often complementary lifestyles: Bantu-speaking agriculturalists, Cushitic pastoralists, Khoisan hunter-gathers, and a non-Bantu-speaking maritime community.

[14] Ralph A. Austen and Daniel Headrick, "The Role of Technology in the African Past" *African Studies Review* 26.314 (1983): 168.

Even by the tenth century, when there existed a local coastwise as well as externally orientated maritime trade network, there is little evidence that Bantu-speakers were involved in oceanic exchange. Kiswahili maritime vocabulary reflects major borrowings from Persian and Arabic that started from the eighth century, indicating that oceanic sailing was then largely alien to them. Also, there are no early literary indications of black Africans having been sea captains, deep-sea fishermen, or maritime traders in the Indian Ocean. There are references in the mid-eleventh century to merchants from Zanzibar trading in Gopakapattana, the capital and emporium of the Kadamba dynasty of West India, but they probably originated from elsewhere as Al-Idrisi commented contemporaneously that "the Zanj have no ships to voyage in, but use vessels from Oman and other countries".[15]

Environmental factors and disease also need to be taken into account. In equatorial and southern IOA, rainfall, which was critical to agriculture and thus to human existence, was a product of complex factors, notably the ITCZ, ENSO, and sea surface temperature anomalies that drive variations in the biannual migration of the ITCZ. Changes in the monsoon, which are heavily affected by ENSO patterns, also play a major role, as does the Indian Ocean Dipole. During the first 500 years CE, a distinct northward shift in the ITZC, and lower sea surface temperatures, resulted in decreased summer rainfall over large parts of East Africa. For example, Mozambique experienced a protracted arid period up to 500 CE, followed by increased rainfall to 800 CE. Records for Lake Tanganyika, a proxy for equatorial East Africa, also indicate major droughts in the last two hundred years BCE and from 200 to 500 CE when it started to experience a period of good rainfall. The same pattern appears for Madagascar. By contrast, interior southern Africa experienced generally good rainfall in the first half of the first millennium CE, except for a dry period around 400 CE.

Human activity may have contributed to climate change. During the first upswing in the IOW global economy from 300 BCE to 300 CE, a combination of iron technology and cultivation of the Southeast Asian complex of crops resulted in significant environmental degradation in East Africa. Iron tools greatly augmented the ability of Bantu-speaking cultivators to clear bushland. However, iron production also

[15] Quoted in G.S.P. Freeman-Grenville (ed.), *The East African Coast: Select Documents from the First to the Earlier Nineteenth Century* (Oxford: Clarendon Press, 1962), 19.

demanded large amounts of wood as fuel. This dictated that forested regions formed the location of intensive iron production, such as to the west of Lake Victoria from about 400 BCE, and the Usambara Mountains and Pare Hills from 100 to 400 CE. Smelting furnaces varied greatly in shape, size and operation, depending in part on the quality of the ore. Unrefined bog iron required huge quantities of charcoal and a long smelting process, favouring larger furnaces. In one case, 88m³ of wood was used to make one metric ton of charcoal that in turn smelted sufficient iron for only four hoes and a few other smaller tools. As iron-making technology developed and the population grew and dispersed, huge quantities of wood were cut and burned to clear agricultural plots for cultivation and produce iron goods. As Peter Schmidt notes:

> Archaeological research in Rwanda, Burundi, Kenya and Tanzania indicates that Early Iron Age (EIA) peoples encroached upon the East African forests between 500 B.C. and 500 A.D. [500 BCE and 500 CE] and that their environmental impact can only be characterized as severe.[16]

By the BCE/CE changeover, 50 per cent of land in parts of sub-Saharan Africa had been deforested in a process and for activities that were, at the time, the largest anthropogenic sources of carbon dioxide emissions. As Bantu-speakers cleared ever-larger areas of virgin forest, such emissions reduced rainfall, which over time diminished agricultural yields to levels that could not sustain human communities, forcing them to move. Between the first and fourth centuries CE, Bantu-speakers migrated down the major river valleys to the present-day Kenyan, Tanzanian, and possibly Mozambique coasts. The protracted arid period from 200 to 500 CE probably accentuated this migration, as people sought well-watered lands with ample sources of wood and iron. By the fourth century, Bantu-speakers had crossed the Limpopo into South Africa. By the mid-fifth century, they had expanded to some 100 km south of present-day Durban along the KwaZulu-Natal littoral characterised by a tropical climate with a minimum precipitation of 800 mm per annum, and iron-ore outcrops, that formed the ideal context for their agricultural and iron-working pursuits. They also expanded rapidly into the northeast interior south of Limpopo River, whereby the close of the fifth century they had formed reasonably large settlements.

---

[16] Peter R. Schmidt, "Early Exploitation and Settlement in the Usambara Mountains" in A.C. Hamilton and R. Bensted-Smith (eds.), *Forest Conservation in the East Usambara Mountains Tanzania* (Cambridge: IUCN Tropical Forest Programme, 1989), 75.

Disease may also have played a critical role in the economic decline of Azania from around 300 CE. Many infections require a minimum host population threshold to survive. Thus hunter-gatherer and pastoral societies with small population densities were less susceptible to certain major infections than more sedentary, higher-density Bantu-speaking agricultural communities. Moreover, cultivated clearances reduced the variety of flora which, coupled with the presence of domesticated animals, encouraged the spread of certain disease vectors. These included the malaria-bearing *Anopheles* mosquito that can breed in any collection of water, from small pools to lakes, and had a proclivity for an environment where crops, cattle, and humans existed in close proximity. Sharply increased outbreaks of malaria could thus result from forest cultivation, and provoke out-migration, particularly in conjunction with soil degradation and decreasing crop yields.

The incidence of malaria, low in arid intervals, as from 200 to 500 CE, increases sharply in periods of heavy rainfall, as in the early 500s. Indeed, malaria could then have assumed epidemic form, and caused high mortality in hitherto untouched communities, such as among the foreign inhabitants of Rhapta and visiting crews, including, perhaps, Austronesians.

Again, the Justinian Plague possibly originated in East Africa. There exist three foci of plague-carrying rodent populations: the Eurasian steppe (from Manchuria to the Ukraine), Himalayan foothills, and Great Lakes region of East Africa. Recent DNA evidence suggests that the three plague pandemics that have erupted over the centuries were caused by *Y. pestis* of Asian origin, but that the strain responsible for the Justinian Plague is probably extinct, and is distant from extant strains associated with the second (fourteenth-century) and third (nineteenth-century) pandemics. Both the second and third pandemics can be traced to plague foci in the Xinjiang region of China, but there is no evidence that the sixth-century outbreak first erupted in Asia, or that it travelled from Asia to Egypt and the Mediterranean. The literary evidence suggests the reverse as it affected progressively North Africa, Europe, Arabia, Mesopotamia, Central and southern Asia, and finally, in 610, China.

Some medieval sources point to Red Sea Africa as a major foci of the plague. Syrian intellectual Evagrius Scholasticus (ca 536–590), an eye-witness to the 542 outbreak, stated that it came from Ethiopia. William McNeill argues that the origin of the plague bacillus was either India, or central East Africa – which Michael Dols considers the source of

the Justinian Plague pandemic. The possibility that the Justinian outbreak originated in East Africa is thus worthy of investigation.

The earliest first-hand accounts of plague in East Africa are
from Uganda in 1877, but many inland East African communities
considered it to have been a traditional and endemic disease. Indeed,
it is generally assumed that plague foci in IOA is ancient, some even
arguing that it was endemic in Egypt in Pharaonic times.[17] It was
probably present in Egypt, Libya, and Syria by the second century CE.
The Justinian Plague may thus have originated in Egypt. From Egypt,
the plague bacillus could well have travelled to East Africa by overland
or maritime routes. It could also have been introduced from Asia by
sea. Had the plague erupted in central East Africa, it would have first
affected major communities of Bantu-speakers which, up to 400 CE,
were concentrated in the iron-working regions near Lake Victoria, the
Usambara Mountains, and the Pare Hills. The Lake Victoria region
was noted by German microbiologist, Robert Koch (1843–1910) as
the epicentre of the 1890s outbreak of bubonic plague, which suggests
that the disease might have been endemic amongst local rodents.
Indeed, Koch declared "the interior of Africa, like Asia, is a plague
center, perhaps since the most ancient times".[18] Traditionally, when
local rats left, or died, villagers in interior East Africa deserted their
villages as through experience they learned that such incidents marked
the start of a plague epidemic.

The oriental rat flea, *X. cheopis*, that carried *Y. pestis*, seems to have
made two separate invasions of East Africa: one down the Nile Valley,
accompanying the Nile (or African grass) rat, *Arvicanthis niloticus*, the
other onto the east coast, accompanying the black rat, *R. rattus*, which
originated in Southeast Asia. Significantly, black rats do not naturally
move more than 200 metres, and are heavily dependent upon human
traffic to travel any distance. Myron Echenberg considers that maritime commerce with East Africa was insufficient for the plague to have
been introduced there until the advent of steamships in the nineteenth
century.[19] However, by the BCE/CE changeover, there was considerable

---

[17] Eva Panagiotakopulu, "Pharaonic Egypt and the origins of plague" *Journal of Biogeography* 31 (2004): 269–75.

[18] Quoted in Facil Tesfaye, "Medical Expeditions and the Scramble for Africa: Robert Koch in Africa 1896–1907" PhD, McGill University (2013), 145.

[19] Myron Echenberg, "'Scientific Gold': Robert Koch and Africa, 1883–1906" in Chris Youé and Tim Stapleton (eds), *Agency and Action in Colonial Africa* (Houndmills, Basingstoke, UK: Palgrave, 2001), 43.

sea trade to Azanian ports, from which there was significant exchange with the interior. R. *rattus* shows a particular preference for grain, so the plague could have been imported on ships to Azanian ports to which, the *Periplus* noted, grain and wine were imported "in considerable quantity, not for trade but as an expenditure for the good will of the barbaroi".[20] The grain, almost certainly wheat, and possibly rice, along with ghee, and cane sugar, may have come from Barygaza in northwest India. R. *rattus* reached Madagascar possibly by 240 CE and by 700 had reached Bosutswe, an ancient settlement in eastern Botswana – indicating an earlier arrival on the Mozambique coast and passage up the Zambezi. It also reached Natal in the eighth century. The black rat could well have made itself at home in Azanian port granaries, notably those of Rhapta, and accompanied consignments of grain and other imported food shipped to hinterland villages. Again, *Y Pestis* could have transferred from the black rat and X. *cheopis* to local rodents and their fleas, which could have carried it along trade routes to the interior.

By contrast, until the twentieth century R. *rattus* was largely absent from the Great Lakes region, the main ancient reservoir of plague foci in East Africa, where the traditional carriers of plague were the southern multimammate rat (*Mastomys coucha/natalensis*) and Nile rat. Another loci of plague is the Lushoto region in the Usambara Mountains, an area that from 100 to 400 CE was intensely exploited for agriculture and iron production, and which had trading connections with the Pare Hills (another focus of early iron production), Tana River, and the coast. The southern multimammate rat is partial to vegetables, grain crops (including sorghum, millet, maize, and irrigated rice), bananas, and cassava. In present-day East Africa, it feasts on maize from April to May, turns to sorghum in mid-summer, then to cotton crops in early autumn. Rats move freely between forest habitats and villages, migration to which increases with greater human disturbance of the forest. Drier conditions restrict rat reproduction and thus population, but both can explode in rainy seasons when significant numbers move into villages in search of food, causing human cases of the plague to erupt. Thus in years of drought, as from 200 to 500 CE, rat numbers and the plague would have been kept in check, but could have increased sharply when a drought was followed by

---

[20] *The Periplus Maris Erythraei*, trans. Lionel Casson (Princeton: Princeton University Press, 1989), 61.

heavy rainfall, such as at the start of the 500s. Rat numbers also rise sharply for about two decades following earthquakes, due to disrupted grain production, supply networks, and storage facilities, as well as degraded housing stock.

Infected rats or humans may travel long distances. At times of natural disturbance that provoke major rat migration, the *Y. pestis*-carrying flea could have travelled along trade routes from interior iron-producing centres to the coast where a plague outbreak would most likely have first occurred in Rhapta, Azania's main commercial "metropolis". A plague epidemic is checked when the mean daily temperature rises above 26.5°C and usually ends when the temperature reaches 29.5°C. On the coast (Mombasa) the average temperature is generally below 26.5°C from May to October. Moreover, during a cool period, such as that which follows a sulphur-rich volcanic eruption, a slight drop in temperature could have enabled a plague epidemic to become endemic. As few as 20 infected animals can trigger an epidemic of plague in a human community. During the trading season, with the arrival of many merchant crews, Rhapta's population may well have risen to 20,000 people. Overcrowding and insanitary conditions would certainly have prevailed, creating optimum conditions for a major epidemic, which could in turn have precipitated the absolute decline of Rhapta by the fourth century. Also, ships carrying ivory, rhino horn, tortoise and nautilus shell, with sufficient grain particles aboard to nourish rats, could easily have carried the plague from Rhapta to Adulis, and subsequently on to Egypt and the Mediterranean world.

5

–

The Second Great Boom in the IOW Global Economy ca 850 to 1250 and its Impact in Northern IOA

Between 850 and 1250, the IOW global economy, including IOA, experienced a marked resurgence. This chapter examines the basis for that revival in the context of human-environment interaction, and its impact in northern IOA. The revival of fortunes in southern IOA is the subject of Chapter 6.

The Upsurge in the IOW Global Economy

Historians have traditionally focussed on the political background to enhanced exchange across the IOW between the ninth and thirteenth centuries. By the early eighth century, conflict between the Byzantine and Sasanian empires had left both exhausted, facilitating the emergence of the new Muslim powers. The rise of Islam is conventionally dated to 618, when Muhammad declared open opposition to the rulers of Mecca and started to establish the foundations of a new religion based on divine revelations, which in turn formed the basis of the Quran. The first Muslim soldiers were desert nomads, groups little affected by centralised powers, or the outbreaks of plague that had started in the 540s. Taking full advantage of the decline of established political entities, and of sedentary peoples severely afflicted by the plague, they captured the two main commercial routes in the Fertile Crescent and Red Sea regions connecting the Indian Ocean to the Mediterranean, and overran the Persian Sassanid Empire. Between 633 and 651, Arab rule was imposed over Iran and Iraq, and in 639

Muslim forces overran Egypt. The Muslim conquest of Sind from 664 to 712, and expansion into northern India, was assisted by an internecine Indian struggle for power in the Doab and Ganges-Brahmaputra regions.

The expansion of Islam was accompanied by an initially fitful economic revival. In the early eighth century, trans-IOW maritime trade recovered, with direct sail by Arab, Persian, and Indian ships from the western IOW to China. However, China experienced an economic decline from the mid-eighth century in part due to a combination of military losses to Muslim Abbasid forces in 751, and major disturbances in Chinese ports in 758, 760, and 878 that resulted in an exodus of foreigners from Yangzhou and Guangzhou. Thereafter, direct contact between the western and eastern IOW sharply declined. At the same time, Srivijaya, a city-state in eastern Sumatra, which in the late seventh century had emerged as a major sea-faring power, was hit in the late eighth and ninth century by a slump in maritime trade, accentuated by growing piracy in the Straits of Malacca.

There followed a major trans-IOW economic upsurge from the tenth to thirteenth centuries. Maritime commerce was encouraged by the Southern Han (917–971) and Song (960–1279) dynasties in China, the Cholas (late 800s to early 1200s) in southern India, and the Fatimid Caliphate (909–1171) in the Middle East. Trans-IOW oceanic trade was further boosted from the 1020s when political instability on the Asian silk route led to many commodities traditionally shipped along it being transferred onto sea routes, both via the South China coast and the overland route from Yunnan, in southwest China, to Burma and India – which in turn stimulated Burmese naval expeditions to Bengal, Malaya, and Sri Lanka.

While conventional histories have stressed these political influences, environmental factors also played a significant role in the upswing in the IOW global economy. From 800 to 1250 there was a marked decline in El Niño events – generally correlated with failure of monsoon rains – and higher temperatures, with stronger, regular southwest monsoon rains, than during the preceding 500 years. This was particularly marked from 700 to 900 in tropical and semi-tropical regions due to a southwards migration of the ITCZ. While this phenomenon led to greater aridity in the lower latitudes of the northern hemisphere from 800 to 1000, thereafter the IOW generally experienced more plentiful rainfall. Greater precipitation promoted agricultural surpluses, demographic growth, craft production, long-distance exchange, and state revenues. This in turn laid the foundations for political stability and for the second major economic boom in the IOW, one particularly marked in tropical and semi-tropical zones from the eighth century, and more generally from about 1000. This second-millennium upsurge was assisted by human adaptation to diseases such as smallpox and measles. Initially these diseases wreaked high death tolls on "virgin" populations, but by about 1000 widespread exposure provided immunity, turning both chickenpox and measles into mild childhood afflictions. Greater, more regular agricultural surpluses also enhanced human health and physiological resistance to disease.

China from the tenth to mid-thirteenth centuries experienced a warmer, wetter, climate, which stimulated agricultural production and population growth. Southern China witnessed intensified production of commercial crops, including hemp, ramie, silk, cotton, and lychees. Moreover, the adoption of fast-ripening rice strains from Vietnam, the planting of double-harvest rice, and improved irrigation techniques, enhanced production of food staples. This in turn attracted migrants from the north, and promoted demographic growth. In total, the Chinese population grew from about 32 million to 121 million between 961 and 1109, demographic expansion being particularly marked in the southeast where the number of households increased from 286,000 to over 1.5 million between 742 and 980. Such developments stimulated the expansion of cities and markets, technological innovation and commerce. The Song regime greatly encouraged economic development, including foreign trade. From 960, it established government agencies in the main ports to promote overseas commerce, boosted the money supply from 996, advancing credit to miners and smelters who supplied the iron for coinage and, from the late eleventh century, increased production of copper coinage that, exported alongside silver, helped the gradual monetisation of the eastern IOW.

In India, improved monsoon rains in the early ninth century, and from about 950 to 1000, and 1075 to 1250, resulted in larger and more regular agricultural surpluses. These stimulated land improvement projects, subsistence and cash crop (notably areca and betel) cultivation, population growth, craft activity, trade, and government revenues. For example, in South India from the eleventh century, temple complexes converted forests to farmland; and in Bengal, expanded agricultural production supported a relatively dense rural

population and specialist textile artisanal sector, leading to a growth
in trade, both maritime (via the Bay of Bengal) and transcontinental
(via the Ganges and Brahmaputra). Cowries, imported into Bengal
in large quantity from the Maldive Islands from the ninth century,
acted as a medium of exchange for both low and high-value commodities, and for property. Indian political authorities taxed, protected,
and through formulation of fiscal policy, facilitated trade. Of notable
importance was the rise in South India of the Chola regime (late-
ninth to late-thirteenth centuries) which promoted the domestic and
international trade networks of South India and northern Sri Lanka
(conquered in 1080), extended political dominance over the Maldives,
and challenged Srivijayan dominance over shipping through the
Malacca and Sunda straits. The Chola also boosted coin printing, and
the circulation of money – including Chinese coins.

In the Middle East, the southward shift of the ITCZ from 700 to
900 brought generally drier conditions, expansion of the desert, and a
corresponding shrinkage in cultivation of desert fringes. Consequently,
the focus of economic power shifted from southern Arabia to the river
valleys of the Fertile Crescent, while Bedouins with their camels and
horses became a significant military influence and dominated regional
trade routes. However, from the tenth to early twelfth centuries, the
region experienced intermittent periods of significantly colder climate, probably accentuated by the Grand Solar Minimum which
peaked from 1040 to 1080. This caused considerable economic, political, and social turmoil. For example, from 919, unprecedentedly
cold weather hit Iraq, and in 926 the Tigris and Euphrates froze over,
creating food shortages and popular disturbances. A further cold spell
from 942 to 946 caused widespread famine in Baghdad, and the flight
of its Jewish and Zoroastrian communities. In 949 another famine
affected Lower Iraq, causing major social unrest. In Iran, the long
cool period precipitated the collapse of the cotton industry, and led
to the southern migration of Turkic pastoralists and emigration of the
Persian scholarly class. However, the region experienced episodes of
relatively plentiful rainfall in the mid-700s, between 900 and 960,
and from ca 1000 to the 1220s, and the climate improved from the
mid-twelfth century. These factors encouraged a gradual expansion
of cultivation – production of barley, wheat, and fava beans peaking
between 1100 and 1350.

Overall, the IOW experienced relatively good environmental
conditions from the ninth to thirteenth centuries. This in turn

stimulated production and trans-IOW trade, which became more structured. Chinese authorities who closely surveyed relations with the early foreign merchant community in Guangzhou occasionally declared a monopoly over foreign trade, and Indonesian courts sometimes commanded a dominant share in merchant shipping. A few Indian princes even formed joint ventures with merchants. In general, however, IOW political authorities protected overland trade in return for tax, but left maritime trade, which entailed considerable capital investment and high risks, to merchant associations. From the eighth century, many Chinese traders sailed overseas, and although in 985 the government barred them from travelling overseas, it could not prevent illegal emigration or movement of foreign-based Chinese: By the thirteenth century, Chinese agents had settled as far west as the Malay Peninsula and eastern India.

In South India, powerful merchant guilds first emerged in the late ninth century on the Malabar Coast. They were probably influenced by Muslim, Jewish, Zoroastrian, and Christian merchant groups from western Asia and the Middle East that had established trading settlements there in the eighth and ninth centuries. Of these, the Ayyavole guild rapidly became the most powerful, gaining vertical control of key craft industries, notably textiles, and forging close affiliations with both mercenary groups and political authorities for whom they acted as tax collectors. A primary function of the guilds was banking – receiving deposits in cash and in kind that they invested in commercial enterprises. They were largely responsible for the monetisation of the economy, and some gained the authority to print their own coinage.

From the ninth century, South Indian merchant associations expanded overseas. They first concentrated on the western IOW, in the Persian Gulf where many settled in Siraf, and in the Red Sea region. From the late 800s they spread into the interior of southern India, to northern Sri Lanka, Java, Bali, and to China where numerous Hindu, Buddhist, and Muslim Indian traders settled in Guangzhou. However, in Java, local rulers and allied merchant groups (*banigrāma*) circumscribed the power of foreign merchants. When Chola power declined from the end of the twelfth century, so did previously dominant Indian merchant influence. By the thirteenth century, Chinese merchants, who from the late eleventh century had again started sailing overseas, outnumbered Indian traders in some Southeast Asian ports.

Persian Gulf merchants also rapidly extended their maritime trading connections, establishing agencies first in the Konkan and Gujarat, by the eighth century in southwest India and Sri Lanka, by the ninth century on the Coromandel Coast, and by the tenth century in Srivijaya, Champa, and China. By the tenth century, Middle Eastern merchants had developed a commenda-type investment contract – i.e. contracts involving two parties (one investing, one travelling) in a nexus of written agreements governing issues such as investment, agency, and risk and profit allocation. The use of the commenda spread west to the Mediterranean, and east to India, Southeast Asia, and China.

In the economic upturn between the ninth and thirteenth centuries, Arab, Persian, Indian, Sri Lankan, Southeast Asian and, in the latter part of the period, Chinese vessels, dominated trans-IOW maritime trade. Until the sixth century, Arab and Persian ships generally sailed no further east than to western or South India, and Indian vessels no further than the Malay Peninsula. By about 850 they were sailing directly to China. Ships from the Persian Gulf sailed to Malabar, then via Sri Lanka and the Nicobar Islands, through the Straits of Malacca to Champa, and on to Guangzhou. The return trip took from 18 months to two years. Probably in response to a massacre in 879 of foreign traders in Guangzhou, direct sail between the Persian Gulf and China ceased, vessels thereafter stopping at Kedah where they transferred western IOW goods onto Chinese and other vessels for distribution to eastern IOW markets, and took aboard commodities from the eastern IOW. The Chinese did not begin to sail to the western IOW until the ninth century, although by the time that maritime relations with the West peaked from 1127 to 1179, Chinese ships were sailing as far west as Quilon (Kollam) on the Malabar Coast.

The upsurge in IOW economic activity was characterised by the emergence of a more integrated trans-IOW exchange system, accompanied by hitherto unparalleled technological innovations, organisational improvements, an expansion in the quantity, value and variety of commodities traded, widespread diffusion of new ideas, and more universal ideologies. The technological advances were most apparent in China which, from between about 750 and 1100 "experienced a series of economic changes roughly comparable to the subsequent patterns of European growth from the crusades to the eve of the French

TABLE 5.1 *Trans-IOW Maritime Trade, Ninth to Thirteenth Centuries*

China				
Imports	**Imports**	**Imports**	**Imports**	**Exports**
cottons (India)	medicinal herbs (SE Asia)	coral (SE Asia)	steel (India?)	ceramics
rhinoceros horn (northeast India; Africa)	ivory (African; Asian)	dates (Middle East)	rugs (Iran)	silk
black pepper (India; Bali)	rattan mats (Vietnam)	pearls (Persian Gulf; India)	coloured glass (Egypt; Iraq)	salt
silks (Southeast Asia)	frankincense (Red Sea)	cinnabar	exotic bird feathers (SE Asia)	copper coinage
perfumes	gharu-wood (SE Asia)	umbrellas (Vietnam)	benzoin (Sumatra)	iron
dyes	tortoise shell (SE Asia; Africa)	benzoin (SE Asia)	pine resin (Sumatra)	lead ingots
drugs & medicines	amber (SE Asia)	cloves (SE Asia),	safflower (Java)	fermented liquor
cardamom (SE Asia)	camphor (Sumatra)	mace (SE Asia)	ambergris (Western IOW)	
pepper (SE Asia)	psoralea (SE Asia)	nutmegs (SE Asia)	limonite (Western IOW)	
sandalwood lac (SE Asia)	storax (SE Asia)	areca (SE Asia)	Indigo (Western IOW)	
laka wood (SE Asia)	myrobalan (SE Asia)	myrrh (Red Sea)	rosewater (Western IOW)	
putchuk (Western IOW)	dragon's blood (? – Socotra)	ivory and sandalwood stupas and statues	gold vessels (temple)	
storax ambergris (SE Asia; Zanj)	myrobalan	gall nuts	malachite	

(*continued*)

TABLE 5.1 (*cont.*)

SE Asia

Imports	Exports	Exports	Exports	Exports
ceramics (China)	benzoin	camphor	gharu-wood	orris root
cottons (India)	areca	safflower	rattan mats	cinnabar
silks (China)	coral	indigo	cardaman	copperas
iron (China)	silks	rhinoceros horn	cloves	alum
gold, silver & copper coinage (China)	medicinal herbs	ivory	mace	arsenic
laquer ware (China)	gold	tortoise shell	nutmeg	borax
arsenic (China)	silk	amber	storax	

South Asia

Imports	Imports	Exports	Exports	Exports
ceramics (China)	horses (Middle East)	black pepper	indigo	medicinal plants
ivory (African; Asian)	cloves (Indonesia)	wootz steel ingots	jewels & precious stones	ebony
rhinoceros horn (African; Asian)	mace (Indonesia)	ivory	putchuk	camphor
cinnabar (Socotra?)	nutmeg (Indonesia)	rhinoceros horn	rosewater	sugar
gold (Zanj)	iron ore/pig iron (Zanj)	safflower	elephants	pearls
		ceramics (Zanj)		

TABLE 5.1 (*cont.*)

Middle East

Imports	Imports	Exports	Exports	Exports
ceramics (China)	cinnabar	turquoise	frankincense	rugs
cottons (India)	cloves (Indonesia)	vermilion	coral	horses
sugar cane (India)	mace (Indonesia)	quicksilver	dates	myrrh
ivory (African; Asian)	nutmeg (Indonesia)	gum arabic	pearls	coloured glass
rhinoceros horn (African; Asian)	copper coinage (China)	pottery	cloth	
mangrove poles (Zanj)	gold (Zanj)			
iron ore/ pig iron (Zanj)	quartz (Zanj)			

Indian Ocean Africa
A/ Egypt

Imports	Imports	Imports	Exports	Exports
ceramics (China)	cloves (Indonesia)	slaves (African; Indonesian)	opium	coloured glass
textiles (India; Iran)	mace (Indonesia)	pearls (Iran)	crystal	madder
black pepper (India)	nutmeg (Indonesia)	dates (Iran)	rosewater	linens
ivory (African; Asian)	frankincense	dried fish (Iran)	dried roses	grain
rhinoceros horn (African; Asian)	myrrh	Chinese coins	papyrus	woollens
cinnabar	quartz (Zanj)		beads crystal	flax

(*continued*)

TABLE 5.1 (*cont.*)

B/ NE Africa

Imports	Imports	Exports	Exports	Exports
ceramics (China)	spices	ambergris	gold	animal skins
coinage (China)	opium (Egypt)	beeswax	ivory	rhinoceros horn
pearls (Iran)	beads	sandalwood	civet musk	tortoiseshell
cloth (Iran; India)	crystal	ebony	slaves	myrrh
rosewater	dried roses	liquid storax gum	frankincense	putchuk
crystal (Egypt)				

C/ Zanj

Imports	Imports	Exports	Exports	Exports
ceramics (China)	ironware	iron ore/pig iron	ivory	aromatic woods
cloth (India)	precious stones	slaves	rhinoceros horn	tortoiseshell
spices	rice	beechwood	ambergris	mangrove poles
perfumes	wine	teak	gold	leopard skins
copper (India)	ceramics (India; China)	quartz (rock crystal)	yellow sandalwood	leather
beads (Middle East; India)		pearls	animal skins	

Revolution".[1] The extraction and refining of iron, copper, lead, and tin increased dramatically. The annual output of iron alone increased from 13,500 to 125,000 tons between 806 and 1078 – compared to

---

[1] Robert Hartwell, "Markets, Technology, and the Structure of Enterprise in the Development of the Eleventh-Century Chinese Iron and Steel Industry" *Journal of Economic History* 26.1 (1966): 29.

British iron production in 1788 of 76,000 tons. In the eleventh century, the Chinese began extensive use of a technique for the partial decarbonisation of cast iron through repeated forging under a cold blast – "the true ancestor of modern Bessemer processes"[2] – in order to produce steel. Metals, notably iron, were used in construction, and the manufacture of a wide variety of products for industrial and military use. Production of gunpowder, alum, salt, quicksilver, and cinnabar also increased markedly, and major advances were made in papermaking and printing.

There was a corresponding growth in the scale of production, and utilisation of animal- and water-driven machinery. The extension of canal systems, especially in the eleventh century, added impetus to production and trade by greatly reducing transport costs across the country.

In India, the greatest technological progress occurred in the textile sector. The draw loom and spinning wheel were developed in the eleventh and thirteenth centuries respectively, facilitating the manufacture of block-printed textiles that were exported in large quantities across the IOW. Furthermore, India was the leading producer of brass and zinc goods. The ninth century witnessed a widespread diffusion, notably in South India and Sri Lanka, of specialised, standardised, and semi-industrial production of wootz, an exceptionally high carbon steel exported for the manufacture notably of blades, including the celebrated Persian-made Damascus steel blade.

Further west, Muslim powers adopted and adapted foreign techniques. At the start of the ninth century, the Persian mathematician al-Khwarizmi (ca 780 – ca 850) introduced Indian positional numerals with index value and zero specifically to assist people in solving problems encountered in money exchange and in commercial contracts. Later, Chinese silk and papermaking techniques were adopted and diffused throughout the Muslim world. From 700 to 1100, the Middle East also experienced what has been termed a "Green Revolution",[3] although it drew heavily on earlier Roman, Byzantine, and Persian practices. Summer crops were introduced permitting all-year-round crop rotation and hence more intensive land use, a greater variety of natural (animal- and green-derived) fertilisation, advanced

[2] Ibid., 54.
[3] Andrew Watson, "A Medieval Green Revolution" in Abraham Udovitch (ed.), *The Islamic Middle East, 700–1900* (Princeton, NJ: Darwin Press, 1981), 29–58.

irrigation techniques including *qanāts*, and cultivation of previously waste land, including near desert (through irrigation) and swampland (through drainage). Authorities granted legal ownership to those who brought wasteland into cultivation, and introduced tax incentives to encourage the use of water wheels or other lifting mechanisms to irrigate land. These innovations enabled extensive cultivation of waterneedy crops such as rice and cotton, brought higher crop yields and promoted demographic growth.

Considerable dissemination, imitation, and substitution of technologies occurred during the upsurge in trans-IOW trade. For instance, from the early eighth century Arab merchants spread Indian agricultural techniques including the cultivation of hard wheat, rice, sugar cane, new varieties of sorghum, spinach, artichoke, eggplant, and cotton – a key industrial crop – throughout the Islamic world and beyond. Indeed, cotton diffusion in Africa largely paralleled the expansion there of Islam. By the twelfth century, Java had adopted Indian textile techniques and the cultivation of safflower and black pepper – supplanting Indian merchants in those products in the Chinese market. Similarly, benzoin, pine resin, and camphor from Sumatra gradually displaced frankincense and myrrh from the Red Sea region in the Chinese market. From the tenth century, Java imported ready-dyed silk from China to which it shipped finished silk textiles, while imported Chinese ceramics stimulated the development of similar styles in Java and Iran by the twelfth and thirteenth centuries respectively.

Islam and the IOW Economy

Islam played a significant role in promoting IOW commercial networks. It encouraged accumulation of personal riches through hard work and frugality, but also stressed redistribution of wealth within the family and, through charitable donations (*zakat*), to the wider Muslim community. Such charity proved an efficient communal insurance in times of uncertainty. Islam condemned debt and usury because of their negative distributive justice and equity. However, money lending was customary, often at high interest rates, permitting traders and others access to credit. As significantly, Muslim powers developed efficient administrative and legal systems. The Umayyads in Syria and Abbasids in Iraq inherited respectively much of the previous Byzantine and

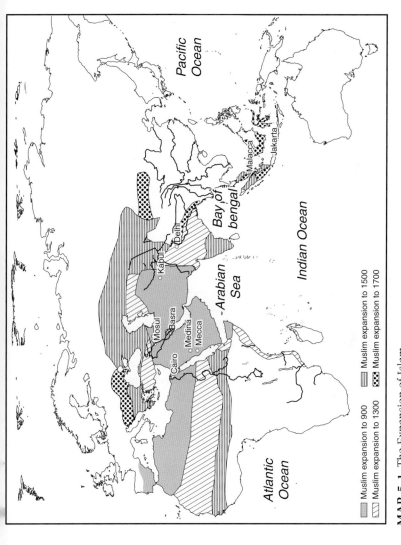

MAP 5.1 The Expansion of Islam

Note: Adapted from http://forums.civfanatics.com/showthread.php?t=61455 (accessed 13/04/12).

Muslim expansion to 900
Muslim expansion to 1300
Muslim expansion to 1500
Muslim expansion to 1700

Persian political and administrative structures, including an effective bureaucracy, postal service, land-based tax system, mints and coinage, and standing army. By the ninth century, Muslim powers had through the "*ulama*", or Muslim religious scholars, also developed a comprehensive legal framework. This comprised a body of law (Sharia) shaped by "consensus" or learned interpretation of the Quran and hadith;[4] "analogy", permitting scholars to incorporate elements from other, notably Christian, Jewish, Zoroastrian, Roman, and Sasanian legal traditions; and "precedent", whereby in the *Dar al-Kufr* (lit. "house of unbelievers" – or lands not governed by the Sharia) pre-Islamic customary law could be recognised.

Such structures were forged in the Islamic heartland (*Dar al-Islam*). Their influence spread through trade networks, both overland into Central Asia and along maritime routes to regions of the IOW as far apart as East Africa and South China. In all major entrepôts along these routes, Muslim commercial agents formed settlements which attracted Muslim clerics. Foreign merchant communities were generally grouped according to belief systems, gathering around religious buildings, with religious authorities governing their internal affairs according to their respective canons. However, the political decentralisation common to much of the region favoured the spread of Islamic legal practice, especially in the largely autonomous mercantile communities that dominated port cities. Moreover, by the tenth century, local authorities in the *Dar al-Kufr*, from Africa to Indonesia, frequently summoned Muslim holy men and scholars for legal advice or adjudication, and otherwise adopted and adapted those aspects of Islam that most enhanced production and trade. Moreover, these Muslim communities maintained commercial and religious networks throughout the wider Indian Ocean world. The result was a loosely coherent and flexible legal framework that governed economic activity across much of the IOW.

A further reason for Islam's success was its espousal of tolerance and universalism. The Quran expressly condemned racism, tribalism, and nationalism, while Muslim powers generally proved relatively tolerant of Jews, Christians, and Zoroastrians, who as "people of the book" (possessing scriptural traditions similar to the Quran) could

---

[4] The *hadith*, which developed by the ninth century, are a collection of traditions about the life of the Prophet (*Sira*) or what he approved – as opposed to the *sunna*, which denotes the way he lived his life and constitutes the second source of Islamic jurisprudence.

be granted the status of *dhimmi* – subject peoples accorded protected status and permitted to practice their religion. The Umayyads (661–750) tolerated and made little effort to convert conquered peoples. Thus initially, in some regions of Persia, conversion to Islam and Arabisation was superficial. This included areas on the western-most frontier of Buddhism and along the trade routes to Central Asia where, despite the Muslim advance, Buddhism survived because its adherents collaborated with Arabs, notably in financing inter-regional trade. Indeed, in Sind, rather than attempt to convert Buddhists, Muslim conquerors categorised them as *dhimmis*.

Islamisation and Arabisation accelerated under the Abbasids (750–1258). However, many non-Muslims continued to thrive. For instance, Jewish merchants resident in Siraf prospered from the mid-ninth century as the port developed into the preeminent Persian Gulf entrepôt. They subsequently migrated, first to Kish (in the late 1100s) and then Hormuz (in the 1300s), when the centre of trade switched to those entrepôts. Moreover, Muslim authorities generally assured security of person and property to merchants visiting or residing in the main trade centres, irrespective of ethnicity, religion, and culture, in return for a tax on their dealings. Thus in 1442, it was commented of Hormuz, then the premier Persian Gulf port:

> Travellers come here from all countries, and, in turn, bring merchandise and can get everything they wish with no trouble at all. There are many people of all religions in this city and no one is allowed to insult their religion. That is why this city is called the citadel of security.[5]

Again, following the conquest of Bengal by Muslim forces in 1204, and settlement there of Sufis, there was no immediate push to convert local Hindus and Buddhists. Mass conversion to Islam, in both the Middle Eastern heartland and beyond, occurred only when core aspects of pre-existing belief systems were accommodated – reflecting a flexibility and pragmatism which in many areas enabled Islam to move beyond being the religion of the conqueror to that of the conquered.

The advantages of conversion to Islam were considerable. Membership of any club based on religion, ethnicity, or other social communality, could help forge bonds of mutual trust and confidence critical to the success of high-risk, long-term, geographically

---

[5] Samarqandī quoted in T.M. Ricks, "Persian Gulf Seafaring and East Africa: Ninth-Twelfth Centuries" *African Historical Studies* 3.2 (1970): 354, n.78.

dispersed trading ventures that required substantial capital investment. Members of initially non-Muslim political and mercantile
classes were particularly attracted to Islam because of its many commercial advantages. It embraced much of the IOW and beyond, and
was characterised by often significant involvement of merchants in
the *tariqa* (Sufi brotherhoods) which greatly promoted Muslim trade
with *Dar al-Kufr* which in turn influenced many local authorities to
embrace Islam. Due to the *tariqa*-merchant alliance, Muslim traders
by the late thirteenth century dominated the main IOW maritime
trade routes between the Red Sea and Indonesia, as well as the overland Silk Road, and had formed settlements in all major entrepôts. For
example, when in the second half of the eleventh century Guangzhou
emerged as China's premier port, Muslim traders settled there in such
numbers that it soon boasted a number of mosques.

Converts to Islam took advantage of the *hajj* and other Islamic
pilgrimages to advance their commercial interests and create or consolidate long-distance trading contacts. Pilgrimages also served to
encourage debate and the dispersion of new ideas, as did the spread
of Arabic as both a lingua franca and written language. The Quran
was quickly transformed from oral to written form after which it was
Muslim practice to demand that all Islamic texts (which Muslims
considered to be the language of God) be written in Arabic. Thus
those wishing to read seminal works of Islamic law, theology, and history had to acquire a thorough understanding of written Arabic. In
the first centuries of Islam, almost all Middle Eastern authors, regard-
less of their ethnic background, wrote in Arabic. Hence, many non-
Arabic languages, including Persian, Urdu, and Turkish, were written
in versions of the Arabic script and contained many Arabic words.
The use of written Arabic, facilitated by the Arab adoption of papermaking (following the capture of Chinese papermakers after the battle
of Talas, in Samarqand, in 751), greatly promoted accuracy in commercial transactions, as well as legal security.

Moreover, from 830, when a school of translators was established
in Baghdad, outstanding Greek, Persian, and Indian scientific works
were translated into Arabic. Chinese influence can be discerned in the
medical works of al-Razi (865–925), ibn Sina (980–1037), and ibn al-
Haytham (965–1039), in pharmacology, and alchemy, as in mathematics (arithmetic, geometry, trigonometry) and its applications in fields
such as astronomy, astrology, geography, cartography, and optics. This
ensured that, from the ninth to eleventh centuries, Arabic became the

language of scientific knowledge. From the ninth to fifteenth centuries the most important centres of scientific learning were based in the Muslim world where knowledge was diffused through universities, schools, mosques, observatories, and hospitals. However, it is notable that, at the height of Arabo-Islamic culture in the ninth and tenth centuries, most cultural luminaries were non-Arabs. Moreover, in the Abbasid east, rulers patronised Persian literature, and Persian-speaking Muslim missionaries spread the Persian language amongst Turkish and Mongol converts to Islam.

Northern IOA in the Second IOW Economic Upsurge

In northern IOA, from Egypt to the Horn, the ninth to thirteenth centuries have usually been analysed in terms of the expansion and impact of Muslim forces. In 639, an Arab army invaded Egypt, and under the Fatimid regime the centre of Islamic commercial and political power moved from Baghdad to Cairo, founded in 973 as capital of the first Fatimite Caliphate. This has led scholars to discuss Egypt, indisputably part of *Dar al-Islam*, and often also the Sudan, in relation to the Middle East rather than Africa. The expansion of Islam, and the clash of Muslim and Christian forces, has additionally set the context for most historical interpretations of Somalia and Ethiopia during this period. The following analysis, by contrast, attempts to set the history of northern IOA in the context of the second great upsurge in the IOW global economy and of human-environment interaction.

Egypt and the IOW Global Economy

As noted, Egypt was of critical importance to the IOW global economy. One of the world's major commercial crossroads, it was a primary supplier of grain to the surrounding region, and of gold, linen, cloth, glass, and tropical commodities, including ivory, rhinoceros horn, and animal skins, to the wider IOW. This made Egypt a primary target for the early Islamic powers. As a former trader to Egypt, 'Amr b. al-'As, who led the Arab invasion of 639, was fully aware of its commercial and strategic importance.

The traditional interpretation is that Egypt prospered under its Arab conquerors, the Fatimids (969–1171), Ayyubids (1171–1250),

and "Turkish" Mamluks (1250–1382), before entering a long period
of decline under the "Circassian" Mamluks (1382–1517). Initially, as
the balance of economic and political power switched gradually from
Iraq and the Persian Gulf to Egypt, the Red Sea and the *Hadhramaut*,
Egypt developed into a principal agricultural, manufacturing, and
commercial hub. Woollen textiles were manufactured in towns in the
Nile Valley, and linens in the Delta and in the Faiyum Oasis (about
100 km southwest of Cairo). In addition to the output of private
weavers, profitable state-run factories manufactured textiles for court
consumption and for trade. Egypt also produced coloured glass that
was exported as far east as China. Other exports included grain, flax,
linen, opium, glass and other beads, crystal, rosewater, and dried
roses. There was a return flow from the eastern IOW of Chinese coins,
porcelain, and slaves (probably Negrito or dark-skinned Indonesians);
from India of coarse Cambay cloth, and some silks, white cloths, furs,
and spices; and from the Persian Gulf of pearls, piece goods, dates,
and dried fish. Egypt distributed Mediterranean goods to the wider
IOW and IOW commodities to the Mediterranean, including spices
and cowries (used to pay for the trans-Saharan gold and slave trades).

In order to stimulate maritime commerce, the Fatimids inaugurated
a major shipbuilding and canal construction programme. They
provided armed escorts for Muslim merchant ships that consequently
dominated much of the Mediterranean, Red, and Arabian seas. They
also promoted commercial exchange with their African hinterland.
Further, the Fatimids encouraged the Karimi, a group of large-scale,
family-run Muslim merchant-banking concerns to settle in Egypt
in the late eleventh century in order to divert the spice trade from
the Persian Gulf. As its international trade boomed, Egypt's primary
entrepôt, Alexandria, was described in 1165 by the Jewish traveller
Benjamin of Tudela as "a commercial market for all nations".[6]

However, the history of Egypt also needs to be set in the context
of human-environment interaction. The climate of northern IOA was
heavily influenced by a combination of factors, most importantly
the ITCZ, IOW monsoons, ENSO, and Indian and Atlantic Ocean
SSTs. Between about 800 and 1250, northern IOA experienced
mixed climatic fortunes. A southward shift of the ITCZ from 700 to
900 resulted in sharply decreased rainfall over Egypt, which led to

---

[6] M. Adler (ed. and trans.) *The Itinerary of Benjamin of Tudela* (London: Henry Frowde,
1993), 76.

the abandonment between 759 and 848 of formerly cultivated desert fringes. By contrast, heavier monsoon rainfall over Ethiopia fed the Nile, making more extensive cultivation possible along the Nile Valley. Up to the mid-tenth century, Egyptian grain harvests were plentiful, which ensured the peaceful behaviour of desert nomads dependent on such provisions. In addition, epidemic disease was largely absent. However, enhanced Nile flows also carried greater amounts of sand, which in the eighth century buried two cities on its Canopic branch.

A period of intermittently intense droughts followed, around 949 and from 953 to 955, and caused food shortages and popular protests. A prolonged drought from 963 to 969 resulted in widespread famine, the death or flight of 600,000 people from Fustat (the first Muslim capital of Egypt), abandonment of large tracts of normally cultivable land including that attached to Christian monasteries, increased nomad raids on Nile settlements, and social unrest. These factors undermined the Ikhshidid dynasty (935–969) and precipitated the Fatimid takeover in 969. The new regime imported North African grain to relieve hunger in Egypt, and in 973 founded Cairo, which became a great centre of Islam. As Arab geographer Al-Muqaddasi (ca 945/946–991) noted:

> Know further that Baghdad was once a magnificent city, but is now falling fast to ruin and decay, and has lost all its splendour ... Al-Fustāt of Misr [now part of Old Cairo] in the present day is like Baghdad of old; I know of no city in Islam superior to it.[7]

However, between 930 and 1470 Egypt experienced highly unstable climatic conditions, with extended low Nile levels from 930 to 1070 and a tenfold rise in droughts between 950 and 1072 compared to the previous 650 years – 11 droughts occurring between 1052 and 1072 alone. The persistent eleventh-century droughts were probably related to extreme El Niño events between 967 and 1096, and a peak in the Solar Minimum from 1040 to 1080, that reduced the intensity of the African summer monsoon and induced frequent failure of Nile summer floods. Very low Nile floods occurred again in 1096, and from 1180 to 1350; and major high floods from 1070 to 1180 and 1350 to 1470. Harvest failures ensued, and famines from 1059 to 1072, in 1181, from 1096 to 1097 and 1199 to 1202, in which numbers of affected people resorted to cannibalism.

---

[7] Al-Maqdisi quoted in Geoff Wade, "An Early Age of Commerce in Southeast Asia, 900–1300 CE" *Journal of Southeast Asian Studies* 40.2 (2009): 232.

These environmental influences had significant economic and political impacts. Famine and disease resulted in desertion of settlements, flight from Egypt, and a sharp decline in population – from an estimated 2.4 million to 1.5 million between 1052 and 1090. Local Jewish and Coptic merchants, who also had major tax-collection interests in landed estates, were hit so badly that by the close of the twelfth century the Karimi had largely superseded them as the intermediaries of trade between the IOW and Mediterranean. Many individual Karimi possessed well over three times the capital held by the average local wholesale merchant in Egypt. From their headquarters in Alexandria, the Karimi established a series of *funduq*, "specialized large-scale commercial institutions and markets which developed into virtual stock exchanges"[8] on the main western IOW commercial routes. Karimi influence expanded in concert with the expansion of the Ottoman Empire, into Asia Minor, and along caravan routes to Nubia, Ethiopia, and West Africa. The Karimi benefitted from a return to benign environmental influences from around 1300 when maximum Nile levels showed a general longer-term increase, and Egypt experienced renewed prosperity and demographic expansion, its population growing from about 2.4 million to 4 million between the end of the twelfth and the mid-fourteenth century.

Ethiopia and Sudan

A southward shift of the ITCZ between 700 and 900 resulted in heavier monsoon rains in the northwestern IOW maritime zone. However, from 967 to 1096, extreme El Niño events brought drought conditions to Ethiopia which experienced a further long arid period between 1180 and 1350, with periods of excessive rainfall from 1070 to 1180 and 1350 to 1470. Such factors were of pivotal significance. Thus while periods of heavy rainfall encouraged extended cultivation, this in turn resulted in significant denuding of slopes in Axum between 600 and 800. Indeed, Ethiopia in general experienced a general decline in soil fertility, agricultural productivity, and population until around 1000 CE. Thereafter, Ethiopia experienced major famines from the mid-thirteenth to mid-fourteenth centuries (in 1252,

---

[8] Subhi Y. Labib, "Capitalism in Medieval Islam" *Journal of Economic History* 29.1 (1969): 85; see also ibid., 82–3.

1258–9, 1272 to 1275 and 1314 to 1344), and a major epidemic in 1261–2.

Environmental factors help explain Muslim expansion into northeast Africa. The southward shift in the ITCZ from 700 to 900, while bringing greater rainfall to Ethiopia, resulted in sharply decreased rainfall further north. Moreover, significant sulphur-rich volcanism from the early eighth to late twelfth centuries resulted in the abandonment of formerly cultivated desert fringes in southern Arabia and Yemen, which encouraged migration across the Red Sea to Somalia and Ethiopia. Yemenites established a sultanate centred on Zeila in the seventh century, and from the ninth century a number of Muslim polities emerged in Ethiopia. Islam had become the dominant faith in Eritrea by the eleventh century and in the east Ethiopian highlands by the mid-thirteenth century. By the fourteenth century, a line of Muslim settlements dominated the main caravan routes from Zeila to the Sudan, from the Red Sea coast to the Rift Valley southeast of the Ethiopian highlands, and to the plateau to the west and south of the highlands – where the Cushitic Sidama elite converted to Islam. By the thirteenth century, the same processes had resulted in the Islamisation of many Somalis, and led to Saylac – an entrepôt on the Somali north coast – developing into an important centre of Muslim culture and learning.

The environmental and human factors noted above inevitably influenced trade. Northeast Africa straddled the northern (Red Sea) termini of the Great Rift Valley and the Atbara and Abbaj (Blue Nile) tributaries of the Nile leading to Sudan and Egypt. It was thus, like Egypt, an important crossroads between IOA and the rest of the IOW. Ethiopia was a traditional source of gold, ivory, civet musk, and slaves. Impoverished highlanders, forced by poverty into slavery, or captured in battle, were particularly abundant in the period up to about 1000 CE, comprising possibly the majority of slaves exported to Lower Iraq in that period. From the twelfth century, probably due to impoverishment, there was a further boom in the export of Ethiopian slaves, a significant number of whom were, by the thirteenth century being shipped to India, notably to Gujarat and the Gulf of Cambay, but also to Malabar and Sri Lanka. Male slaves served predominantly as soldiers. For instance, in ca 1333, Ibn Battuta reported a corps of 50 "Abyssinian" [slave] soldiers aboard a vessel in Ganhar, Gujarat, and others at Calicut. Thousands were also shipped to the Deccan in the early 1400s, and in the late 1400s to Bengal and the Indian west coast. In Bengal, an Ethiopian slave named Shahdaza seized the throne in 1486 under the name Barbak Shar – starting a period of rule by Habshis (a term derived from the Arabic "Ḥabashī" meaning "Abyssinian", used for African and Ethiopian slaves in pre-British India) that endured into the first decade of the sixteenth century; and on the Indian west coast, Ethiopian slaves seized control of the off-shore island of Janjira (165 km south of present-day Mumbai) from the 1490s.

Somalia exported, chiefly through Aden, frankincense, animal skins, rhinoceros horn, tortoiseshell, myrrh, putchuk, liquid storax gum, ambergris, gold, beeswax, sandalwood, and ivory. In high demand in IOW markets, these commodities were exchanged for Chinese coins and porcelain, Iranian pearls, piece goods, dates, and dried fish, Indian silks, white cloth, coarse (Cambay) cloth, and spices, Egyptian opium, and (probably Egyptian) glass and other beads, as well as crystal, rosewater, and dried roses.

The maritime trade of northeast Africa was dominated by merchants from Siraf until the port was devastated by an earthquake in 977, following which Yemeni merchants competed fiercely with those of Kish – the Iranian port that succeeded Siraf – for a trade with northeast Africa that was stimulated by rising demand for African commodities in India and China. Imports into China from the Africa-Arabia-Persian Gulf area increased 943 per cent between 1049–53 and 1175, much of it for African ivory, frankincense, rhinoceros horns (used to neutralise poison, and in aphrodisiacs), and tortoiseshell (used to manufacture girdles). *Chau Ju-Kua* (1170–1228), a Song dynasty supervisor of maritime trade, stated that the best rhinoceros horn, and the finest and largest quantity of tortoise shell, came from the Berbera coast. He also considered Socotra, a renowned source of dragon's blood, to be part of the region. In the thirteenth century, Arab geographer, Yāqūt al-Hamawī (1179–1229), described Mogadishu, on the Indian Ocean coast of Somalia, as a major entrepôt for sandal-wood, ebony, and ambergris.

Islam in Northern IOA

Many Eurocentric histories portray Islam as a monolithic politico-religious institution with a Middle Eastern core that dominated much of the IOW until undermined by the technologically superior, more adaptable, and modernising forces of Europe. Such histories consider that in IOA, the chief economic impact of Muslim intervention was the creation of a heinous slave export trade. However, the expansion of Islam in IOA needs to be reevaluated in the context of both human-environment interaction and the IOW global economy. Muslim armies, government institutions, and law created a Pax Islamica over vast regions, providing a hitherto unparalleled degree of security and protection under which merchants of all nationalities and religions prospered. Because Muslim holy men worked closely with merchants, Islamisation generally advanced with the Muslim trading frontier. Sufi orders were particularly important in spreading Islam in sub-Saharan Africa. Arabic became the political and commercial *lingua franca* over much of the western IOW, but Arabicisation did not necessarily follow Islamisation. In most of northeast and East Africa, Muslims spoke local languages, while Kiswahili developed as the *lingua franca* of the East African littoral as it did later, in the nineteenth century, in much of the East African interior. Also, linguistic and cultural communal-ities meant vibrant commercial relations were generally maintained with non-Muslim communities.

In Egypt, the chief aim of Muslim rulers was to maximise state revenue. Consequently, as was the case with governments in many other parts of the *Dar al-Islam*, they adopted a pragmatic and tolerant attitude to other religions. Although Egypt became predominantly Muslim by the thirteenth century, Arabs initially refrained from pros-elytisation. By 690, possibly half of registered adult male Christians had converted to Islam, but this was a reflection less of pressure by Muslim rulers than a nominal adhesion to Christianity enforced by the prior Roman regime on a population that believed in trad-itional local gods such as Isis. Moreover, from about 700, Islamisation proceeded slowly. For example, the first Arab governor of Egypt followed his Byzantine predecessors in ratifying the appointment of Coptic Church patriarchs. However, adhesion to the church declined sharply following the 1347 to 1349 plague epidemic which caused high mortality among monks and abandonment of monastic estates. Some non-Muslims were appointed to important official positions. In the early caliphate, Christian officials administered the naval centres of Alexandria, Dumyat (Damietta), and Rosetta. The state protected politically loyal merchants of other faiths (notably "of the book"). Alexandria and Cairo, in particular, attracted traders of non-Egyptian origin, including Ethiopians. As in other IOW entrepôts, each merchant community had its own quarters. In the 1160s, 7,000 Jews worshipped at two major synagogues in Fustat (Old Cairo). Moreover, this tolerance was extended to the indigenous population. By the fourteenth century, there was extensive intermarriage and a breakdown of local ethnic prejudice in Egypt.

Nevertheless, the attraction of conversion to Islam was great. First, Egypt became the focal point of Islamic learning. By the 1160s, Alexandria, which possessed a long-established reputation as a cultural centre, had developed twenty academies and a vibrant community of scholars, some of whose works, translated into Arabic, had a considerable influence on Islamic science. The geographer, al-Hamawī, noted of the scholars and alchemists of Alexandria Museum:

> The place of their sessions is like stairs, where they sit divided into classes. On the lowest level sat the alchemists, making gold from silver by chemical means. Next to these stairs there was a spring of water able to cure leprosy.[9]

Cairo similarly developed advanced scholarly institutions, including the observatory, established in 996, and al-Azhar University, "the oldest university in the world",[10] founded in 988. Such establishments also transformed Cairo into an international centre of scientific learning. Following the restoration in Egypt of the orthodox Sunni regime under Saladin in 1169, the Mongol destruction of Baghdad in 1258, and the establishment of the caliphate in Egypt in 1261, Cairo became the world centre of Sunni scholarship. Islamisation was facilitated by Egypt's role as a major producer of papyrus parchments, used by all caliphs until the tenth century, and subsequently of paper. From the thirteenth century, Al-Azhar wielded enormous influence over developments in Islam in both the *Dar al-Islam*, and in the *Dar al-Kufr*. Its scholars constantly reevaluated the realities of the religious frontier in Africa, notably the need to accommodate various cultures and religions. Al-Azhar was connected to other IOA centres of Islamic learning, including Kutranj, on the Blue Nile in Sudan, and Lamu on the Swahili coast. It also attracted IOA students: those from Ethiopia were housed in a special hostel (*riwaq al-jabartiyya*) maintained by the Ethiopian Islamic community.

---

[9] Yaqut quoted in P. Donini, *Arab Travelers and Geographers* (London: Immel, 1991), 22.
[10] Donini, *Arab Travelers*, 23.

Islamisation increased as the Muslim trade network flourished and imperial frontiers expanded. For example, gold and pilgrims regularly flowed from West Africa to the Sudan, and on to Egypt or across the Red Sea to Jeddah and Mecca. Muslim merchants also travelled up the Nile and returned with equatorial products, including Sudanese ivory, rhinoceros horn, and slaves. Indeed, so important were the resources of northeast Africa, the Sudan, and sub-Saharan areas beyond, that the Egyptian imperial policy sought to bring those regions under its control through military subjugation, commercial dominance, and colonial settlement.

However, Egypt's imperial expansion did not assume the uniformly military or antagonistic form conventionally ascribed to it. Proselytisation in Lower Egypt was significant from 716, but proceeded slower further south. From the seventh century, Arab merchants, miners, pilgrims, and nomads visited Nubia, a tributary state of Egypt, and some stayed. Consequently, the northernmost Nubian kingdom of Maris became Muslim and was assimilated into Egypt. Following the sack in 1272 of the Red Sea port of 'Aydhab by Christian forces from Makuria, Nubia was brought under Egyptian rule and settled by Arab 'Urbān soldiers from Upper Egypt. The 'Urbān subsequently expanded south into lands with higher rainfall and, in the mid-1300s, Egypt imposed an Islamic puppet dynasty in Makuria. Nevertheless, adherence to Islam, as previously to Christianity, remained nominal. Somalia became predominantly Muslim by 1200, but the converted, rulers and subjects, maintained aspects of traditional indigenous beliefs and practices. This pattern was duplicated in other IOW regions, such as the Sudan where the veneration and exclusion of the local monarch continued to be practised.

In northeast Africa the expanding Muslim frontier inevitably created tensions, but again did not assume the rigidly aggressive form often assumed. Muslims accorded Ethiopia special status. Not only were Christians "people of the book", but from 615 to 628 Axum had granted refuge to 100 of Muhammad's followers fleeing persecution by the Prophet's Meccan opponents. In consequence, Christian Ethiopia was deemed to be *Dar al-Hiyad* (or *Dar al-Sulh*), a region with a non-Muslim government, but distinct from the *Dar al-Kufr* in that it was considered to be at peace with Muslims and exempt from *jihad*. Moreover, despite rivalry, Ethiopian, "pagan", and Muslim traders interacted commercially. Thus "pagans" to the south of the Ethiopian highlands traded with the small Somali Muslim states that possessed important IOW links. Moreover, overall Muslim commercial dominance did not prevent "Christian" commercial influence from expanding in the 1300s along a north-south axis between the Dahlak Islands and the river Awash. As significantly, by the late 1600s, sufficient numbers of Oromo – a pastoral people who expanded into much of southern Ethiopia from the early 1500s – had converted to Christianity and become sedentary agriculturalists, for Emperor Iyasu I (1682–1706) to settle them along the northern edge of the river Abbai (Blue Nile) as a buffer against further incursions from "pagan" Oromo.

The relatively cordial relations between the different religious communities in northeast Africa stemmed from a commercial rationale, religious tolerance, and shared linguistic and cultural traits. Moreover, in a pattern repeated elsewhere, merchant and political elites often learned Arabic but Arabicisation did not necessarily follow conversion. Most converts to Islam in northeast Africa retained indigenous languages and cultures common to their non-Muslim neighbours. In addition, the Christian hierarchy in Ethiopia maintained good relations with the Islamic regime in Egypt in order to retain its close links with the Coptic Church whose patriarch in Alexandria continued to appoint the bishop in Ethiopia until the 1950s.

6

Southern IOA and the Second Upsurge in the IOW Global Economy

From the ninth to thirteenth centuries, three southern IOA "civilisations" emerged – the Swahili, Great Zimbabwe, and early Malagasy. There is considerable debate as to their origins, interrelationships, and linkages to the wider IOW, as well as to African and exogenous influences on them. This chapter examines these debates within the context of human-environment interaction and the second great upsurge in the IOW global economy.

Environmental Factors

Equatorial East Africa is affected by multiple climatic factors, including the ITZC, ENSO, and Atlantic and Indian Ocean sea surface temperatures (SSTs). From around 750 to 940 CE, littoral regions of the equatorial zone experienced increased rainfall as a result of a southward migration of the ITZC. However, the evidence points to aridity over much of the rest of southern IOA. Between about 540 and 890, the equatorial interior was hit by severe drought that resulted from weak El Niño events and low western Indian Ocean SSTs. Indeed, lake levels in equatorial East Africa continued to be relatively low up to the late thirteenth century. The evidence suggests that major drought also affected Mozambique between 800 and 900, while from about 900 to the thirteenth century, SSTs indicate an extended weak negative Indian Ocean Dipole (IOD) that is associated with generalised drought in East Africa. Drought also affected central Madagascar from 600 to 800, southeast Madagascar between 600 and 1200, and eastern South Africa from 800 to 1000. By contrast, western regions of central East Africa, affected more by Atlantic climatic influences, and southern Africa in general, experienced severe drought to about 890, but thereafter plentiful rainfall until 1300.

The Swahili Civilisation

By the eleventh century, a "Swahili" (lit. "coastal dweller" or "people of the coast" – from the Arabic *sahil*, meaning "coast") civilisation had emerged in Zanj (former Azania), comprising numerous small Islamic city-ports stretching from the Benadir coast of Somalia in the north to Sofala in the south, and extending westwards to the Comoro Islands and northwest Madagascar. As noted in Chapter 4, the currently dominant view rejects the traditional interpretation that Persian, Arab, and possibly Indian traders and settlers created the Swahili civilisation, arguing instead that the Swahili language (Kiswahili) and culture is predominantly of Bantu African origin, and that Bantu-speakers developed the maritime culture that is at the heart of the Swahili political economy.

However, new evidence suggests that from the ninth century, when IOW global trade started to rebound, foreign settlers and merchants rather than local peoples were chiefly responsible for the recovery of East African maritime trade. As the ITZC migrated southwards from 700 to 900, and significant sulphur-rich volcanic eruptions occurred from the early eighth to late twelfth centuries, numbers of Arabs and Persians fled growing aridity in their homelands for better-watered littoral of East Africa. Others, such as followers of Zayd ibn 'Alī (695–740), great grandson of the Caliph, Ali ibn Abi Talib (601–661), who was the son-in-law of the prophet Muhammad, left due to religious persecution. Typically, these migrants sought protected locations with secure anchorage on the East African coast, generally in river mouths or on offshore islands. These settlements practised little agriculture, which expanded only from the fourteenth century when parts of the neighbouring continental littoral were brought under cultivation – which suggests a large Bantu-speaking presence on the coast only from that time. In later centuries, agriculture was practised on both the mainland and interior of larger islands by "Swahili", many of whom had little or no knowledge of maritime skills.

Arab geographers Al-Istakhri (mid-tenth century) and Al-Muqaddasi (late tenth century) commented that the Zanj were non-Muslim. However, Islam, which first appeared in East Africa from the late eighth century, spread rapidly along the Swahili littoral due to the influence of Muslim settlers whose links to the wider IOW gave them considerable economic, political, and social influence. In a number of locations along the Swahili coast, Muslim immigrants became political rulers, while Muslim religious leaders were generally venerated. From the early tenth century, as Arab immigration intensified, the Swahili elite increasingly replaced wooden-framed mud and thatch buildings with permanent structures that included mosques constructed in the Red Sea tradition – i.e. finely squared porite block walls bonded in red mud, with floors and walls covered in coral lime. They also adopted Shirazi models of administration, and asserted Shirazi ancestry. From the twelfth century, many of the African political and merchant elite in Swahili port cities converted to Islam, and learned at least basic spoken and written Arabic. Their connections with the wider IOW were further facilitated through trade and the *hajj* which their access to maritime transport enabled them to perform more easily than African Muslims from sub-Saharan West Africa.

However, as in northeast Africa, Arabisation was not an automatic concomitant of conversion. Kiswahili remained the mother tongue of local Muslims and non-Muslims. Indeed, many foreign merchants and hinterland Africans in regular commercial contact with the Swahili ports adopted Kiswahili as a second language, while Muslim holy men and scholars used Kiswahili when teaching, to the degree that Islamisation in East Africa was associated with the spread of Kiswahili, not Arabic. Although official manuscripts were mainly written in Arabic, *Kiarabu*, the old Swahili script based on Arabic letters, was used on coins and tombstones as early as the eleventh century, and thereafter in trade documents, correspondence, genealogical lists, and chronicles.

Swahili merchants participated fully in the general growth in maritime commerce. Two distinct trading hubs existed: a northern network centred on the Lamu Archipelago, and a southern network incorporating Mozambique, the Comoros and Madagascar. From the tenth to twelfth centuries the preeminent settlements were Shanga, Pate, and Manda, in the Lamu Archipelago. These centres were linked initially to the Persian port of Siraf, a principal IOW entrepôt, and later Kish and Mormuz. Other important settlements in the northern sector of southern IOA included Mombasa, Pemba, and Zanzibar. However, as previously noted, because the influence of the monsoons diminished at about 12°S, overseas traders also established resident agents at more southerly locations along the East African coast, such as Mafia and Kilwa, as well as on the Comoro Islands and in northwest Madagascar.

During the Baghdad-based Abbasid dynasty (750–1258), Persians were the dominant foreign traders along the East African coast. They expanded their commercial frontier south to a lengthy littoral they called *Bilad as-Sufala* ("low-lying land") with a capital, "Sofala", near Beira in Mozambique, adjoining Hwfl/ Waq-waq (possibly Madagascar, the Comoros, or part of the African mainland then inhabited by Khoisan-speakers) which reputedly possessed the most valuable export commodities. East African commerce was as important to Siraf as trade with East Asia. From the eleventh century, Persians probably traded as far as Pondoland (in present-day South Africa), and learned of a treacherous sea route around the Cape into the Atlantic. Moreover, while most foreign merchants dealt with coastal entrepôts, at least one enterprising Sirafi ventured into the interior: Al-Masudi (d. 956), who visited East Africa at least twice, the last occasion being in 916/17. He provided the earliest detailed written account of Zanj, noting that ships sailed regularly from the Persian Gulf (Oman and Siraf) directly to the main Zanj port of Qanbalu (probably Unguja, i.e. Zanzibar Island). The round-trip from Sohar in Oman to Sofala was nearly 12,000 km (to China it was 16,000 km). From the eleventh century, Zanj-Egyptian trade also flourished. This is reflected in the influx into Zanj of Fatimid coins and, by the thirteenth century, keen *Karimi* merchant interest in East Africa. Again, from the late twelfth century, Zanj-Indian commerce grew dramatically, as did mostly indirect trade with China.

Imports into Zanj included Middle Eastern beads, Iranian perfumes, kitchenware, precious stones, and wine, Indian rice, spices, cotton cloth, copper, ironware, beads, and pottery, and Chinese porcelain. These stimulated the local manufacture of coarser varieties of pottery, the adoption of cotton cultivation and cotton-cloth making technology (the loom and spindle-whorl), as well as the production of coinage (found in large quantities at Mafia and Kilwa), first in silver and later in copper.

The most valuable Zanj exports were ivory, rhinoceros horn, tortoiseshell, ambergris, and gold – shipped down the Zambezi from the highland interior. Ivory was in demand in Egypt, the Mediterranean,

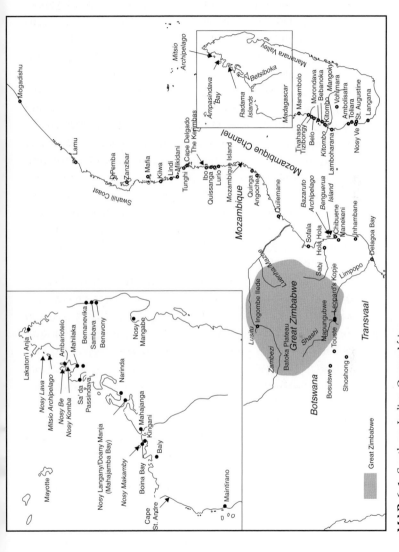

MAP 6.1 Southern Indian Ocean Africa

Note: Produced by Carl Hughes, IOWC.

and especially China, where regional sources were inferior and declining. By Tang times (618–907), Chinese sources of rhinoceros horn, valued for its alleged curative and aphrodisiacal properties, had sharply diminished due chiefly to deforestation. China was a significant market for tortoiseshell and ambergris for ornamental and pharmaceutical uses, as well as for perfumery. Other East African export staples included yellow sandalwood, leopard skins used to manufacture saddles and rugs in Muslim countries and in China, timber that in Siraf, for instance, was used for boat and house construction, aromatic woods, and small (oyster) sea pearls from the Bazaruto Islands. Also, rock crystal (quartz) was manufactured into beads on the coast (e.g. Lamu) for export, or shipped to Egypt and Iran to be manufactured into medallions, jewellery, and mosque lamps. Further, millet, rice, and meat served as commodities in coastal trade. In addition, Zanj exported slaves, although their number is contested (see Chapter 12). Zanj staples in demand in India and China were initially transported via Oman, but from about 900 were increasingly shipped to India where goods for the eastern IOW were transshipped – chiefly in the Gujarati port of Somnath until its destruction in 1038.

This late first to early second-millennium upswing in Zanj maritime trade stimulated Swahili shipbuilding, notably of lateen-rigged (a triangular sail attached to a long yard at an angle of 45° to the mast) dhows with cotton sails, and square-rigged *mtepe*-style vessels (wooden ships the planks of which were sewn together with coir and fastened with wooden pegs) with huge coconut mat sails. This in turn promoted sail-making from locally produced coir (coconut fibre) and cotton (grown, e.g. on Kilwa). Most Swahili boats were used in coastal and western Indian Ocean trade, although Arab and Indian merchant vessels dominated the Arabian and Red seas. Swahili merchants used chiefly non-Swahili ships to travel to the eastern Indian Ocean. Thus even at the start of the sixteenth century, traders from Kilwa, Malindi, Mogadishu, and Mombasa, as well as from Egypt and Ethiopia, sailed to Southeast Asia aboard Gujarati ships.

"Great Zimbabwe" and Intra-Southern IOA Exchange

Enhanced maritime trade greatly strengthened coastal-interior linkages. In the northern Zanj sector, the Lamu Archipelago, located at the southernmost reach of the regular monsoon, was a natural meeting place for north-south maritime and coastal-interior trade. From the ninth century, Lamu exported pottery from Wenje, about 100 km inland and, from about the mid-tenth to late eleventh centuries, quartz, probably from Kitui, about 350 km inland. Lamu possibly also traded with large centralised polities practising agriculture, cattle-raising, and ironwork, that emerged between the thirteenth and fifteenth centuries at Kibengo, Munsa, Mubende, Bigo, and Ntusi, significant interior settlements located between Lakes Albert and Victoria.

However, communication with the deep interior was easiest and of greater significance via the Zambezi River on the Mozambique ("Sofala") coast. The volume and value of foreign trade with Mozambique was such that, by the late thirteenth century, Kilwa had emerged as a major southern IOA entrepôt. It dominated exchange between the wider IOW and IOA trading posts south of Cape Delgado, and hence well beyond the reach of the monsoons, such as Chibuene in the Bazaruto Archipelago, Sofala, Angoche, Quilemane, the Kerimba Islands and, from the mid- to late fourteenth century, Mozambique Island. From these ports, trade routes ran deep into the plateau interior. Strong, regular coastal-interior linkages developed and, from around 900 CE, major inland concentrations of power and trade emerged. Such developments reflected both revived maritime trade and improved climatic factors. A period of greater rainfall from around 850 induced agro-pastoralists to spread into previously marginal areas, such as the fringes of the Kalahari, and the Shashi-Limpopo basin where from 900 to 1300 large, hierarchical centres emerged.

The most famous inland complex was Great Zimbabwe which developed at the head of the Zambezi and lasted from about 1050 to 1500. Associated settlements emerged in Zimbabwe, Mozambique, Botswana, and the Transvaal. One such settlement was Leopard's Kopje, at the Shashi-Limpopo confluence, but the most notable was Mapungubwe from ca 900 to 1250, the focus of a regional empire that, at its height, probably dominated an area equal to that of the nineteenth-century Zulu kingdom. From the eleventh to thirteenth centuries, hierarchical polities also arose in central eastern Botswana, including Bosutswe, Shoshong, and notably Toutse from where ivory, cattle, and skins flowed via Leopard's Kopje to the coast. By the early sixteenth, settlements associated with the Great Zimbabwe tradition extended over some 50,000 km^2 of territory. They also spread to southern Mozambique where, from the late 1100s to early 1600s, the Zimbabwe-style stone town of Manyikeni constituted a cotton spinning, iron-smelting, and iron tool manufacturing centre. Related trade settlements included Hola Hola on the Sabi River, Benguerra Island where local Early Iron Age pottery and imported Chinese porcelain have been discovered, and Chibuene on the peninsula south of the Bazaruto Islands which from the ninth century possessed Arabian and Persian Gulf connections and was linked to Manyikeni.

Great Zimbabwe experienced major geographic and demographic expansion. At its peak from 1350 to 1450, it ruled an empire three to six times greater in size than that of Mapungubwe, and its capital may have boasted a population of 10,000. Great Zimbabwe developed specialist mining and metal-working sectors, and engaged in vigorous inter-regional exchange of salt and metals (notably copper and iron in raw and manufactured forms) for grain, cattle, and game. Such internal networks might have existed independently: The Portuguese claimed that the Congo possessed a well-established, sophisticated system of long-distance exchange, with standardised units and a currency system, unconnected to overseas trade. However, relations between the East African coast and the interior were also long-standing, and rising overseas demand for IOA products strengthened Great Zimbabwe-coastal linkages via the Limpopo, Zambezi, and Mazowe rivers.

Major commodities shipped from the coast to the interior included glass beads (supplementing regionally produced gold, ostrich eggshell, and snail-shell beads), cowries and other marine shells, cloth, and ceramics. Unlike those of Zanzibar, "Zhizo" style beads, which passed through Chibuene to interior southern Africa, probably came not from Sri Lanka but from the Persian Gulf, possibly from Sohar. These imports flowed notably to inland centres such as Mapungubwe, Great Zimbabwe, Ingombe Ilede, and Toutse. The return flow of commodities to the coast comprised chiefly ivory and gold, and secondarily animal skins, copper (in part to produce a Swahili currency), and iron. Growing IOW demand for African ivory, due to falling supplies in Asia and the higher quality of African tusks, stimulated specialised elephant hunting, long-distance porterage, and ivory-working. Ingombe Ilede, located near the confluence of the Zambezi and Lusitu rivers, where large elephant herds roamed, developed into a significant ivory-working centre, as did the Batoka plateau (in present-day southern Zambia). Gold had been exploited and traded from early times. However, unprecedented growth in international demand, notably from time of the Abbasid Empire (750–1258) in the Middle East, and from the early 1300s in East Asia and Europe, stimulated greater production of gold in both West (Guinea) and East Africa. More than 200 Early Iron Age gold mines operated in Botswana. Gold was exported in nuggets, as dust (carried in porcupine quills), and in processed form. At Mapungubwe, for example, it was fashioned into beads, metal sheet, bangles, and bracelets.

The Malagasy Civilisation

In the late nineteenth and early twentieth centuries, Gabriel Ferrand and Alfred Grandidier, leading French authorities on Madagascar, advanced opposing theses concerning the origins of the Malagasy, the timing and route of their migration to the island, and their relations with East Africa. These theories have formed the basis for ongoing scholarly debate. Ferrand argued that from the seventh to thirteenth centuries CE, when Srivijaya, based at Palembang in Sumatra, flourished, Indonesian mariners involved in long-distance trade sailed along the northern rim of the Indian Ocean to East Africa from where separate or mixed Indonesian and African groups migrated to Madagascar. Grandidier countered that, since all Malagasy spoke variants of the same language of Austronesian origin, they must all have originated from the Malayo-Polynesian region. Thus the ancestors of the first dark-skinned Malagasy were Southeast Asian Negritos. Grandidier argued that continental Africans, lacking the maritime skills to cross the Mozambique Channel, formed a significant proportion of the population of Madagascar only during the nineteenth century, as victims of the slave trade. In 1951, Otto Dahl made a major contribution to the debate by demonstrating that the Malagasy language was closely allied to Manyaan, spoken in Kalimantan, in southeast Borneo. Dahl's argument is supported by K. Alexander Adelaar who specifies a historical origin for Manyaan speakers in Banjarmasin, a river port situated at the junction of the Barito and Martapura rivers. However, DNA evidence indicates that the Manyaan contributed little to the Malagasy gene pool, the main contributors to which were, on the male side, from East Borneo, South Sulawesi, and the Lesser Sunda Islands, and on the female side from eastern Indonesia, notably North Maluku, South Sulawesi (Bugis) and Lesser Sunda Islands (Bajau).

Estimates for the timing of the departure of the proto-Malagasy from Southeast Asia, and of human settlement of Madagascar, vary enormously. Between about 1500 BCE and 1500 CE, in the largest dispersal of its kind prior to the European "Voyages of Discovery", Austronesians colonised previously uninhabited islands between Easter Island, in the eastern Pacific, and Madagascar, some 26,000 km distant, in the western Indian Ocean. Estimates as to when the proto-Malagasy left Southeast Asia vary even more, from 3000 BCE to the thirteenth century CE. Dahl initially argued that, due to the paucity of Sanskrit influence on the Malagasy language, the proto-Malagasy must have left around 400 CE. Adelaar, backing Ferrand, argues rather for a departure at the end of seventh century, linked to the emergence of Srivijaya, and settlement of Madagascar in the eighth century. Adelaar contends further, on the basis of linguistic evidence, that contact between Malagasy and Malay speakers continued for some time after the colonisation of Madagascar to which the Arabic script was introduced from Southeast Asia, not the Middle East.

Scholars also differ as to the route taken. Some associate the proto-Malagasy migration with early trans-Indian Ocean connections, as in the successive dispersal of Southeast Asian boat forms (double canoes, single outriggers, and double outriggers), and coconut cultivation, to South Asia (India, Sri Lanka), and the western Indian Ocean (Swahili coast, Comoros, Madagascar). Waruno Mahdi, who argues that this process started as early as between 1000 and 600 BCE, contends that on return voyages Austronesians diffused sorghum to Indonesia by about 1000 BCE, and to China by the BCE/CE changeover. A number of scholars also associate early Austronesian voyages west with the spice trade, referencing a passage in Pliny's first century CE *Natural History* to long-distance mariners reaching the Red Sea region on rafts with highly prized cinnamon (see Chapter Three). Jan Christie concurs that from about 500 BCE, the Javanese were involved in regular maritime exchange with both eastern India and South China, importing stones (for tool making) and metals in return for spices and sandalwood from eastern Indonesia, and that from the first century CE, such trade contacts included the Mediterranean. Indeed, challenging the conventional emphasis on the role of Arabs, Persians, and Indians in early IOW shipping, Pierre-Yves Manguin and Mahdi argue that Southeast Asians probably dominated maritime trade in both the eastern and western IOW until at least the seventh century. It is thus entirely possible that during the first upsurge in the IOW global economy from 300 BCE to 300 CE, Southeast Asians sailed to East Africa and Madagascar.

The majority view is that the proto-Malagasy voyaged across the northern rim of the Indian Ocean to East Africa before crossing to Madagascar. However, on the basis of the diffusion of lashed-lug boat-building techniques, Manguin contends that they followed a direct equatorial route 4,800 km across the Indian Ocean via the Maldives. He also argues that they sailed in large boats. A third-century CE Chinese description of Southeast Asian ocean-going *jong* indicates that they were over 50 metres in length, rose 4 to 5 metres above the water line, had four masts, sailed direct and fast even in rough seas, and could carry between 600 and 700 people and possibly 1,000 tons of cargo.

The question of an early Southeast Asian presence in East Africa is unresolved. Most Afrocentric scholars point to an absence of archaeo-logical evidence for such presence, and argue that the Southeast Asian complex of plants and animals (see Chapter 2) was probably introduced into East Africa by Indian and Middle Eastern intermediaries. They further contend that cultural manifestations conventionally attributed to Indonesians, such as the outrigger canoe and sewn boat, were inde-pendent adaptations by Bantu-speakers who not only initiated foreign trade but, using iron technology, built large ocean-going boats with which they settled offshore islands and visited Madagascar. Overall, however, the evidence points to the presence of Southeast Asians on the East African coast by the BCE/CE changeover. They were adept high-sea mariners and engaged extensively in trans-IOW maritime exchange. Given the vibrant economy of East Africa around the BCE/CE change-over, when the Southeast Asian complex of plants and animals entered the region, it would have been surprising had they not sailed there. A lack of archaeological remains says little given that Southeast Asian mariners traditionally lived on their boats, travelled in family groups, and raised their children on board ship. Even close to land, they plied coastal waters, estuaries, and lagoons, leaving their boats only to culti-vate crops on neighbouring land, and to trade and raid. They thus left little archaeological or DNA record of their presence in East Africa, although there is intriguing evidence of Austronesian Y chromosome (father to son) DNA input in northern Zanzibar Island.[1]

---

[1] Himla Soodyall, results of DNA testing on the "Origins of the Malagasy" Project, with Gwyn Campbell and Sylvester Kajuna, in Soodyall to Kajuna, Johannesburg, 18 August 2014.

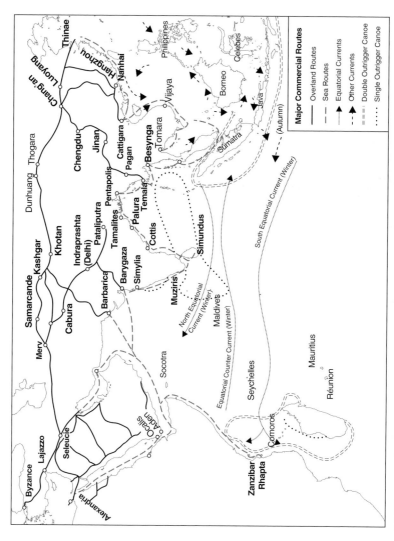

MAP 6.2 Indian Ocean World Currents, Outrigger Canoe Distribution, and Early Major Trade Routes

Note: Produced by Carl Hughes, IOWC.

FIGURE 6.1 Ninth-century Javanese Ship with Outriggers (from Borobudur)

Note: From James Hornell, "Indonesian Influence on East African Culture" *Journal of the Royal Anthropological Institute of Great Britain and Ireland* 64 (1934): 323.

Major debate also surrounds the first human settlement of Madagascar. Robert Dewar claimed evidence for human Stone Age occupation of sites on the northern Malagasy coast dating to between 2400 and 1461 BCE, and in the southwest from 805 BCE. However, these postulated dates are exceptionally early, and cut marks on animal bones may have had non-human causes. Other research on allegedly human-modified animal bones and landscapes (charcoal and pollen levels) points to human activity during the BCE/CE change-over, but there is, as yet, no indication of permanent human settlement at that time.

Indeed, there is considerable evidence that Madagascar was first permanently settled during the second boom period in the IOW global economy from the ninth to thirteenth centuries when Southeast Asian mariners, under the auspices of Srivijaya, dominated trans-IOW maritime trade from China to the Red Sea and East Africa. By then, high-sea Javanese *jong*, averaging from 400 to 500 tons (one built about 1513 was possibly 1,000 tons), constructed with several layers of planks lashed together with coir, were over 60 metres long, lay 1.8 to 2.1

metres in the water and could, like earlier Southeast Asian ocean-going vessels, transport over 1,000 people in addition to cargo. The economic upswing from the ninth century resulted in strong demand for both high-value products, such as cloves, nutmeg, and mace from the Spice Islands, and camphor from Borneo, and more mundane commodities such as high-quality pig iron from Zanj. Thus, following the collapse of East African trade in the mid-first millennium CE, Southeast Asians again started sailing to the region. For example, in 945–946, a large Southeast Asian fleet raided the coast of southeast Africa and offshore islands in search of ivory, tortoise shell, leopard hides, ambergris (for sale in Southeast Asia and China), and reputedly for strong, docile, African slaves (it is implied for themselves). Again, in the twelfth century, large amounts of Sofala pig iron was shipped via Southeast Asia to India. Southeast Asian ships sailing in East African waters also called at Madagascar. Thus in 1154, Arab geographer Al-Idirisi wrote, in what was certainly a reference to Madagascar, "the people of the isles of Zabag [Sumatra and Java] come to the land of Zanj on small and large ships ... for they understand one another's languages".[2] Moreover, Javanese mariners had charted the route to the Cape of Good Hope and beyond before the first European vessels sailed to the IOW. In western Indian Ocean waters, the Malagasy used outriggers: In 1228, one such outrigger fleet overshot its target of Kilwa and reached Aden.

Roger Blench considers that Southeast Asians settled Madagascar sometime between the fifth and seventh centuries. However, there would have been little incentive to do so as the IOW global economy, notably that of East Africa, was then experiencing a major slump. The first concrete proof of permanent human settlements, on Nosy Mangabe and in the Mananara Valley of northern Madagascar, date, as do those on the Comoros, to the eighth or ninth century, while the first firm evidence for an expansion of livestock, of African origin, is in the northwest of the island and dates to about 870. This accords with Adelaar's contention, on linguistic grounds, that Indonesian migration to Madagascar occurred after the arrival of significant Muslim influence in Southeast Asia from the late ninth century. Recent DNA evidence also supports the view of an Austronesian migration to Madagascar in the late first millennium CE. The most accurate genetic

---

[2] Quoted in Paul Kekai Manansala, *Quests of the Dragon and Bird Clan* ([North Carolina?]: Lulu.com, 2006), 99.

data to date indicates that the founding settlement, on the northwest coast, comprised a maximum of 20 households, totalling around 500 people, either genetically mixed, or half Austronesian and half African. In South Madagascar, evidence points to human settlement and sub-sequently incorporation into long-distance trade from around the start of the second millennium. Interestingly, DNA analysis demonstrates that 62 to 65 per cent of present-day Mikea, Vezo, and Taimoro of southern Madagascar are of predominantly Bantu-speaking African descent, compared to some 42 per cent of Merina. The Bara of South Madagascar also claim African origin.

The motivation for settling Madagascar is unclear. Colonisation of uninhabited new land is almost invariably very difficult. Pull factors certainly existed. Although Madagascar possessed no ivory, the chief regional export, it had valuable marine and coastal resources. However, push factors probably predominated. The expanding Muslim commercial frontier may have persuaded Austronesian mariner-traders to leave the East African coast and settle in Madagascar. More likely, malaria played a dominant role. Bantu-speakers who by the eighth century formed the majority of the East African coastal population, carried the sickle-cell gene which offered protection against malaria. However, Southeast Asians, who possessed no such protection, would in East Africa have suffered high mortality from malaria. This may have induced them to incorporate significant numbers of Bantu-speakers onto their ships as sailors, and migrate from East Africa to the Comoros and Madagascar. Centuries later, when the non-sickle-cell-carrying proto-Merina reached Madagascar, they were propelled to leave the malaria-infested lowlands of Madagascar for its high plateau interior, which remained malaria free until probably the early nineteenth century.

Settler activity was shaped by customary skill sets, and by geographical constraints, notably the mountainous central plateau and southern desert. As much of the coastal environment of Madagascar, notably of the island's northern sector where the first migrants landed, was akin to that of Indonesia, the Southeast Asian component of the first settlers probably adopted in Madagascar a lifestyle similar to that of their homeland. They possessed Iron Age technology and traditionally practised a mixture of lagoon or estuary gathering and fishing – exploiting tidal channels and mangrove forests for crabs, molluscs, bivalves, pearl oysters, coral, and cowrie shells; hunting sea turtles and trepang (sea slugs or sea cucumbers, much in demand in China); and fishing. Also, women wove palm-leaf mats and sails, and men cut mangrove bark for tannin, and mangrove timber for firewood. Madagascar possessed ample numbers of turtles and tortoises (including, initially, giant tortoises) the shells of which were in great demand across the IOW, as well as whales valued for their oil, ambergris used in perfumes, and mangrove poles employed in the Middle East for construction. They also found there pygmy hippopotami, valued for their horns and, until they were hunted to extinction probably in the mid to late first millennium CE, "elephant birds", ostrich-like ratites (including *Aepyornis maximus* which weighed about 500 kg) whose feathers and eggshells formed valuable commodities. In addition, the early occupants of the Mananara Valley (eighth to twelfth centuries) manufactured earthenware pottery, iron, and soapstone (chlorite schist) vessels and beads.

Small, generally hybrid Afro-Indonesian communities, spread gradually along the coasts of Madagascar and into the interior, exploiting marine and riverine resources, cultivating sugarcane, manioc, banana trees, and pandanus (a palm-like tree), and raising zebu cattle on hinterland plains. One intriguing issue is the provenance of maize, first domesticated about 4300 BCE in highland Mexico, and diffused through Central America and the Caribbean. It is conventionally believed that Europeans carried maize to West Africa shortly after 1500, and to East Africa sometime after that. However, in December 1506, inhabitants of Sada (modern-day Anorontsangana), in northwest Madagascar, showed Portuguese visitors "maize in abundance".[3] This was possibly only the third time since 1503 that the Portuguese had landed in Madagascar, and the first time in this particular location, so the indigenous population could not have adopted maize from them. Moreover, by 1514–15, Portuguese vessels were transporting to Mozambique provisions purchased in Madagascar, including maize. Additionally, when they visited the Philippines in 1521, the Portuguese found maize growing locally which indicates the possibility that Southeast Asians may have introduced maize into both Island Southeast Asia and Madagascar – where in the northeast it

[3] A. and G. Grandidier, *Histoire physique, naturelle et politique de Madagascar*, vol. 5 Histoire politique et colonial. T.1 De la Découverte de Madagascar à la fin du règne de Ranavalona 1ʳᵉ (1861) (Paris: Imprimerie Paul Brodard, 1942), 10.

surpassed rice as the staple food crop. This in turn augments the argument for a pre-1500 "trans-Pacific diffusion" in which Polynesians carried boat forms and the chicken east to South America and the sweet potato, bottle gourd, and maize to Southeast Asia.

The main external relations of the first Malagasy were probably with the southern Swahili trading network centred on the Mozambique coast, and through that to the wider IOW. However, between the eleventh and fifteenth centuries, Madagascar became increasingly integrated into the entire Swahili trading network, and was visited directly by Indonesian fleets. Madagascar's northern coasts, the first settled, were easily accessible from the Comoros and, during the northeast monsoon, to vessels from southwest and South Asia that, in the cool season, could either return on the trade winds or sail via northwest Madagascar to the Comoros and East Africa. These commercial linkages grew from the ninth to thirteenth centuries, as Madagascar experienced considerable population growth. From the fourteenth century, Islam and Swahili architectural styles reached the island, and a number of trading centres emerged, all connected to Kilwa, Malindi, and Mombasa. They possessed hierarchical societies with Swahili (called "Antalaotra" in Madagascar) political and commercial elites. Mahilaka, in Ampasindava Bay, on the northwest coast, developed into a large walled town with stone buildings and at least one mosque, inhabited by between 5,000 and 10,000 people. By 1500, major settlements, some with populations of 6,000 to 10,000, existed near river mouths and in major bays along the west and northwest coasts.

Malagasy exports included rice, livestock (from the twelfth century), soapstone, gum copal resin, and coral stone to East Africa; mangrove poles, rice, tortoise shell, crystal quartz, and possibly gold, silk, and spices such as ginger, to the Persian Gulf and Arabia; slaves to the Middle East and Indonesia; and possibly iron ore or pig iron to Indonesia and India. Imports included Cambay beads and cotton and silk cloth; Middle Eastern pottery, glass vessels, silver, gold, and probably pearls; Chinese ceramics (from the 1300s), silver coins and jewellery; and spices, possibly of Indonesian origin. Further, by the late 1200s, Comorian cotton goods were shipped, possibly via the Maldives, to Southeast Asia. Of Madagascar's maritime ties to western IOW markets, Ibn Majid commented in 1489–90 that, at the start and end of the kaws (nominally the SW monsoon but usually, in this region, a southeasterly wind), "a fleet of ships set out from Komr [Madagascar] for Zanj, Mrima, Hormuz and India".[4]

From the tenth to thirteenth centuries, as the IOW economy boomed, further migrations occurred from Southeast Asia to Madagascar, probably directly across the Indian Ocean. Thereafter, regular Indonesian migration to the island petered out, although maritime contact between Southeast Asia and Madagascar persisted into the fifteenth, and possibly sixteenth century. The ancestors of the present-day Merina of the high plateau constituted one of the last major waves of incoming Indonesian migrants, although their settlement might have been involuntary – the result of a shipwreck. The first indications of a human presence in the highlands date to the early second millennium CE, of permanent human occupation to the mid-fourteenth century, and of sizeable communities, to the fifteenth century. While most scholars argue that the proto-Merina arrived in the twelfth century – the date of the last textual evidence for "Indonesian" voyages to Madagascar – indigenous traditions indicate that they reached Madagascar at the start of the sixteenth century. Migration from East Africa to western Madagascar also continued. For example, in 1613 there existed Bantu-speaking communities in northwestern Madagascar, possibly comprising refugee slaves.

In sum, considerable controversy surrounds the origins and development of the Swahili, Great Zimbabwe, and Malagasy civilisations. The traditional view that the Swahili and Great Zimbabwe civilisations were created by foreigners, has been largely discredited. Afrocentrists argue that the Swahili civilisation was the product of a long history of Bantu-speaking expansion and enterprise. However, there currently exists insufficient evidence to support the view that Bantu-speakers transformed themselves into a maritime people, or that they formed any significant settlement on the East African coast prior to the eighth century CE. The evidence rather points to a downturn in the IOW global economy from about the third century CE, associated with adverse environmental factors, that was particularly marked in the East African region. Economic recovery from the late eighth century, notably from the tenth century, associated with more favourable environmental events, revived trade links between the East African littoral,

---

[4] Quoted in James Hornell, "Indonesian Influence on East African Culture" *Journal of the Royal Anthropological Institute of Great Britain and Ireland* 64 (1934): 317; see also ibid., 318.

Middle East, and Southeast Asia, as between the East African coast and deep interior, notably with the Great Zimbabwe complex. From the mixture of cultures on the East African littoral, the Swahili civilisation emerged and flourished, spreading to the Comoro Islands and to northwest Madagascar, where the first permanent human settlement of the island also occurred at the start of the second upswing in the IOW global economy. This initially comprised both Southeast Asian and African elements, although later migrations to the island were in origin distinctly African or Indonesian – one of the latter forming the proto-Merina of the highland interior of Madagascar.

7

Uncertainties and European Intrusion: The IOW Global Economy, 1300 to 1830

In the mid-thirteenth century the IOW global economy entered an extended period of turbulence that endured into the early nineteenth century. To date, this period has been analysed in the historiography in two distinct parts, following Eurocentric temporal paradigms. The first, under the umbrella term of the "Middle Ages" or later "Middle Ages" has largely been interpreted in terms of political disturbances indigenous to the IOW. The second, on which the bulk of pre-nineteenth century IOW historical works has concentrated, is conventionally termed the "Early Modern", and focusses on the European impact on the region from 1500 to 1800. However, conventional approaches largely neglect the critical historical role of environmental factors and of human-environment interaction. This chapter reasserts the significance of human-environment interaction, and within that framework reassesses the period up to 1500, prior to the advent of Europeans into the IOW, as well as the European impact between 1500 and 1830. Chapter 8 is devoted specifically to the European impact on Indian Ocean Africa in this same period.

Human-Environmental Context in the Greater IOW, 1300 to 1500

From around 1300, the advent of generally adverse environmental factors ended the extended economic boom the IOW had enjoyed between the ninth and thirteenth centuries. These adverse elements were particularly marked from the mid-fourteenth to early fifteenth century, late sixteenth to early eighteenth century, and again from the late eighteenth to early nineteenth century. It is here posited that the nature and impact of these environmental changes were critical to historical developments within the IOW, including Africa's relationship to the wider IOW.

Whereas from about 900 to 1300 the monsoon system was strong and precipitation relatively regular and abundant, thereafter the northern hemisphere cooled, weakening the monsoon system to the extent that the southwest monsoon rains experienced frequent failure. Subsequently, a southward movement of the ITCZ promoted generally cool arid conditions from 1300 to 1700 over much of mainland southern Asia. Volcanism also had a major influence. The ten most powerful volcanic eruptions (volcanic flux magnitude of over 14 kg km^{-2}) since 1000 BCE occurred between 1253 and 1816. Six of these erupted within a century, between 1235 and 1334. The largest ($f \approx$ 100 kg km^{-2}), in about 1258, had a sulphate concentration eight times that of the 1883 Krakatoa eruption. By contrast, the years 1258 and 1453 were the IOW's wettest between 1300 and the mid-1800s, and induced major flooding in some regions. A further three volcanic eruptions in 1235 (previously unsuspected), 1274, and 1334, were comparable to the 1815 Tambora eruption in volcanic flux magnitude ($f \approx$ 26.3 kg km^{-2}). Such eruptions resulted in reduced temperatures for two to three years, and harvest shortfalls often accompanied by famine and disease.

From about 1300, China entered a prolonged period of economic and political turbulence. Excessive rain and floods in the early 1330s caused widespread destruction. They also forced rodents to flee their natural habitats, which in 1333 resulted in an outbreak of bubonic plague in inner China. Considerable social and political turmoil ensued and economic activity in general declined. The prior period of economic expansion in Song China (960–1279) also came at significant environmental cost. For example, metal-working – copper production alone reached a peak of 13,000 metric tons a year – resulted in the release of great quantities of environmentally harmful emissions. Again, demand for wood for domestic and industrial construction led to such deforestation that many workshops in North China switched for fuel from wood to coal and coke. Deforestation, combined with demand for exotic animals, also heavily impacted wildlife. Distribution of rhinos, highly valued for their horns, was restricted to diminishing

regions of the south and west. Rhinoceros horn was increasingly
imported, initially chiefly from Indochina, and from the eleventh century, sources further west, including Southeast Asia and Africa. The
same was true for ivory and tortoise shell.

However, Chinese maritime trade with the wider IOW was also
increasingly disrupted. In the early twelfth century, Chinese vessels
became more active in IOW, but from 1127, government maritime
trade policy became more restrictive, and when Mongol invasions
provoked the fall of the Southern Song in 1279, Chinese sea trade
with the wider IOW progressively diminished. The Mongol administration made efforts to revive such connections by re-establishing
a maritime trade bureau in Quanzhou in 1278 and sending an envoy
to India in 1281. There were also missions from the Malabar Coast to
China between 1279 and 1314, as well as an Indian trading presence in
Quanzhou. However, the Yuan regime taxed foreign merchants double
the rate it charged Chinese traders, and in 1284 imposed a government
monopoly over foreign commerce. A Muslim rebellion from 1357 to
1366 severely affected Chinese ports, notably Quanzhou, the most
important centre of trade with the wider IOW, and in 1368 the Ming
banned foreign trade, with the result that many foreign merchants left
China. In the late fourteenth century, the regime's increasing opposition to private trade, combined with growing political insecurity, led
Southeast Asians, for example, to explore new markets in India and
further west. At the start of the fifteenth century, the Ming changed
tack, promoting an aggressive policy of maritime expansion, but this
ended abruptly in the 1430s.

In the late thirteenth century, Southeast Asia, like China, also
suffered repeated Mongol invasions that led in 1288 to the collapse of
Pagan in Burma and attacks on Java in 1292–3. Political and economic
insecurity was heightened by the growth of piracy that adversely
affected shipping in the Straits of Malacca. Such factors contributed
to a sharp drop in maritime trade from the late thirteenth century,
the disintegration of the Strivijayan thalassocracy, and the decline
of Cambodia and Champa. Environmental forces accentuated economic and political insecurity. From the 1320s, mainland Southeast
Asia experienced generally weak summer monsoons and long, cool
arid periods that adversely affected wet-crop agriculture, and thus
undermined the regional economy. For example, mega droughts
from the 1330s to 1360s, and a shorter, more intense drought from
the 1400s to 1420s, broken by occasional excessive rains, were major

contributory factors in the collapse of the intensive irrigated cultivation system supporting the Khmer capital of Angkor.

By contrast, Southeast Asian islands generally experienced ample rainfall, and the regional trading "empire" of Majapahit, based in Java, flourished in the fourteenth century. However, drought and famine probably affected Java in 1426, certainly eastern Java from 1450 – when it critically undermined Majapahit. Nevertheless, an upswing in sea trade stimulated the emergence by the 1430s of Malacca as a major trading hub connecting the eastern and western maritime zones of the IOW: In the early 1500s, Portuguese writer Tomé Pires claimed that 84 different languages were used within Malacca's foreign merchant community.

Further west in South Asia, a southwards shift in the ITCZ induced generally weak summer monsoons and long arid periods, often associated with El Niños, from the 1320s to about 1700. Drought and famine occurred from 1198 to 1210, and from the mid-thirteenth to early fifteenth centuries (broken by catastrophic floods in 1292). Drought, famine, and high food prices provoked rebellion in the Delhi Sultanate from 1334 to 1335, and droughts between 1396 and 1408 caused the depopulation of large parts of the Deccan. Drought also promoted the military expansion of the Delhi Sultanate into southern India, and adversely affected maritime trade and major merchant networks such as the Ayyavole. Trade between the Kalinga, Karnataka, and Konkan (Aryya) coasts and eastern Java declined, although Cambay, on India's west coast, remained a major centre of IOW maritime exchange, Ibn Battuta commenting in 1324 that "the greatest part of its inhabitants are foreign merchants".[1]

In the Middle East, cooler and more arid conditions prevailed from the mid-1300s due to southward ITCZ migration, increased El Niño events, or both. Consequently, rainfall and groundwater sources proved increasingly insufficient to sustain peasant communities overwhelmingly dependent on a single crop of winter wheat or barley. Growing aridity also provoked tribal raids on agricultural settlements. By the end of the thirteenth century, following the sack of Baghdad, there was a marked decline in Muslim political, cultural, and economic life in the core of the empire, and from the late 1300s the main western terminus for trans-IOW maritime trade shifted from the Persian Gulf

[1] Ibn Battuta, *The Travels of Ibn Battuta*, trans. Samuel Lee (London: John Murray, 1829), 164.

to the Red Sea region. Increasing aridity and insecurity also provoked significant emigration, including that of many Yemeni Arabs to northeast Africa, notably to Ethiopia and Somalia. A plague epidemic in 1438–9 also caused significant Yemeni migration to East Africa and Somalia – where it promoted the Islamic Audel expansion into Oromo territory. Such factors formed the context for a sharp decline in the population of the Middle East from the fifteenth century.

IOA and the Environment, 1300 to 1500

Northern IOA

The economic decline of Egypt from the late 1300s is largely ascribed to Circassian Mamluk policy, notably the imposition of state monopolies, refusal to invest in new techniques, and high taxes. Agricultural and industrial production decreased dramatically, as did the population. At the same time, however, the shift in the axis of trans-IOW maritime commerce from the Persian Gulf to the Red Sea region stimulated the foreign trade of Egypt. As a result, a marked fall in state-controlled production and trade occurred only in the fifteenth century, well after the economy in general had slumped. This points to other, notably environmental, contributions to economic decline. Egypt experienced decreased Nile floods and increased aridity from 119 to 1245 and 1282 to 1340 that resulted in harvest failures and major famines in 1228, 1263–4, 1293 to 1295, 1297, and 1304, in which many humans and the draught animals upon which they depended, died. The famine of 1293 to 1295 was so severe that some people resorted to cannibalism.

These lengthy arid periods were punctuated by episodes of exceptional rainfall, as in 1298 when many buildings were destroyed. In 1302, a severe earthquake erupted, provoking a tidal wave that hit Alexandria, destroying many buildings, and caused the Nile to burst its banks. From 1340 to 1469, Egypt experienced an almost continuous wet period, with disastrous floods from 1372 to 1374, and in 1394 and 1403, interspersed by occasional low Nile floods, as in 1427, 1429, and 1450. Both excessive and low Nile levels provoked famine which was almost always followed by outbreaks of epidemic disease. Again, in 1437, a swarm of locusts ravaged animal feed, resulting in starvation and a severe epidemic amongst livestock. The death of animals

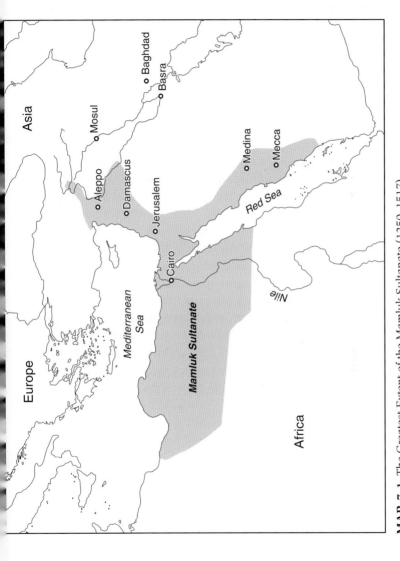

MAP 7.1 The Greatest Extent of the Mamluk Sultanate (1250–1517)

Note: Adapted from Suzan Yalman, "The Art of the Mamluk Period (1250–1517)" Metropolitan Museum of Art –www.metmuseum.org/toah/hd/maml/hd_maml.htm (accessed 12/04/12).

deprived the peasantry of meat, transportation, and the animal power required to work irrigation devices and mills.

The Black Death pandemic of 1348–9, which cyclically reoccurred, had disastrous consequences. It decimated the population of both commercial centres such as Alexandria, hit first in 1347, and the peasantry. Overall, the Egyptian population fell from about 4 to 3 million between 1300 and 1500. Such was the mortality in Upper Egypt that the irrigation infrastructure and basins regulating the flow of the Nile fell into disrepair. Consequently, formerly cultivated land returned to scrubland that was progressively occupied by Bedouin pastoralists. Another result, notably from about 1350 to 1502, when Nile flows were well above average, was excessive flooding in Lower Egypt. The economy showed signs of revival when plague epidemics relented, as during the reign of Sultan Barquq (r. 1382–99), but in the early 1400s Egypt experienced an economic decline that undermined the Karimis, severely curtailed tax revenues, and critically eroded the economic and political structure of the Mamluk state. This left Egypt open for the Ottoman takeover in 1517.

Most histories of northeast Africa from the thirteenth to fifteenth centuries focus on the continued advance of Islam which led to the emergence of centralised Islamic states such as Adal which, at its zenith in the 1500s, extended from the port-city of Zeila, on the Gulf of Aden, to the Ethiopian highlands. Islamic influence also spread south along the Somali east coast, Barbosa (ca 1518) commenting that Mogadishu "belonged" to the "Moors" and that "All the people speak Arabic".[2] From the fifteenth century, Sufi mystics settled in the Benadir hinterland and Islamisation of Somalia advanced steadily in subsequent centuries.

Again, it is important to emphasise the environmental context. Ethiopia experienced an extended arid period from 1200 to 1321, characterised by frequent droughts – which hit again in the 1370s. Coupled with continued soil degradation, greater aridity induced a high frequency of famines, notably in 1252, 1258–9, from 1272 to 1275, and sometime between 1314 and 1344. There followed a period of relatively good rainfall from 1350 to 1470, although droughts hit again in the early 1400s, and a severe famine in 1435–6. Epidemics erupted following some famines, as in 1261–2, and sometime between

---

[2] Barbosa quoted in Hādī Hasan, *A History of Persian Navigation* (London: Methuen, 1928), 137–8.

1344 and 1372 and between 1454 and 1468. Famine and disease caused high mortality, the famine of 1435–6 reputedly depopulating entire provinces. Further, in 1414 an exceptionally cool northern hemisphere summer, associated with a sulphur-rich volcanic eruption, probably underpinned the socio-economic and political disturbances that precipitated the 1415 Ethiopian invasion of the Muslim kingdom of Ifat, in Somalia.

Despite such adverse environmental factors, Ethiopia continued to participate in IOW exchange. It exported gold, ivory, civet, horses, provisions, gum arabic, frankincense, myrrh, and madder via Aden to Muscat and India. The major import was cloth. Ethiopian merchants were initially fully engaged in overseas commerce. For example, they were noted in the Persian Gulf entrepôt of Hormuz in 1442, seventy years later on Gujarati ships travelling to and from Malacca, and in ca 1518 in Bengala at the mouth of the Brahmaputra River in northeast India. However, as early as 1512, Arabs from Aden and the Hadhramaut had come to dominate Ethiopian foreign trade.

Southern IOA

The climate history of southern IOA from 1300 was complex. Northern Hemisphere cold events, associated with a southward shift in the ITCZ, generally result in drought over most of sub-Saharan Africa except for South Africa where wetter conditions prevail. However, the southward migration of the ITCZ is also linked to more frequent and intense El Niño events which induce greater rainfall in eastern Africa with above average rainfall as far west as Lake Edward. Lake records indicate that from around 1400 in the interlacustrine region and the equatorial zone to its east, generally cold-moist versus warm-dry episodes gave way to a long period of heavier precipitation. For much of south-central Africa, the evidence is also of enhanced rainfall from about 1400. By contrast, in western and northern regions of East Africa, an extended wet period up to 1300 was succeeded by a long, cool arid interval. Records for Lake Edward, to the north, where unstable air flows from the Atlantic meet drier air from the Indian Ocean, indicate severe droughts from 1000 to 1200, and after 1400. To the south, Lake Malawi also became progressively drier from 1400. Southeast Africa similarly suffered drought. Mozambique experienced generally arid conditions from 1300, as did Natal from about 1320, except for a decade of good rainfall in the 1480s. The southwards shift of the ITCZ to below 12°S meant that the northern reaches of Madagascar experienced much the same climate as coastal equatorial East Africa: increased rainfall with postulated prosperity, agricultural expansion, and population growth. By contrast, regions further south, in common with sub-tropical southern Africa, experienced the reverse. If conditions in Mozambique can be taken as a proxy, central western Madagascar also experienced generally arid conditions from 1300, as did the island's central plateau.

Southern IOA, including Madagascar, continued to form part of the trans-IOW commercial exchange system. The Swahili commercial zone that developed from around 800 CE expanded down the East African coast to Sofala, and eastwards to embrace the Comoros and northwest Madagascar by around 1000 CE. By then, Kilwa had emerged as the major entrepôt for the southern section of the western Indian Ocean network, including Madagascar. It had direct links to Aden, Hormuz, and notably Cambay in Gujarat, while Gujarati Muslim and Hindu (Banyan) traders were active along the Swahili coast. However, Langani (Old Massalajem) in Mahajamba Bay, and Boina (New Massalajem) in Boina Bay, also had regular trade relations with Zanzibar, Malindi, and Pate, while in 1514, the Portuguese even found Malindi "Arabs" in Matitanana, in southeast Madagascar.

African and Malagasy products were of considerable significance to the IOW economy. Chinese ships under Admiral Zheng He (1371–1433) visited Malindi in 1405–6, and Mogadishu and Brava between 1417 and 1419 and again in 1421–2. Although the Chinese fleet there-after disappeared from the Indian Ocean, Egyptian, Arab, Persian and Indian ships continued to visit eastern Africa, while Africans were heavily engaged in exchange with the wider IOW. For example, in 1442 traders from Zanzibar were noted in the Persian Gulf entrepôt of Hormuz, while seventy years later it was noted that merchants from Kilwa, Malindi, Mogadishu, and Mombasa voyaged to and from Malacca. Further, Swahili coast exchange with the wider IOW was considerable. It exported chiefly gold, ivory, and wax in return for white and coloured cloth, beads, rice, millet and wheat – much of it from Cambay. In addition, prior to the Portuguese arrival in 1505, Kilwa exported "Flasks of very good perfume ... and a large quantity of glass of all types and all kinds of cotton piece goods, incense, resin, gold, silver, and pearls."[3] Pires (ca 1512) noted that merchants from Cambay and Arabia (mostly from Aden) exported Swahili coast staples from Kilwa, Malindi, and Mombasa, to Zeila and Berbera to be exchanged for horses that probably formed part of the extensive trade in Arabian and Persian horses to India.

European Impact, 1500 to 1800

The majority of works on IOW history focus on the European impact from 1500, stressing the assertion of European military, commercial, and ultimately political ascendancy. This process started with the European "Voyages of "Discovery" which sixteenth-century Spanish historian, Francisco López de Gómara (1511–66), termed "the greatest event since the creation of the world, apart from the incarnation and death of him who created it".[4] In one such epic voyage, Vasco Da Gama (1469–1524) rounded the Cape of Good Hope in 1497 and "discovered" the Indian Ocean. With papal blessing, the Spanish and Portuguese, the first significant European presence in the extra-European world, divided the globe between them. The Spanish, who claimed everything west of Brazil as far as the Philippines, found major gold and silver sources, in Peru and Mexico respectively, established settler colonies in temperate regions, and slave plantations in tropical and semi-tropical zones. Local resistance was minimal due to superior European military technology, and to the introduction of Old World diseases that decimated large numbers of indigenous Americans.

For the IOW, Portuguese King Manuel in 1501 adopted the title "Lord of the conquest, navigation, and commerce of Ethiopia, India, Arabia and Persia", claimed all land and sea between Brazil and China, and in 1505 established the crown-dominated *Estado da India* ("Portuguese State of India") to direct his IOW enterprise. Subsequently, the states of northwestern Europe contested Portuguese claims to the IOW. England and Holland did this through forming board-governed chartered companies, the English East

[3] Quoted in G.S.P. Freeman-Grenville, *The East African Coast. Select Documents from the First to the Earlier Nineteenth Century* (Oxford: Clarendon Press, 1962), 106–7.
[4] Quoted in J.H. Elliot, *The Old World and the New, 1492–1650* (Cambridge: Cambridge Unioversity Press, 1970), 10.

India Company (henceforth EIC), and the *Vereenigde Oost-Indische Compagnie* ("United East India Company" – henceforth VOC) in 1600 and 1602 respectively, and France through the crown-governed *Compagnie des Indes orientales* ("East India Company" – henceforth *Compagnie*) established in 1664. These companies accepted mercantilist economic theory according to which the world's wealth, counted in precious metals, was finite. Europe lacked significant gold and silver deposits, so European states sought positive trade balances to promote the inflow (in payment for exports) and curb the outflow (to pay for imports) of precious metals. Self-sufficiency became a major political objective. Moreover, as the stock of precious metals was finite, international trade was considered to be a zero-sum affair. Therefore, rulers promoted the companies as national enterprises to which they granted trading monopolies over vast regions of the globe, as well as naval and military protection, in order to promote national trade, and capture overseas sources of precious metals and commodities.

The traditional viewpoint is that European fleets swept indigenous IOW merchants aside, reducing them to the role of "peddlers", dominated all major trade commodities, and in IOA ruptured all entrepreneurial African connections to the wider IOW. European success was due to superior shipping and military technology, and mercantilist practices. The *Estado* declared monopolies over gold and spices, the IOW commodities most valued in Europe, and attacked indigenous, mainly Muslim, competitors. Through implementing a pass system and establishing fortified trading posts at key locations, it also attempted to control traffic on the main shipping lanes. The Dutch later eroded Portuguese dominance only to be challenged in turn by the French and English. European power was at first limited largely to the maritime sphere and armed settlements strategically placed on key sea lanes. But with the implosion of Mughal power from the early eighteenth century, Europeans expanded into the South Asian peninsula where, by 1800, England had become dominant and thus the leading European continental power in the IOW.

However, revisionist work increasingly demonstrates that European predominance has been overrated. The following section critically assesses conventional historical interpretations in the context of environmental factors, the frailty of European trading structures and practices, and the resilience and continued vitality of indigenous IOW commercial networks.

The Environmental Context

Adverse environmental events associated with what is commonly referred to as the "Little Ice Age" characterised much of the period of European incursion into the IOW from 1500. For example, the sixteenth to mid-seventeenth centuries witnessed the most extreme La Niña activity between 1525 and the present day. Up to 1700, the southward shift of the ITCZ continued to promote generally cool arid conditions over much of mainland southern Asia. The Tibetan glacier record, which is sensitive chiefly to the monsoons, indicates two warm intervals, one in the sixteenth and the other in the eighteenth century. A severe cold period coincided with the Maunder Minimum of weakest solar irradiance (characterised by sunspots) between 1645 and 1715, when global air temperatures were 0.5°C to 0.8°C lower than today. An inordinate number of natural disasters occurred during this cold era (the peak of the "Little Ice Age"). From 1638 to 1643, a series of major volcanic eruptions hit the eastern IOW: Java's Mt Raung in 1638; Japan's Mt Komagatake in 1640; and Indonesia's Mt Kelut and Philippine's Mt Taal in 1641(and possibly Indonesia's Mt Awu in 1640 and 1641); and New Guinea's Mt Karkar in 1643. A further, previously unsuspected volcanic eruption, occurred in ca 1690.[5] Each eruption created a sulphuric dust veil in the atmosphere that led to surface temperatures dropping by some 0.2°C to 0.3°C for up to three years – with resultant crop failures, food shortages, epidemics, and economic, social, and political disturbances.

In East Asia, a long arid period gripped China from 1440, lasting in northern China until about 1700, and in central and southern China until the 1850s. China experienced particularly cool periods from 1470 to 1560 and 1620 to 1740, broken by warmer episodes from 1560 to 1620. The years 1586 to 1589 and 1638 to 1641 were generally characterised by extreme drought, punctuated by episodes of torrential rainfall and floods, and famine. In addition, volcanism almost certainly played a significant role in the collapse of the Ming dynasty in 1644. Severe frost from 1654 to 1676 killed orange cultivation in the Jiangxi province of southeast China. Overall, between 1585 and 1645,

---

[5] Dave G. Ferris, Jihong Cole-Dai, Angelica R. Reyes, and Drew M. Budner, "South Pole Ice Core Record of Explosive Volcanic Eruptions in the First and Second Millennia A.D. and Evidence of a Large Eruption in the Tropics around 535 A.D." *Journal of Geophysical Research* 116. D17308 (2011) DOI:10.1029/2011JD015916.

there was a 40 per cent decline in population. In a further famine from 1702 to 1704, millions of people died and cannibalism occurred.

In Southeast Asia, El Niño-induced aridity provoked famine and socio-economic turmoil in the 1500s and 1600s. In the sixteenth century, famines occurred frequently between 1559 and 1597, and in mainland Southeast Asia resulted in a shift of population and political authority from the interior to the coast. Again, Java generally from 1600 to 1679 and in 1686–7, and eastern Java from 1450 to 1650 and 1700 to 1750, experienced drought and El Niño-like conditions. In Banten and Mataram from 1625 to 1627, drought was followed by famine and epidemics. In Java, a cholera epidemic erupted after an El Niño-provoked famine from 1629 to 1633 in which year harvest failure throughout the Indonesian Archipelago provoked widespread revolt. A malaria epidemic from 1656 to 1658, in the midst of a series of El Niño events and drought in the 1650s and 1660s (the most adverse environmental events of the seventeenth century in Southeast Asia), caused high mortality. Overall, the population of the Philippines fell by about 56 per cent between 1640 and 1690, that of Mataram in central Java experienced continuous decline from 1651 to 1755, and that of the Amon and Lease islands in the Central Maluku group halved between 1640 and 1670.

Adverse environmental conditions also affected South Asia from 1500. The indications are that the western Himalayas, eastern Pakistan, and most of northern India, experienced lower temperatures, and possibly lower monsoon rainfall, for considerable periods between the mid-sixteenth and early nineteenth centuries; and higher temperatures and precipitation from 1730 to 1780. Drought and famine often followed periods of low monsoon rainfall, which were in turn often associated with El Niños (as indicated in Table 7.1). A major famine occurred in Gujarat from 1556 to 1559 in which many died, villages and fields were abandoned, and cannibalism occurred. The late 1590s were also marked by plague. In El Niño-induced famines from 1628 to 1631, up to 3 million people died in Gujarat, some 30,000 in Surat alone from 1630 to 1631. Following the drought of 1770 in Bengal and Bihar, the harvest failed, famine ensued, a smallpox epidemic erupted, and some 10 million people died. Survivors fled to Nepal, cultivation was abandoned, political security collapsed and brigandry became endemic. In a famine from 1788 to 1794, possibly related to the impact of the Laki eruption of 1783 on the monsoon rains, an estimated 11 million people died in India and many villages were deserted, while in 1792 alone up to half of the population of the northern Circars, in Madras Presidency, perished.

TABLE 7.1 *South Asia: Selected Adverse Environmental Influences, 1550 to 1835*

Event	Year
Lower Temperatures	1550–53, 1558–61, 1569–76, 1622–28, 1637–40, 1650–72, 1776–96, 1815–17, 1832–35
El Niño-associated Drought & Famine	1576–78, 1594–8, 1614–16, 1623–24, 1628–33, 1660–62, 1685–88, 1702, 1707–9, 1727, 1788–96

Moreover, in El Niño-induced droughts, normally active water courses turn to stagnant pools, permitting mosquito populations to explode with, in consequence, a radical increase in cases of malaria. The first recorded malarial epidemics in India occurred in the mid-seventeenth century. Cholera epidemics also broke out, probably in 1633, and in 1781 (Madras), 1783 (Uttar Pradesh), and 1790 (Madras). The first major cholera pandemic of 1817 (starting in Bengal), erupted during rains that followed an extensive drought, possibly related to the 1815 eruption of Tambora, and to El Niño events.

The Middle East experienced a generally colder, drier climate during the period 1500 to 1800. There appears to have been a severe drought around 1500. Environmental conditions worsened from the mid-1590s with a series of freezing winters and droughts reaching peaks during the Maunder Minimum from 1645 to 1715, and again from about 1780. These reduced agricultural production and led to the abandonment of arid lands, with intensified nomadic raids on remaining settlements. One of the impacts of these events was continuous population decline. However, these conditions affected the western and central regions of the Middle East more than Iran where, although it appears that cultivation of marginal lands at altitude was abandoned, relatively benign climatic conditions assisted agricultural production at lower altitudes, promoted population growth, stimulated trade, and provided a sound financial base for the Safavid regime (1501–1736).

European Impact

It is in this context that the European impact needs to be considered. European companies operating in the IOW faced enormous structural, logistical, and environmental problems. Distances from Europe were so great that companies were obliged to construct operating bases with quasi-executive powers within the IOW: Portugal in India (Cochin in 1505, Goa from 1510), the VOC in Java (Batavia from 1618), the French *Compagnie* in India (Pondicherry from 1674), and the English East India Company (EIC) in India (Bombay from 1687, Calcutta from 1773). Given the size of their operations, and inter-European and European-IOW hostilities, these company headquarters were necessarily manned by large bureaucracies and garrisons. Although the Portuguese had a maximum of 7,000 employees in the IOW at any given time, by the end of the seventeenth century the VOC employed 30,000. Company headquarters possessed military defences, as well as docks with boat-building and repair facilities. In addition, the companies established a network of strategically situated and fortified commercial bases throughout the IOW. The building, maintenance, and protection required for such structures was costly, particularly given often adverse environmental and disease factors, endemic hostilities, and boat losses.

Europeans in the IOW experienced high mortality rates. First, sea voyages from Europe to the region were lengthy. Those to India typically took from six to seven months, and to Indonesia eight to nine months (compared with two to three months to North America), rendering European voyagers to the IOW more susceptible to diseases such as scurvy, dysentery, and dropsy (hydrops/edema). One of the first Dutch fleets to the IOW returned in 1597 with only a quarter of its original crew alive. Mortality aboard English ships was lower due to the habit of cleaning the decks regularly with a mixture of vinegar and water, and of airing accommodation.

Also, before sound mapping of IOW waters was achieved in the late nineteenth century, losses from shipwrecks en-route was high. Sea lanes round the Cape of Good Hope and through the Mozambique Channel were particularly affected by violent storms, as in the cyclone season were the Mascarene-Madagascar maritime zone, Bay of Bengal, and South China Sea. Provisions comprised some 30 to 40 per cent of the cost of EIC voyages in the seventeenth century, yet accounts of voyages testify to the frequent chronic shortage of food aboard ship. This heightened the vulnerability of crew to sickness that in turn resulted in chronic manpower shortages – which affected ship-handling. Manpower losses could reach 50 per cent or more. In 1677, of about 2,000 Portuguese emigrants who sailed for Sofala, most died of disease, probably en-route or shortly after arrival. Of the 171,000

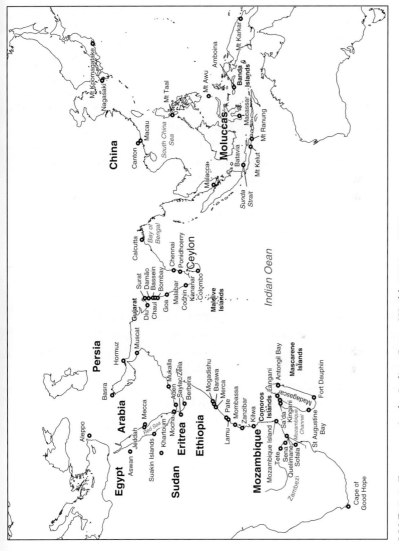

MAP 7.2 Europeans in the Indian Ocean World, 1500 to 1750

Note: Produced by Carl Hughes, IOWC.

149

Portuguese who between 1497 and 1590 sailed to the IOW, about
17,000 (9.9 per cent) were lost to disease and shipwrecks on the out-
bound voyage. These were high attrition rates for a country with a
population of about one million.

   In addition, the IOW comprised mainly disease-friendly tropical
and semi-tropical zones. While most indigenous populations had
built up resistance to local diseases, Europeans proved highly vulnerable. Of major significance was malaria. Roughly 80 per cent of
Europeans in affected zones died within six months, while survivors
experienced recurrent debilitating bouts of the disease (often referred
to as "the fever"). In some cases, malaria was unwittingly facilitated by
European innovations, such as the Dutch-style canals of Batavia that
proved amenable to mosquito breeding. Europeans were only able to
settle malarial areas permanently in any number after the widespread
adoption of quinine in the late nineteenth century. Amoebic dysentery
was another major killer. Tropical diseases meant that European personnel in coastal trading posts experienced high turnovers, and most
attempts to found settlements, or advance into the hinterland, were
doomed to failure.

   Moreover, as trade was considered to be a zero-sum affair,
Europeans consistently engaged in conflict. For example, the
Dutch Republic was at war with European foes for much of the
period between 1598 and 1708, while England and France and thus
the EIC and *Compagnie*, were at war from 1744 to 1748, 1756 to
1763, and 1795 to 1815. This also meant that, during hostilities, most
East Indiamen of the warring countries were obliged to sail in large
convoys, the speed of which was determined by their slowest vessels,
and which suffered delays if scattered by storms or forced to make
unscheduled stops for provisions, repairs, or because of sickness
aboard. Again, European troop mortality on campaigns was probably on a par with early nineteenth-century rates: overall, some 69 per
1,000 troops died during British military expeditions in India from
1800 to 1856 – almost triple the rate in Europe – while Dutch troops
in Indonesia from 1819 to 1828 experienced a mortality rate of 170
per thousand. Western ships were generally larger and better armed
than most IOW vessels, but this did not guarantee success during conflict. For example, Ming forces in 1521–2 twice repulsed Portuguese
fleets at Tunmen (Tãmão), near present-day Hong Kong. Indeed, the
momentum of Portuguese attacks on IOW shipping and trading communities quickly faded due to heavy losses of ships resulting from

storms and enemy attacks, and of men due to shipwrecks, disease and warfare. Thus, the number of Portuguese vessels entering IOW waters decreased sharply from 507 in the first half of the sixteenth century (30 alone in 1505) to 268 in the period 1551 to 1600. While this was compensated for in part by an increase in the average size of ships – the tonnage of the *nao*, the standard Portuguese vessel, rose over time from 400 to up to 2,000 – the loss of one home-bound ship often represented for the Portuguese 20 per cent of that year's trade; and the Portuguese lost 31 ships from 1500 to 1580, 35 from 1580 to 1610, and 64 from 1610 to 1650. In their turns, the Dutch VOC lost a total of 244 ships, or almost 16 per cent of their East Indiamen, and the English EIC 231 vessels or 5 per cent of the total. While sailing times and safety improved over time, the EIC still lost 124 ships in the eighteenth century, an average loss of one ship every 9.7 months. In total, a European "Indiaman" had an average life of only four return voyages (8–12 years) and overall, European mortality rates were so high that, up to the nineteenth century, being sent to the IOW was widely viewed as tantamount to a death penalty.

Mercantile Structures and Exchange

For the European companies, trade was the only means to cover costs and generate profits. Mercantilist theory dictated that this be secured through monopolies of the most valuable commodities, initially precious metals and spices. Supplies of southeast African gold, and Japanese silver were quickly eclipsed by the far greater quantities discovered and exploited by the Spanish in South and Central America. Of the major IOW spices prized in Europe, black pepper was found in Malabar, in southwest India, cinnamon in Sri Lanka, and cloves and nutmeg in the Moluccas or "Spice Islands", in Indonesia. The Portuguese captured approximately half of the spice trade to Europe. However, Muslim trade accounted for the rest shipped to the Mediterranean chiefly via Basra (Iraq) and Aleppo (Syria), and the Portuguese failed to impinge on the more valuable inter-regional spice trade. Indeed, in the first half of the seventeenth century, the Portuguese willingly granted passes to Gujarati ships sailing from Surat to Aceh because they hoped to purchase some of their return cargoes of pepper and other spices, and until at least the late eighteenth century, only indigenous networks tapped supplies and markets deep in the continental hinterlands of the IOW. For example, the European market took only about 10 per cent of IOW spices, the remainder being carried by indigenous merchants to markets within the region, chiefly in China, India and Mesopotamia.

In the seventeenth century, the Dutch gained supremacy in the IOW over the Portuguese, and came close to establishing monopoly control over some spices. Nonetheless, they did so at great cost. Failing to oust the Portuguese from the Malabar "black pepper" coast, the Dutch nevertheless tapped sufficient Indian and Sumatran sources for pepper to comprise over half the total value of VOC shipments to Europe until the mid-1600s. Despite this, no European power achieved total control over pepper because sources were varied, confined to the hinterland, and producers resisted monopoly purchase agreements. By 1658, after expelling the Portuguese from Sri Lanka, the Dutch gained a large degree of control over cinnamon and, by 1670, imposed a near monopoly over Indonesian nutmeg, mace, and cloves through confining cultivation of cloves to Amboina and nutmeg (and its derivative, mace) to the Banda Islands. However, they could not maintain too high a price in Asia – the market for approximately one-third of fine spices – lest demand there fall. Between 1613 and 1657 the Dutch destroyed many spice bushes in order to limit production, and many local vessels. In 1629, most of the indigenous population of Banda were deported, and replaced with Dutch settlers and slaves. The Dutch also periodically attacked other communities in the region including, from 1667 to 1669, the spice smuggling centre of Macassar.

However, within a few decades, the prestige, and thus price of spices, started to decline. This was due to the rise in demand in Asian and European luxury markets during the early 1700s for high-status tropical goods, such as tea, opium, and cotton piece goods and also, by the mid-1700s, for coffee, cocoa, alcohol, and tobacco. In addition, Europeans started to eat more imported foods, notably asparagus, spinach, artichoke, tomato, pimento, and melon. Monopolies were steadily eroded by the smuggling and diffusion of seeds and plants, and by the increasing use of substitutes. For example, "long nutmeg", slightly inferior in quality to the true Banda Island variety, was cultivated on other Indonesian islands and often successfully substituted for true nutmeg. Similarly Chinese cassia circulated as an inferior substitute for cinnamon. In addition, the cost of suppressing indigenous producers and traders was high. Consequently, by the end of the seventeenth century, VOC monopoly control over major IOW commodities had been undermined. In addition, successive Anglo-Dutch wars from 1652 to 1654, 1665 to 1667, and 1672 to 1674, eroded Dutch naval power and VOC finances. Further Anglo-Dutch conflict from 1780 to 1784 pushed the VOC to the verge of bankruptcy. In 1790, the company was 81 million guilders in debt, in 1796 it was nationalised by the Batavian Republic, and in December 1799 it was dissolved.

Possibly as damaging to the monopoly companies was the volume of unofficial European trade. Due to a combination of inadequate and/or irregular pay and profitable commercial opportunities within the IOW, many company employees, from the highest commanders to the lowliest soldiers, engaged in private trade, with or without authorisation. For instance, in 1732, the VOC Council of Seventeen commented that company ships carried such quantities of smuggled goods that there was little room for legitimate cargo; and in total, three VOC Governor Generals were dismissed for illicit trading. Smuggling by company employees and others, including slaves aboard ship, further undermined company attempts to monopolise key commodities, and increased supervision costs.

Privateers, frequently ex-company employees, entered unlicensed commerce, often in collaboration with indigenous IOW traders. Benefitting from a knowledge of company tactics and plans, privateers enjoyed much lower overheads and generally far better access to local markets than official company agents. Sometimes, in recognition of their inability to control private trade, and in an attempt to revive flagging company fortunes, European monopoly concerns relaxed their regulations. For example, King Pedro II (1668–1706) declared freedom of commerce for his subjects in the IOW to which he encouraged emigration from Portugal. However, the *Estado da India* was by then so undermanned that it could do little to prevent trading by Portuguese privateers. These included deserters who in the sixteenth and seventeenth centuries accounted for an estimated 50 per cent of the Portuguese presence in the IOW. In 1681, the *Compagnie* also permitted private French shipping. Again, in the 1780s and early 1790s, private concerns were responsible for some 75 per cent of British exports to India. Moreover, European pirates were periodically active in the IOW, operated widely, and could react far more quickly than companies to fluctuations in trade, preying off European and indigenous vessels alike. This forced companies to provide costly escorts for their vessels and those of their indigenous allies, and even to cooperate with one another. For instance, the French and British combined to suppress pirates who from 1690 to 1720 successfully operated from various points on the coast and offshore islands of Madagascar. In total, therefore, unofficial European activity heavily eroded company profits.

Indian Ocean World Commercial Networks

Revisionist historians such as K.N. Chaudhuri and Anthony Reid have argued convincingly against the Eurocentric interpretation of European dominance and for the continued vitality of Asian commercial systems. Possessing a sophisticated trans-IOW maritime trading network which had operated from the BCE/CE changeover, Asians enjoyed a head start on European traders. Moreover, they knew of the Cape route into the Atlantic prior to 1500. Thus in early 1512, the Portuguese met a Javanese pilot who had the directions to the Cape marked on a map, while in 1462 Ibn Majid noted that south of Sofala "the land ends and turns towards the north west"[6] and that it was possible to reach the Mediterranean following that trajectory. The centuries-old indigenous IOW trading infrastructure continued to dominate maritime commerce until at least the eighteenth century, and overland exchange until colonial times. European aggression was episodic, limited in geographic range, and largely failed to suppress indigenous commercial structures and trade. IOW waters were far too vast for any single power to control, and Europeans failed to establish more than a few precarious settlements on the coastal fringes of the IOW until the EIC advance in India from the late eighteenth century. With the exception of the Dutch in seventeenth-century Indonesia, European companies had insufficient ships, manpower, and local knowledge, to prevent indigenous traders from bypassing patrols. Should European powers impose intolerably high taxes or other conditions, IOW traders simply switched to alternative ports and routes – as, for example, sailing from China through eastern Indonesia to Java, and following the southern equatorial route across the Indian Ocean via the Maldive Islands.

---

[6] Quoted in Gabriel Ferrand, "A propos d'une carte javanaise du XVe siècle" *Journal Asiatique* 12 (1918): 168.

Indigenous IOW merchants thus diffused certain key commodities to IOW markets by maritime and overland routes independently of Europeans. One example was coffee, which in the first half of the fifteenth century spread from Kaffa, in Ethiopia, its original centre of production, to Yemen, where it was consumed as a stimulating beverage, and subsequently diffused to Mecca and Medina by 1475, and to Cairo by the close of the fifteenth century. Following the Ottoman conquest of Egypt in 1516, coffee consumption spread to Syria by 1534, and subsequently throughout the Ottoman Empire. IOW merchants similarly diffused coffee, probably by both overland and maritime routes, from Yemen and Arabia to the Iran and India by the start of the seventeenth century. By the eighteenth century, the *tujjar*, Muslim long-distance merchants based in Egypt, gained a monopoly over the coffee trade (their chief source of wealth, just as previously spices had been for the *Karimi*) from Mocha, which under the Ottomans replaced Aden as the chief southern Red Sea port. Indigenous merchants, notably Armenians, also dominated the valuable export trade in Iranian silk to the Ottoman Levant. Indigenous IOW merchant activity thrived even in European-dominated centres. For example, the foreign merchant community in Portuguese Goa included traders from elsewhere in India (Malabar, Kananar, Gujarat), Iran, Arabia, and Ethiopia. Contrary to the conventional view, large inland polities, notably those of the Chinese, Mughals, Safavids, and Ottomans, were not indifferent to foreign trade. They promoted internal security, communications, commerce, often encouraged monetarisation of the economy, and fostered linkages between land-based and maritime trade networks. For example, the Mughals of northern India boosted bullion imports, minted coinage, and in 1572 captured Gujarat in large part because it was a major producer of IOW commodities and a leading IOW maritime entrepôt. It was unnecessary for land-based empires to commit to building, manning, and maintaining a fleet when they possessed or could attract skilled maritime people – such as the coastal Gujarati.

Indeed, European companies, suffering from a combination of high mortality, limited resources, commercial competition, and regional disdain for Western manufactures, were increasingly obliged to enter "country trade" – intra IOW exchange – in order to generate sufficient revenue to pay for their IOW exports to Europe. For example, from 1543 to 1640 the Portuguese entered the trade exchanging Chinese silk and gold for Japanese silver and copper. In its turn, the VOC shipped Indonesian spices and Japanese silver to India in return for

Indian cloth which, with Bengali opium and raw silk, they exchanged in China for silks and porcelain.

From the outset, Europeans depended on local pilots to guide their vessels, notably along dangerous coasts and in river estuaries. Shipwrecks and damaged vessels often forced European concerns to charter IOW ships, sometimes entire fleets. Further, Europeans increasingly used local wood to construct ships. Thus many of the largest Portuguese ships were built, at the royal arsenal in Goa or under contract at shipyards in Cochin, Bassein, or Damão, of Indian teak which proved cheaper and more durable because it was resistant to the teredo worm that ravaged European timber in tropical waters. Also, given high European mortality rates, companies frequently hired indigenous IOW sailors, commonly termed 'lascars' in the Indian Ocean, to man their ships, and local auxiliaries to supplement their depleted garrisons. Moreover, given the scarcity of European women, it was common for many Europeans to forge unions with local females. Indeed, from 1510, Afonso de Albuquerque, Governor-General of Goa from 1509 to 1515, officially encouraged the formation of a Luso-Indian community by subsidising marriages between Portuguese residents and Hindu brides. In some cases, local "wives", official and unofficial, also served as translators and local commercial agents for their European partners.

European engagement in the country trade necessitated even greater cooperation with local IOW authorities and commercial agents. Thus, the Moguls granted the Portuguese access to Gujarati cotton goods, required to pay for Goa's East African purchases and for Europe-bound cargoes, in return for the right to trade with, and carry *hajj* pilgrims to, the Red Sea region. Europeans likewise increasingly relied on indigenous commercial and military services. For example, despite Rome's prohibition of relations with non-Christians, Portuguese authorities in Goa borrowed from Hindu and Jain financiers, and came to depend on Hindus as tax collectors; while in 1683, a Mughal army saved Portuguese Goa from Marathas forces. Private European traders became even more involved with IOW traders, some to the extent of jointly financing commercial ventures. Such collaboration also encouraged European trading posts to accept IOW merchants.

In sum, the ongoing vitality of exiting Asian commercial networks and trade, and the problems faced in the IOW by Europeans, meant that the latter failed to obtain the economic and political paramountcy in the region that traditional Eurocentric histories have claimed. Europeans did not succeed in establishing more than fragile footholds in the continental hinterlands of IOW maritime zones until the late 1700s. They failed to impose durable control over the chief IOW commodities in demand in Europe, or the main sea lanes. Their trading companies were top-heavy, with costly bureaucracies and armies, and their personnel suffered high mortality due to disease, shipwrecks, and almost perpetual conflict. They also faced severe competition from private Western and indigenous traders. Moreover, European commodities were largely unappreciated in IOW markets. In order to stem the continued flow of silver bullion to pay for IOW merchandise, Europeans increasingly entered country trade. As their human, financial, and material resources were limited, and they lacked intimate knowledge of regional languages, customs, and geography, they of necessity forged alliances with local authorities and indigenous commercial agents. Indeed, a strong argument can be made that Europeans were dependent upon indigenous commercial networks which remained dominant in the IOW until at least the late eighteenth century.

As significant were the forces of human-environment interaction. Between the fourteenth and nineteenth centuries, the IOW global economy suffered protracted periods of stagnation, most notably in the late fourteenth and in the long seventeenth century, due to a complex interplay of human and environmental factors. These included heightened volcanism, significant climatic fluctuations, harvest failures, pestilence, civil disturbances, and political upheavals. Such events undermined production and trade, and periodically pushed thousands of desperate people to migrate, or into slavery. These factors are little considered by conventional histories that have too easily interpreted indigenous societies and trading systems as inherently weak and European trading companies as structurally and technically superior and economically dominant.

8

The European Impact in Indian Ocean Africa, 1500 to 1830

This chapter examines the European impact in IOA from 1500 to 1830 within the environmental context. The dominant academic viewpoint is that Africa was marginal to the wider IOW economy. Most historians now reject traditional Eurocentric approaches that consider African history to have started with the arrival of the Europeans, most notably from the imposition of colonial rule. Nevertheless, while historians of Africa argue for the economic dynamism of Africans prior to 1500, most concur that thereafter IOA made a negligible contribution to the IOW global economy. They stress the primacy of external forces, notably Arabs and Europeans, whose production and export of slaves formed Africa's chief contribution to the external Atlantic and IOW global economies. This, in turn, laid the basis for the colonial takeover and economic underdevelopment of IOA. There is, however, an urgent need to revisit these views.

Environmental Factors in Indian Ocean Africa

Most histories of the European encounter with Africa from 1500 pay scant attention to the environmental context which, nonetheless, greatly affected European-African relations and imposed major constraints upon European activity in Africa. It is thus important to discuss the environmental context for the European encounter with IOA. In general, from 1500, IOA was afflicted by a series of prolonged droughts. Nile River and Great Lakes records indicate that from the early 1500s much of northeastern Africa, East Central Africa, and Madagascar experienced increased aridity that resulted in food shortages, periodic famine, and migration. The following sections examine environmental factors at work during this period in Egypt, Ethiopia, and the southern section of IOA and, within this context, the European impact in IOA.

Egypt

From the mid-1590s, Egypt experienced major periods of drought, notably from about 1625 to 1799, most of them associated with ENSO events, and which often resulted in harvest shortfalls, and famine. These long, arid periods were punctuated by occasionally excessive rain and floods which damaged irrigation systems and sometimes caused considerable human and animal mortality. Years of drought (and drought followed by excessive rainfall) also often triggered outbreaks of disease. For example, droughts in 1621, in the 1690s, and in 1718, were closely followed by plague epidemics. Attempts to curb the spread of plague, as in 1579 when the sultan ordered the governor of Alexandria to prevent anyone from sailing for Istanbul, proved futile. Alexandria alone experienced 59 plague epidemics between 1701 and 1844. Livestock were also badly affected by epizootics, notably in the eighteenth and first two years of the nineteenth century. In addition, a number of lethal parasitic diseases plagued people living along the Nile, where peasants were commonly afflicted with swollen legs – probably elephantiasis (*Lymphatic filariasis*), caused by parasitic worms spread by mosquitoes – and with Guinea worm infestation. In addition, gastrointestinal and pulmonary infections appear to have been responsible for most deaths, notably of infants, in Cairo and Alexandria.

Adverse environmental factors, food shortages, and disease caused a sharp decline in animal and human populations from the late sixteenth century, which in turn undermined the ability to maintain irrigation systems, and caused agricultural production to fall. They also induced flight from affected areas, social and political protest, and sometimes acute breakdown of law and order. In 1659, during one such prolonged crisis, Mamluk soldiers rebelled. In the 1690s, soldiers again rioted, and in 1695 killed Yasif al Yahudi, the Jewish master of the Alexandria mint, chief tax collector, and financial advisor to the governor, when he tried to increase taxes on coffee, houses, and shops. Again, in 1698, Hawwara Bedouins refused to pay their taxes. In 1786, in the middle of a major environmental crisis, the sultan's forces invaded in an attempt to suppress the rebel Mamluks (Beys). However, they succeeded only in pushing the rebels into Upper Egypt, and exciting popular revolt, and in 1787 they evacuated Egypt. Protracted droughts from 1794 also provoked popular uprisings, and collapse of central authority leading to rampant theft and brigandry. The French invasion and occupation from 1798 to 1801 accentuated the general crisis and from 1799 to 1800 Egypt was hit by famine and an epidemic of plague.

Ethiopia

From 1500 to 1675, Ethiopia experienced a generally wet period, punctuated by sometimes intense droughts that resulted in harvest failure. Six severe famines occurred between the early 1500s and 1630, and during a three-year drought from 1557 to 1559, some people turned to cannibalism. Conditions worsened from 1675 with the onset of a long, arid period, characterised by major droughts between 1694 and 1750, in 1800, and from 1826 to 1827, interrupted by episodes of excessive rainfall in 1801, 1817, 1818, 1822, and 1829. Growing aridity accelerated soil erosion. Intense droughts, sometimes followed by years of excessive rainfall, and accentuated by locust plagues, caused harvest failure and induced famine. Outbreaks of disease frequently followed famine. At least five major epidemics hit Ethiopia in the sixteenth and seven in the seventeenth century. It also experienced smallpox epidemics in 1768–9. At the same time, the lowlands suffered from endemic malaria, and elephantiasis and dysentery were commonplace.

Drought in Arabia provoked significant Arab emigration to Ethiopia, as in 1507–8 and from 1539 to 1541. However, the migrants found similarly adverse environmental conditions in northeast Africa. This resulted in fierce competition between migrants and local communities over fertile land and water sources, and helped fuel a bitter conflict between Muslim and Christian forces from 1527 to 1600. The severe droughts of the early 1500s also propelled a massive expansion of Oromo pastoralists northwards into southern Ethiopia, where guerrilla tactics and the use of horses enabled them to push into central

TABLE 8.1 *Indian Ocean Africa: Adverse Environmental Factors, 1500 to 1830s (estimated dates)*

	Drought	Excessive Rains	Famine	Epidemics
Egypt	1621, 1641, 1694–7, 1718, 1791–2, 1794–6	1711, 1743, 1745, 1801, 1818, 1822, 1829	1621, 1641, 1694–7, 1791–2, 1794–6, 1799–1800	1620s, 1690–1844
Ethiopia	1518, 1520, 1553, 1557–9, 1641, 1650, 1694, 1715–16, 1750, 1800, 1826–7	1801, 1817, 1818, 1822, 1829	1520s, 1590–1610	mid-1520s, 1558, 1611, 1616, 1618, 1633, 1683, 1693, 1694, 1701, 1709
Great Lakes Region	1725–29, 1749–55, 1761–9, 1785–92, 1808–26			
SE Africa	1527–30, 1543–4, 1580, 1688, 1700, 1789, 1790–1810s			
Southern Africa	1600, 1700			
Central Madagascar	1692–5, 1702, 1708–16, 1790s–1810s		1696–1703, 1747, 1755–6	early 1790s, 1817, 1833–5

Ethiopia from about 1545, and from 1559 to 1568 into Somalia where they caused the Audel Empire to fragment.

Southern IOA

From 1500 to 1750, in coastal equatorial East Africa, ITCZ-ENSO interactions possibly triggered El Niño-like conditions and increased rainfall with postulated prosperity, agricultural expansion, and population growth, although a universally cold interval occurred around 1709. The Great Lakes region experienced an extensive period of significant rainfall until about 1750, punctuated by severe droughts, as probably occurred from 1725 to 1729. However, Uganda's northern interlacustrine zone experienced drought, famine, and major strife in around 1544 and 1625, as possibly did the equatorial coastal region. From the mid-eighteenth century, the climate abruptly changed, and the entire equatorial region was until 1840 affected by major droughts, that were followed by famine, disease, high human and animal mortality, mass migration, and depopulation.

Regions to the north and south of the equatorial zone continued to experience drought into the nineteenth century. Records for Lake Edward, to the north of the equatorial zone, indicate severe droughts from 1400 to 1750. To the south, Lake Malawi became progressively drier up to 1780. Lake Tanganyika levels were also generally low between 1550 and 1800. In southeastern Africa, Mozambique experienced arid conditions, with severe droughts from about 1580 until the 1810s, notably around 1700 and in the 1790s. Natal experienced good rainfall from 1588 to 1595, 1786 to 1796, and 1812 to 1819, but arid conditions with periodically major droughts from 1490 to 1570, 1675 to 1770, and after 1810. Southern Africa generally experienced a cold and dry climate from 1690 to 1740, a wetter period from 1740 until the 1790s, and then another cold arid interval until about 1830.

During the LIA, the ITCZ shifted significantly more to the south in the austral summer, to below 12°S, to affect the northern reaches of Madagascar. This area thus experienced much the same LIA climate as coastal equatorial East Africa. From 1500 to 1800, northeast Madagascar experienced a significantly wetter climate than today, while eastern Madagascar generally experienced relatively good rainfall from 1570, broken by arid periods from 1594 to 1617, 1724 to 1746, and 1785 to 1799. Northwest Madagascar, described in 1613–14 as well-watered, fertile and populous, was affected by alternating periods of very wet and arid periods with, from 1700 to 1750, a particularly high frequency of El Niño events. The region was affected by dry intervals centred at around 1600, 1650, 1700, and 1770.

The central plateau experienced more arid conditions, with intense drought in the early 1690s, in the first two decades of the eighteenth century, and from the 1790s to 1810s. Oral traditions indicate three severe famines occurred in the central highlands. The first, the

Tsimiofy (lit. "do not peel"), occurred probably from 1696 to 1703 or 1708 to 1716; the second, the *Mavovava* ("yellow mouth") in ca 1747, and the third "younger famine" in 1755–6. Smallpox also affected the highlands following increased exposure to foreign trade from the late eighteenth century. The first major smallpox epidemic occurred sometime between 1791 and 1794, with others erupting in 1817, and from 1833 to 1835.

If conditions in Mozambique can be taken as a proxy, the central west coastal region of Madagascar experienced generally dry arid conditions from 1300 with severe droughts from about 1580 until the 1810s, notably around 1700 and in the 1790s. Possibly related is an epidemic that occurred in western Madagascar in 1701. The southwest and south-central west coastal regions of Madagascar probably experienced much the same climatic variations as Natal, with generally arid conditions from the 1490s to 1810s, severe drought around 1600, from 1690 to 1740, and from the 1790s to 1810s. Reports from St Augustine Bay, in southwest Madagascar for 1638, 1650, 1663, and 1709 to 1711 describe the region as sparsely populated, lawless, impoverished, and with few cattle. Drought could well have motivated the Sakalava expansion northwards from 1649 to 1650 to dominate the southern reaches of Menabe which were better watered and could provide pasture for their cattle.

European Impact in IOA

European companies attempted to impose monopolies over the IOA commodities most valued in Europe, and attacked indigenous, mainly Muslim, competitors. Thus the Portuguese assailed Kilwa in July 1505 and enslaved 200 of its Muslim residents. However, European companies and individual merchants in IOA faced major environmental constraints, and generally failed to impose more than short-lived economic, military, or political sway.

Of major significance were tropical diseases from which the Portuguese in Mozambique suffered such high mortality that they often lacked sufficient soldiers to maintain the main garrison on Mozambique Island. When the Dutch attacked Mozambique between 1604 and 1607, they found only about 60 soldiers defending the fort. In 1632, the Viceroy of Mozambique was so short of men and supplies that he entertained an alliance with Malagasy chiefs, while

in 1667 Jesuit priest Manoel Barreto recommended abandoning
Mozambique, which he described as a graveyard for the Portuguese,
for Madagascar. However, tropical diseases were as prevalent in
Madagascar. For example, few Europeans present in lowland zones
of the island during the rainy season escaped the ravages of malaria which not only killed many but, through recurrent bouts,
incapacitated most who survived the initial attack of the disease. Thus
Dutch attempts from Mauritius from 1639 to 1642 to found trading
posts in Antongil Bay, in northeast Madagascar, and English efforts
to establish colonies under John Smart at Augustine Bay in 1645–6,
and in 1649–50 under Robert Hunt on Nosy Be (Assada), all failed
largely due to local hostility and the ravages of malaria. Subsequently,
most Europeans learned to avoid Madagascar during rainy season
between November and April.

Moreover, possession of more advanced military technology did
not guarantee Europeans military success. Conventional interpretations of the Portuguese intervention in Ethiopia from the mid-
sixteenth to mid-seventeenth centuries credit the superiority of their
weapons with the failure of the Muslim attack on Christian Ethiopian
forces allied to the Portuguese. Thus the artillery employed by 400
Portuguese soldiers under the command of the younger brother of
Vasco da Gama proved decisive in the Ethiopian victory over Ahman
Grañ at Wayna-Daga in 1543, as it did in maintaining Ethiopian military superiority when subsequently 170 Portuguese soldiers were
integrated into the imperial army. However, from 1539, Turks and
Arabs supplied Muslim forces in Ethiopia with matchlocks and artillery. Moreover, initial Muslim success was due to a superior cavalry
armed with swords rather than firearms. Indeed on open ground,
possession of matchlocks and artillery offered little advantage over
traditional weapons – bow and arrow, and short and long spear
backed by a shield, dagger, axe, club and sling. This was shown in the
Ethiopian repulsion of a Turkish invasion force employing cannon and
matchlocks in 1557, and expulsion of a Turkish force from Debarwa,
in the highlands, in 1559. Similarly, from the late 1500s, guerrilla
tactics enabled the Oromo to outmanoeuvre Ethiopian forces who
employed set formations, and matchlocks which were awkward to
carry and place, and took time to re-load. Additional technological
advances did not necessarily help. Thus Ethiopians generally rejected
the flintlock, introduced in the early eighteenth century, due to its

cost, and the difficulty of repairing its firing mechanism and replacing the flint.

Likewise, the Portuguese venture in eastern Africa was, ultimately, largely unsuccessful. From the early 1500s, Portuguese fleets attacked Swahili bases in East Africa and northwest Madagascar, and Portuguese soldiers founded forts at Kilwa (1505), Mozambique Island (1507), and Mombasa (1593). From the start, however, their hold on the northern Swahili coast was precarious. First, sixteenth- and seventeenth-century Oromo expansion from the southern reaches of Ethiopia into Kenya provoked major social and economic chaos along the littoral opposite the Lamu Archipelago, causing local populations to flee to coastal towns such as Mombasa, Lamu, Siyu, and Pate. Second, Ottoman-Egyptians in the 1580s, and Omanis from the 1660s, launched maritime attacks on Portuguese positions on the East African coast, and from 1690 the Omanis established dominance along the littoral north of Mozambique. Again, largely due to disease, the Portuguese failed to make much military progress or found durable settlements in interior East Africa, while in Madagascar where in 1506 they sacked the Muslim ports of Sada, Langani (Nosy Longany in Mahajamba Bay) and Kingani, Portuguese dominance was fleeting and Muslim trade quickly recovered.

By 1700, the Portuguese presence in East Africa was largely restricted to Mozambique Island and Sofala – where in 1722 there were only 26 "Portuguese", almost all Creoles and *degredados* (criminals exiled to unhealthy parts of the Empire). The Portuguese maintained a presence only through local alliances, often cemented by marriage to African women, some of whom also acted as their translators and commercial agents. From such associations emerged the *prazo* system, whereby large fiefs originally held by descendants of Portuguese settlers became progressively more African. The *prazo* created trading and raiding networks that channelled some commodities such as slaves to Mozambique Island for export, although certain African groups, such as the Yao, bypassed the Portuguese and traded directly with Swahili-governed ports.

European vessels were also vulnerable to attack from European rivals. For instance, in July 1622, an Anglo-Dutch fleet sank four Portuguese ships in the Mozambique Channel. In addition, for about a century after being chased from the Caribbean, European pirates set up bases in northern Madagascar and the Comoros, areas largely unaffected by the droughts that gripped most surrounding regions, from where they inflicted significant losses on European and IOW merchantmen in the western IOW. As early as 1635, English pirates operating from Mohilla and Anjouan were hounding Indian vessels in the Red Sea. From 1685, they established a base on the island of Nosy Boraha (Ste Marie) off the northeast coast of Madagascar where some married into local elite families. In 1694, Thomas Tew engaged in a piratical campaign from Madagascar that earned each member of his crew £1,200. The following year, he allied with Avery (alias Bridgman), another English pirate, to capture a large ship owned by Aurangzeb, the Mughal Emperor of India (r. 1658–1707) returning from the Red Sea. The same year and on the same route, Abdul Ghafur, a merchant prince from Surat, lost a ship with a cargo worth two million rupees. Ghafur and other IOW ship-owners hired European companies to provide their vessels with armed escorts, but proved unable to stem the piracy. Consequently Ghafur suspended all trade and successfully claimed compensation from the VOC. Other pirates used different offshore and coastal bases such as "Masselage" in Boina Bay in the northwest, and St Augustine in the southwest. Their numbers fluctuated, many indubitably dying of malaria. From Réunion, it was noted that there were only 30 pirates at Madagascar in 1709, and by 1714 very few. However, their numbers were augmented by pirates chased from the Caribbean by European naval ships, and they continued to inflict considerable damage in the western Indian Ocean. In 1721, John Taylor seized off Mauritius the Portuguese Indiaman *Nossa Senhora do Cabo* and its cargo that included diamonds valued at about £500,000. Again, in April 1722, pirates over-came the Dutch garrison at the Cape and occupied the fort for ten weeks before sailing away accompanied by 18 VOC deserters. After a combined Franco-British fleet was launched against them in 1722, piracy in Madagascar declined, although as late as 1730 some 300 pirates were reputedly still based on the Malagasy coast and islands.

IOA Economies

As indicated above, the economic fortunes of European companies and merchants in IOA fluctuated considerably between 1500 and 1830 and, as elsewhere in the IOW, indigenous commercial structures remained vibrant and competitive. Moreover, there are signs that production, and flows of commodities, people and expertise led to increasing integration of both intra-IOA exchange and of IOA into the wider IOW global economy.

Northern IOA

The new Ottoman rulers of Egypt faced drought in 1518–19, and a damaging flood in 1521, but for most of the rest of the sixteenth century were blessed with relatively good climatic conditions, albeit punctuated by arid periods. For example, rainfall was sufficiently abundant in the 1500s to permit Bedouins to occupy large tracts of desert for pasture. The Ottoman-Egyptian regime promoted local manufacturing and agriculture. Most artisans, who comprised between 20 and 40 per cent of the population, were engaged in small-scale cloth production, but larger scale manufacturing units also existed, notably oil presses and sugar refineries, producing for local elite and foreign markets. Further, the government countered the depopulation that had characterised the preceding Mamluk period by promoting immigration from neighbouring, especially North African, countries, and encouraging soldiers to settle and cultivate land in Upper Egypt.

In order to tap Sudanese gold and slaves, and ivory and other produce from regions to its south, the Egyptian Ottomans expanded their imperial frontiers steadily into Nubia and the Sudan – from Aswan to the second Nile cataract in the 1550s, and by 1583 to the third cataract, 600 km from Khartoum. Beyond lay the Funj and Tajur sultanates, the most easterly of a chain of Islamic states that, marking the *Dar al-Islam-Dar al-Kufr* frontier, stretched westwards to the Atlantic. At its peak in the seventeenth century, Funj controlled the trade of the entire region from the Red Sea westward to Kordofan.

Although Egypt initially suffered from a Portuguese blockade of Red Sea traffic, its foreign trade, conducted chiefly with the rest of the Ottoman Empire and Syria, and secondarily with the Red Sea region and wider IOW, quickly revived. Because Egypt straddled a major commercial crossroads, much of this comprised transit trade. Some two-thirds of goods flowing to Egypt from the Red Sea was re-exported to Turkey and Europe, and by the eighteenth century, 20 per cent of Egyptian imports from Syria were re-exported (primarily to Europe, North Africa, and the Sudan), as were one-sixth of imports from Europe (to the Red Sea and the Sudan). Barbosa in ca 1518 noted that goods from the eastern and western IOW, including spices, were shipped to Jeddah to be exchanged for copper, quicksilver, verdigris, saffron, rosewater, scarlet cloth, silks, camlets, taffetas, gold, and silver. From Jeddah, eastern IOW commodities were carried in small craft to Suez, then by camel to Cairo. There, some were transported to Alexandria for distribution, alongside Arabian coffee, African gums, coarse cotton, untanned hides, dyes, natron, and rice, to Mediterranean markets. In return, Egypt received cloth, arms, furs, and wrought silk from Istanbul, raw silk from Syria, oil from Morea, Crete, and Syria (for the making of soap), and textiles, paper, iron, lead, and gold and silver coinage from Italy and France. Egypt produced and exported silk, linen, and cotton textiles, and (primarily for imperial Ottoman markets) gold, slaves, and provisions. For example, by 1700 almost all imports by sea to Jeddah, the primary port of the Hijaz, came from Egypt, and half comprised provisions destined for Mecca and Medina.

Much of the conventional literature about the impact of Europeans focusses on the spice trade. In the Red Sea region, as in the Persian Gulf, the Portuguese diverted some IOW spices onto the Cape route to Lisbon and Antwerp. However, they possessed insufficient resources to capture the entire trade, and their aggressive tactics disrupted traditional IOW-Levant commerce. The net result was that diminished supplies of IOW commodities, including spices, reached Europe where, consequently, prices rose in the early 1500s – pepper, for example, by between 30 and 38 per cent. Moreover, the indigenous spice trade quickly recovered, assisted by the Ottomans whose navy in 1505 secured the Red Sea route, a control solidified by the Ottoman conquest of Egypt in 1517. Ottoman-Egyptian forces subsequently expanded along the southern littoral of the Red Sea, in 1524 seizing Suakin which controlled the caravan trade in gold, slaves, and ivory from the Funj sultanate, in 1548 Zeila, and in 1557 Eritrea. Although Ottoman-Egyptian attempts from the 1580s to subdue the Ethiopian highlands failed, their fleets expelled the Portuguese from Aden in 1548 and Muscat in 1552, and harassed them at Diu in 1538 and at Aceh in Sumatra from 1565 to 1567. Excluded from the Red Sea, Europeans were obliged to use the more dangerous Cape route where ship losses were sometimes substantial. For example, from 1500 to 1650 over fourteen Portuguese vessels were lost off South Africa; in 1722, ten VOC and three EIC ships went down in a single night; in 1723, two VOC ships were wrecked; in 1729, five vessels were lost; and in 1737, eight out of nine ships in a VOC fleet were wrecked. Moreover, in the eastern IOW, indigenous merchants diverted traffic from the Portuguese-dominated sea lane across the northern rim of the Indian Ocean, onto the southern equatorial route from Indonesia through the Maldives to the Red Sea. Consequently, Portuguese shipments to Europe of spices, chiefly pepper, fell from 33 to 50 per cent between the early 1500s and 1700, while by 1588 indigenous vessels were transporting from Aceh to the Red Sea, and thence to Europe, from 1.6 to 2 times more spices than the maximum ever shipped by the Portuguese.

In the seventeenth century, despite domestically adverse environmental factors, Egyptian trade with the wider IOW rose as the large Muslim states of West and South Asia (Ottoman, Safavid, Mughal, and Deccan) imposed peace and security, production costs fell, and European demand for eastern goods was stimulated by the inflow from the Americas of precious metals and by profits made chiefly from the slave and sugar trades. Similarly, northeast African merchants, notably from Saylac until its decline in the mid-1600s, Berbera, Mogadishu, Merca, and Barawa, prospered from booming exports to IOW markets of coffee, gold, ivory, frankincense, ostrich feathers, civet, and Ethiopian slaves.

Alexandria played an initially pivotal role in Egypt's regional and long-distance trade. Tomé Pires noted of the port in ca 1512:

> The merchandise which these people take to India comes from Venice in Italy. It comes to Alexandria, and from the Alexandria warehouses it comes by river to the factors in Cairo, and from Cairo it comes in caravans with many armed people. It comes to Tor, but this is not often, because on account of the nomad robbers they need many armed people to guard the merchandise. But at the time of the Jubilee (Jubileu), which is held every year in Mecca on the first day of February, when many people come, [the merchandise] is sent to Mecca with them. And from there it comes to Jidda and from Jidda it comes to the warehouses they have in Aden and from Aden it is distributed to Cambay, Goa, Malabar, Bengal, Pegu [Burma] and Siam.[1]

However, Alexandria, which was hit by general economic crisis and chronic monetary instability from 1585 to 1690, and a collapse in the spice trade between 1620 and the 1650s, was badly affected from the 1780s by a deep economic recession, out-migration, and increasing domination of Egypt's Mediterranean trade by the rival port of Rosetta.

---

[1] Pires (1512) quoted in P. Francis (Jr.), *Asia's Maritime Bead Trade 300 B.C. to the Present* (Honolulu: University of Hawai'i Press, 2002), 171.

Eastern and Southern IOA

In East Africa, one of the first Portuguese goals was to impose a monopoly over "Sofala" gold, to which end they established coastal strongholds at Sofala and Mozambique Island, and launched expeditions up the Zambezi where they built forts at Sena and Tete. However, in order to access interior trade routes, the Portuguese were obliged to accept indigenous protocol whereby the *mussambazes*, a group of African traders, conducted regional commerce, and local chiefs supervised the markets. Disease depleted the numbers of Portuguese who thus proved incapable of preventing indigenous traders moving to the coast staple exports, including ivory and gold, along routes that bypassed the Europeans. In addition, the Portuguese naval presence was too limited to effectively control the East African coastline. Thus a report for October 1514 indicates that large IOW ships continued to sail from Cambay to the Swahili ports between Mogadishu and Mombasa where their largely cloth cargoes were transshipped onto smaller vessels for transport to independent ports in Mozambique, such as Angoche.

Moreover, the Portuguese could do little to stem the advance of the Muslim trading and settlement frontier in the western Indian Ocean. Muslim, predominantly Hadhrami and Yemeni, migration to southern IOA occurred in two big waves, between 1250 and 1500, and again from the 1700s, and was propelled chiefly by adverse environmental conditions in the Red Sea area. Ottoman control of the Red Sea also permitted significant Arab migration between 1500 and 1700, much of it passing via Pate to locations along the Swahili coast and in the Comoro Islands. Some of these migrants were warriors who left Ethiopia around 1570 due to the failure of their jihad against the imperial Ethiopian army. In all, they considerably invigorated East African economic and cultural life. A European report for 1569 indicates that by then Pate had a significant trade with Mecca and other overseas markets, including India. It was renowned for its silk cloths which the Portuguese purchased with ironware, beads, and cotton cloth, and sold elsewhere along the Swahili coast. However, Muslim traders, operating chiefly from Pate, also dominated regional trade. This included by the early seventeenth century a vigorous traffic in slaves. However, the trade appears to have fluctuated considerably, and other commodities, notably ivory and gold from East Africa, and ambergris, sandalwood, ebony, turtle shell, cattle, and rice from the Comoros and northwest

Madagascar were arguably more valuable export staples than slaves (see Chapter 12). The staple imports into southern IOA were cloth, beads and, from the early seventeenth century, firearms.

Portuguese influence in East Africa was further weakened by the continued expansion there of Islam in which *tariqa* (Muslim brotherhoods that developed from Sufi orders), and Muslim traders associated with them, played key roles. B.G. Martin estimates that between 1500 and 1800, possibly 60 to 80 per cent of African Muslims became members of a Sufi order. Those affecting IOA mainly derived from bases in Iraq, Syria, Iran, and Central Asia. The influence of the *tariqa*, and of larger Muslim traders, was augmented by ordinary Hadhrami and other Arab migrants who on the Swahili coast engaged primarily in overseas trade, agriculture, and craft production. Thus Martin notes that:

> there are hints that the Muslim commercial empire partly destroyed by the Portuguese after 1500 was in part established by *sharif* migrants throughout the Indian Ocean, and that their social and religious prestige helped them very considerably in expediting trade.[2]

This was the case, for example, of the Ba 'Alawis in Lamu, Pate, and the Comoros. Similarly, some of the Jamal al-Layl Sayyid clan, and its Al- Qadri sub-lineage, settled as craftsmen at Pate and Lamu in 1543–4, and by 1650 in the Comoros. Indeed, the vibrancy of indigenous IOW commerce with East Africa caused the Omani in the 1660s to launch maritime attacks on Portuguese posts along the East African coast that culminated in the 1699 expulsion of the Portuguese from Mombasa. Declining Portuguese influence and an increased relationship with the Hadhramaut and Oman, bolstered along the East African littoral both Islamic influence and a renewal of Swahili culture reflected, for example, by the development from ca 1700 of Kiswahili as a written language.

An examination of the coffee trade further demonstrates the increasing integration of IOA into a wider IOW system of production and commercial exchange. In 1855, explorer Richard Burton noted that coffee, originally from Ethiopia, was cultivated there "in the gardens about the town [Harar], in greater quantities among the Western Gallas, and in perfection at Jarjar, a district of about seven

---

[2] B.G. Martin, "Arab Migrations to East Africa in Medieval Times" *International Journal of African Historical Studies* 7. 3 (1974): 379.

FIGURE 8.1 Harar from the Coffe Stream (1855)

Note: Richard Francis Burton, *First Footsteps in East Africa; or an Exploration of Harar* (London: Longman, Brown, Green, and Longmans, 1856), 340–1.

days' journey from Harar on the Efat road".[3] Burton noted further that it was shipped in quantity to Aden, but the nearby Yemeni port of Mocha was until the early nineteenth century its main centre of distribution – to Egypt, the Near East and Turkey. By the early 1700s, significant demand for coffee had also developed in southern Europe. From 1714, French company ships started calling at Mocha from where they offloaded beans at Réunion where a "ball" of *Mocha* quickly became a standard money locally, and by 1723, there existed 100,000 trees each of which, when mature, produced an annual average of three to five pounds of beans. In France, Réunion *Mocha* quickly gained a reputation for quality second only to Arabian *Arabica*. Planters defied the *Compagnie*'s monopoly and sold most beans clandestinely: In 1725 the entire harvest of some 40,000 pounds was sold to interlopers, an indication that total sales were considerably higher than official coffee exports to France – registered at 3,400 pounds in 1724, 23,800 pounds in 1726, and 120,000 pounds in 1727. Until the 1790s, Réunion and the French Caribbean colonies, notably St. Dominique, were responsible for much of world coffee production. A devastating cyclone in 1805 induced Réunion planters to diversify into tobacco, cotton,

---

[3] Richard Burton, *First Footsteps in East Africa, or an Exploration of Harar* (Köln: Könemann, 2000), 241.

spice, and especially sugar cane cultivation, although until *Hemileia vastatrix*, introduced from Sri Lanka in 1878, ravaged Réunion *Mocha*, coffee was the second most important cash crop behind sugar cane.

Réunion planters also experimented with coffee on the east coast of Madagascar, possibly from the 1790s. In 1820, a coffee plantation was established on the French offshore island of Ste. Marie (Nosy Boraha). However, it failed to prosper and coffee emerged as a major crop in Madagascar only from the mid-1820s after the adoption of autarky by the Merina court which subsequently monopolised all major exports. In 1825, the large Réunionnais firm of Julien Gaultier de Rontaunay (1793–1863) engaged to plant 150,000 bushes and in 1840 another Réunion planter signed an eight-year crown contract for a coffee plantation – both in the Mananjary region on the east coast. By mid-century, de Rontaunay, who also introduced coffee cultivation into the Malagasy highlands, was annually exporting some 500 kg of Malagasy *Mocha*.

Most histories of the western Indian Ocean emphasise the role of the Comoros and Madagascar as provisioning bases for European ships to and from the IOW. However, recent claims that Madagascar played an essential role in early globalisation in the period 1600 to 1800 through supplying European shipping with water, rice, and cattle from all regions of the island, are misplaced.[4] They ignore the political economy of the island and the environmental factors (discussed earlier in this chapter) at work during the period under review. The central plateau did not possess cattle in any quantity, nor produce sufficient surplus of provisions to export, until the early nineteenth century, while most of the southern reaches of the island were too arid to guarantee supplies of provisions. Only the very northern reaches of the island received sufficient rainfall to produce ample provisions, but a combination of malaria and local animosity ensured a generally hostile, often fatal reception for Europeans calling there. Consequently, Madagascar was of little significance in the European provisioning trade. Thus only some 3 per cent of European ships sailing to and from the IOW during the seventeenth and eighteenth centuries called at Madagascar for provisions. As Huw Bowen notes, only during four decades in those two centuries (the 1630s, 1640s, 1760s, and 1770s) did 20 per cent or more of EIC ships heading for India touch at Madagascar and/or sailed through the Mozambique Channel, and of these over 90 per cent headed primarily for Anjouan, generally their first port of call,

---

[4] Jane Hooper, *Feeding Globalization. Madagascar and the Provisioning Trade, 1600–1800* (Athens, Ohio: Ohio University Press, 2017).

where their captains forged generally excellent relationships with local authorities, found safe anchorage, and secured plentiful provisions of fruit, cattle, goats, fowl, and fish.[5] By contrast to the Europe-IOW maritime traffic, the Comoros and northwest Madagascar did prove essential sources of foodstuffs for some IOW settlements afflicted by adverse environmental factors, notably droughts. Thus Portuguese posts along the East African coast often depended for supplies of rice, maize, cattle, and water on chiefly Muslim authorities in the Comoros and northwest Madagascar – regions that from 1500 to 1800 largely escaped the drought that afflicted much of the rest of Madagascar, as well as East and southern Africa. They also purchased there cloth (including bark cloth), sandalwood, timber for masts, and slaves. The frequency and regularity of such exchange is reflected in the spread of the Portuguese language. In 1591, James Lancaster used a Portuguese interpreter in the Comoros where, in 1602, Martin found "many individuals who speak Portuguese".[6] Other western IOW regions similarly sought provisions from the Comoros and Madagascar. In 1607, William Finch noted that the ruler of Socotra had "two good Frigats" that he employed to trade with the Comoros and Malindi for rice and maize.[7] Again, from 1630 to 1632, when India, notably western India, was hit by a devastating drought that led to widespread famine, disease, high mortality, depopulation, and dramatic fall in economic activity, EIC ships based in India sailed to the Comoros for provisions.

In sum, most conventional histories consider that the arrival of Europeans in the IOW ended Africa's participation in the wider IOW global economy, except as a source of slaves. This interpretation of Africans as passive, and exploited by external forces, is explicable in terms of the heavily Eurocentric historiography. It also offers an explanation for the ease and rapidity of European colonial conquest of Africa in the late nineteenth century. However, such views are in urgent need of revision. First, the role of IOA needs to be set within

---

[5] H.V. Bowen, "Britain in the Indian Ocean Region and Beyond: Contours, Connections, and the Creation of a Global Maritime Empire" in H.V. Bowen, Elizabeth Mancke, and John G. Reid (eds.), *Britain's Oceanic Empire. Atlantic and Indian Ocean Worlds c.1550–1850* (Cambridge: Cambridge University Press, 2012), 55–6.

[6] Quoted in Malyn Newitt, *A History of Mozambique* (Bloomington: Indiana University Press, 1995), 173.

[7] "Observations of William Finch, merchant, taken out of his large Journall" in Samuel Purchas (eds.), *Hakluytus Posthumus or Purchas His Pligrimes containing a History of the World in Sea Voyages and Lande Travells by Englishmen and Others*, vol. 4 (Glasgow: James MacLehose and Sons, 1905), 13–14.

the wider context of the IOW global economy. Between the fourteenth and nineteenth centuries the IOW global economy experienced major turbulence due to a complex interplay of human and environmental factors. Conventional histories have largely ignored or underestimated particularly the environmental forces at work, and have too easily interpreted African societies and trading structures as insufficiently robust to resist European military and commercial superiority.

Europeans failed to establish secure settlements in IOA except at the Cape of Good Hope and, from the mid-eighteenth century, on the Mascarene Islands. A tenuous Portuguese presence on the East African coast largely collapsed from 1699 when they abandoned Fort Jesus, Mombasa, after an occupation of 106 years. Moreover, Europeans were largely unaware of the continued vitality of Swahili ports and their exchanges with the wider IOW, and of production and trade in interior sub-Saharan IOA and in Ottoman and Ethiopian realms to their north. Overall, the indications are that for most IOA peoples, the economic vibrancy of the pre-1500 era continued. Indeed, through introducing New World food crops, such as cassava, peanuts, and possibly maize, Europeans inadvertently enhanced the diet of Africans, promoting overall health, demographic growth, and colonisation of new lands. Domestic commerce was fuelled by regional specialisation and division of labour, involving chiefly the exchange of cattle, iron products, grains, salt, textiles, and slaves. In the northern sector of IOA, tropical produce such as ivory and rhino horn, as well as slaves, continued to flow through the Sudan to Egypt and Ethiopia. At the same time, the Ottoman hold over the Red Sea and connections with the wider IOW enabled it to compete with Europeans in the supply of Indian pepper and textiles to European markets. Imports into northern IOA included cloth, notably Indian cottons, beads, pottery, and hardware. Some of these commodities were carried by African merchants. For example, Ethiopian traders were noted in sixteenth-century Goa. The same products were exchanged in East Africa where ivory, the most valuable export, was obtained mainly from African traders in the interior. On the coast, import and export commodities were handled chiefly by Swahili, Arab, and Indian vessels that plied between ports in the western IOW. And in Madagascar, which had no ivory or rhino horn, but was famed for its turtle shell, drought-induced migration towards the northwest, and integration into the Swahili maritime trading network, provided the basis for the rise of the Sakalava kingdoms.

9

–

The International Economy and Indian Ocean Africa

Most histories of the nineteenth-century IOW focus on European economic and colonial expansion, and on the East African slave trade. Several studies also stress the increased incidence, dispersion, and impact of disease. However, few of these studies place their analyses within the context of radical changes in human-environment interaction in the long nineteenth century that dramatically affected European-IOW relations. First, the West experienced revolutions that facilitated unprecedented population growth, gave rise to an ever-burgeoning cycle of technological innovations, and fostered major overseas investment. These in turn laid the basis for the emergence of a truly international economy that, in the IOW, opened up huge commercial possibilities. Second, the IOW generally experienced arid conditions until the mid-nineteenth century, followed by a sharp rise in temperatures and rainfall interrupted by periodically harsh droughts. It is against this background that the impact of the rise of the international economy on IOA is analysed, as are the topics treated in the remaining chapters of this volume.

The innovations which underlay the Industrial Revolution, ca 1750 to 1830, marked a radical turning point in the history of the IOW, including IOA. First, the West progressively rejected mercantilism. In *The Wealth of Nations* (1776), Adam Smith argued that wealth could be created, trade be mutually beneficial and that, rather than promote prosperity, monopolies, protectionism, and colonies were ruinously expensive. There was no clearer reflection of the validity of Smith's assertions than in the history of mercantilist activity in the

IOW where, by the time his book appeared, European charter companies were teetering on the verge of bankruptcy. Additionally, the Industrial Revolution, which coincided with financial and commercial revolutions centred on London, sparked the first of an unceasing explosion of technological innovations. Together, these changes offered the possibility, for the first time in history, of escaping Malthusian cycles of economic and population growth, overextension, and collapse. They transformed Britain into the world's major exporter of capital, skilled labour, iron and steel goods, cheap textiles, and coal, and a major importer of food, industrial raw materials, and "exotic", often tropical goods, such as ivory and sugar. Britain's adoption by 1840 of laissez-faire and free trade, and the increasing application of steam-powered transport, further promoted cross-border movements of capital, labour, and commodities. Britain's capital exports helped promote industrialisation primarily in Western Europe and North America, thus enormously expanding economic growth and wealth in the Atlantic basin. This in turn stimulated inter-regional trade and investment, laying the foundations for the development of a truly international economy that had, by the close of the nineteenth century, incorporated all bar the most isolated areas of the world into one interrelated economic system.

Such developments fundamentally altered Europe's relationship with the IOW. The conventional viewpoint is that Europeans already monopolised the most valuable commodities, and that indigenous IOW maritime commerce further declined from the early 1700s due to competition from European privateers. Growing European commercial dominance helped to undermine the three IOW Islamic empires (Ottoman, Safavid, and Mughal) which, Ashin Das Gupta argued, led to a collapse of law and order, and accentuated the decline in indigenous IOW trade. Finally, the technological innovations associated with the Industrial Revolution consolidated European military and political supremacy over indigenous IOW societies which they opened, for the first time, to the forces of modernisation.

In this view, the only debatable issue is that of timing. The economies of the large indigenous IOW states, China and the three large Islamic powers, were based on traditional land-generated tax revenues to which Europeans remained essentially indifferent until the late eighteenth century when the EIC became the ruler of increasing swathes of continental South Asia. However, scholars such as André Gunder Frank and Om Prakash have argued that European economic paramountcy was achieved only in the nineteenth century when industrially produced cheap yet good-quality goods created for the first time a mass market in the IOW for European manufactures. This in turn stemmed the traditional flow of precious metals from Europe to the IOW. Certainly, it was only from 1815, with victory over France in the Napoleonic Wars, that Britain gained unparalleled dominance in the Indian Ocean – henceforth a "British Lake". The security emanating from *Pax Britannica*, the adoption of free trade, and growing demand in the industrialising West for tropical products, greatly stimulated plantation agriculture and commercial exchange in the IOW. It also encouraged the expansion of European and North American trading networks into the IOW.

From the mid-1700s, the eastern IOW experienced a trade boom based on a huge surge in Chinese demand for exotic imports such as trepang, rattan, wax, agar, and slaves, which were exchanged for Chinese earthenware, ironware, porcelain, and silk. Western traders became increasingly involved because of growing European demand for tea, and intra-IOW demand for guns and opium – although VOC and Dutch "burgher" trade, heavily concentrated on spices, declined. At the same time, elite IOW and European demand underpinned specialist textile production in India, which in Bengal remained largely rural, but in Gujarat gave rise to a complex urban infrastructure centred on the industrial centre of Ahmadabad and the port cities of Surat and Cambay. Further west, the Persian Gulf and Red Sea traffic rebounded and indigenous production and commerce experienced a notable upswing.

The West's dominance was even more marked in Africa, which most scholars consider to have remained peripheral to global production and exchange. Historians of nineteenth-century Africa focus chiefly on the slave export trade, the intrusion of modern capitalist forces, European colonisation, and the forcible imposition of a modern economic infrastructure. Thomas Metcalf contends that even with the onset of colonialism, Indians rather than Africans seized the economic and social opportunities opened up by empire in IOA. Revisionist historians are beginning to challenge these views, arguing for greater continuity between pre- and post-industrial eras, and for greater African participation in developments in the wider world. However, most scholars underrate the environmental context, notably that the nineteenth century witnessed the end of the LIA and, in its closing decades, dramatic climatic turbulence. Such elements greatly influenced human activity.

The Environment

As noted, the interplay of various factors, including the Asian monsoons, ITCZ, ENSO, Indian Ocean Dipole (IOD), and volcanism, drives climatic variations in the IOW. The ITCZ stayed southward of its modern position during the LIA with resulting weaker monsoons over Asia. In the mid-nineteenth century, it shifted northwards, inducing stronger, more regular monsoons, although they occasionally failed, causing major droughts. ENSO patterns also strongly influenced monsoon rainfall. Up to the early nineteenth century, monsoon failures generally coincided with El Niños, and strong monsoons with La Niñas. However, these correlations did not always hold true for the period from the 1820s. ENSO records indicate a prolonged cool event from 1863 to 1875, although the 1860s and 1870s are the only two decades to consecutively register La Niña conditions 80 per cent of the time. Also, the 1870s and 1890s witnessed an increase in the proportion of strong to extreme El Niño and La Niña events. The most severe El Niño events of the past 150 years occurred between 1876 and 1878, when the rains failed, and monsoon Asia generally experienced major famine in which many millions of people died – an estimated six million in India alone in 1877.

Sulphur-rich volcanic eruptions similarly have global teleconnections, and can trigger ENSO events. A single volcanic eruption can cause significant cooling for a few years. Sustained volcanism over an extended period, as from 1810 to 1816, 1822 to 1825, 1853 to 1856, 1872 to 1877, and in the 1880s, had a longer-term cooling effect. The IOD also has wide ramifications. In the boreal summer and fall during positive IOD events, a cold sea surface temperature anomaly, linked to intensified southeasterly trade winds, forms in the eastern Indian Ocean where it helps induce drought in western Indonesia and southern Australia.

Simultaneously, warm sea surface temperature anomalies occur in the western Indian Ocean, helping to intensify precipitation in East Africa. Opposite although generally weaker patterns prevail during negative IODs.

TABLE 9.1 *ENSO Events 1797 to 1899*★

Year	El Niño	Strength	La Niña	Strength	Year	El Niño	Strength	La Niña	Strength
1797			★	medium	1850			★	weak
1798	★	weak	★	weak	1851			★	medium
1799	★	strong			1852	★	weak		
1801			★	very strong	1853	★	very strong		
1802			★	very strong	1856	★	medium		
1803	★	strong			1857	★	medium	★	weak
1804	★	weak			1858	★	medium		
1805			★	very strong	1860	★	weak	★	very strong
1806	★	very strong			1861			★	very strong
1807	★	strong			1862			★	medium
1808			★	very strong	1863			★	very strong
1809			★	strong	1864	★	weak	★	weak
1810			★	strong	1865	★	medium		
1811			★	strong	1866	★	very strong	★	medium
1812	★	strong			1867			★	strong
1813			★	medium	1868	★	very strong	★	strong
1814	★	weak			1870			★	very strong
1815	★	weak			1871			★	very strong
1816	★	weak			1872			★	medium
1817	★	strong			1873			★	very strong
1819			★	strong	1874	★	weak	★	strong

Year	*	Magnitude
1820	*	strong
1823	*	medium
1824	*	medium
1825	*	medium
1829	*	weak
1832	*	weak
1833	*	strong
1837	*	strong
1838	*	weak
1840	*	weak
1841	*	weak
1843	*	weak
1844	*	medium
1845	*	very strong
1846	*	weak
1847	*	strong
1848	*	weak
1849	*	medium

Year	*	Magnitude
1875	*	strong
1876	*	weak
1877	*	very strong
1878	*	weak
1879	*	extreme
1880	*	very strong
1881	*	medium
1884	*	weak
1885	*	strong
1886	*	medium
1887	*	very strong
1888	*	very strong
1889	*	weak
1890	*	strong
1891	*	very strong
1892	*	strong
1893	*	very strong
1894	*	extreme
1896	*	medium
1897	*	strong
1899	*	strong

* J.L. Gergis et al., "A History of ENSO events since AD 1525: implications for future climate change" *Climate Change* 92 (2009): 368–9.

TABLE 9.2 *Volcanic Eruptions of VE4 or Over**

Year	Volcano	Coordinates	VE indice	Impact
1800	St. Helens, USA	46.2°N 122.2°W	4	
1808/9	?	?	?	
1810	?	?	?	
1812	Soufriere, St. Vincent	13.3°N 61.2°W	4	
1813	?	?	?	
1814	Mayon, Philippines	13.3°N 123.7°E	4	
1815	Tambora, Sumbawa, Indonesia	8.3°S 118.0°E	7	
1816	?	?	?	
1818	Colima, Mexico	19.4°N 103.7°W	4	
1818	Beerenberg, Jan Mayen	71.1°N 8.2°W	4	
1822	Papandayan, West Java	7.4°S 107.7°E	4	
1822	Usu, Japan	42.5°N 140.8°E	4	
1823	?	?	?	
1825	Isanotski, Aleutian Island	54.8°N 163.7°W	4	
1831	?	?	?	
1835	Coseguina, Nicaragua	13.0°N 87.6°W	5	
1845	Hekla, Iceland	64.0°N 19.7°W	4	
1849	Purace, Columbia	2.4°N 76.4°W	4	
1853	Usu, Japan	42.5°N 140.8°E	4	
1853	Chickurachki, Kurile Island	50.3°N 155.5°E	4	
1854	Sheveluch, Kamchatka	56.8°N 161.6°E	5	
1856	Komaga-take, Japan	42.1°N 140.7°E	4	
1861	?	?	?	
1869	Purace, Columbia	2.4°N 76.4°W	4	
1872	Sinarka, Kurile island	48.9°N 154.2°E	4	
1873	Grimsvotn, Iceland	64.4°N 17.3°W	4	
1875	Askja, Iceland	65.0°N 16.8°W	5	
1877	Suwanose-jima, Japan	29.5°N 129.7°E	4	
1880	?	?	?	
1881	Nasu, Japan	37.1°N 140.0°E	4	
1883	Krakatau, Sunda Strait	6.1°S 105.4°E	6	
1883	Augustine, Alaska	59.4°N 153.4°W	4	
1884	?	?	?	

TABLE 9.2 (*cont.*)

Year	Volcano	Coordinates	VE indice	Impact
1886	Tarawera, New Zealand	38.2°S 176.5°E	5	
1888	Bandai, Japan	37.6°N 140.1°E	4	
1889	Suwanose-jima, Japan	29.5°N 129.7°E	4	
1890	?	?	?	
1899	Dona Juana, Columbia	1.5°N 76.9°W	4	

* R.S. Bradley and P.D. Jones, "Records of Explosive Volcanic Eruptions Over the Last 500 Years" in idem (eds.), *Climate Since A.D. 1500* (London: Routledge, 1992), table 31.1; Jihong Dai, Ellen Mosley-Thompson, and Lonnie G. Thompson, "Ice Core Evidence for an Explosive Tropical Volcanic Eruption 6 Years preceding Tambora" *Journal of Geophysical Research* 96.D9 (1991): 17,361–17,366.

In the 1800s, much of northern hemisphere IOW experienced cool, arid conditions until mid-century. For example, eastern China experienced severe droughts from 1780 to 1820, while northwest China was particularly arid in the 1820s. From 1825, temperatures across the IOW generally started to increase, although there were exceptions. For instance, South China experienced exceptionally cold weather from 1876 to 1895. Moreover, the East Asian summer monsoon weakened, and there was a protracted arid period characterised by El Niño activity between about 1856 and 1878. From 1830 to 1900, temperatures in the southern hemisphere were generally lower, and the climate in the tropics experienced far greater decadal variance, than in the twentieth century.

Longer-term climatic change was complicated by shorter-term factors. Strong ENSO effects, associated with severe droughts followed in consecutive years by unusually heavy rain, were experienced from 1844 to 1846, 1876 to 1878, and 1899 to 1900. Again, high volcanic dust veil marked the years 1783 to 1788, 1832 to 1838, and 1884. ENSO events and high dust veil indexes correlate with crop failures, food shortages, and disease – the spread of which was facilitated by communications improvements and increased migration. For example, cholera, endemic in Bengal, was from 1817 carried by British troops to Nepal and Afghanistan, and from 1820 to 1822 travelled with British ships to Sri Lanka, Southeast Asia, China and Japan, as well as to Muscat from where it dispersed to the Persian Gulf and to East Africa. By 1831 cholera was established in Mecca: Between 1831 and 1912, it broke out 40 times during the *hajj*, pilgrims carrying it to every part of the Muslim world, from Indonesia to East and West Africa. A similar pattern developed with other killer diseases such as smallpox and malaria. Venereal disease, which was rarely as dramatic but severely affected health and fertility, also spread rapidly throughout the IOW. Only from the mid-twentieth century did the spread of modern medicines and effective treatment begin to counter this pattern.

The spread of virulent diseases had considerable demographic impact in the IOW. Cholera killed approximately 13 per cent of Cairo's population in 1831, and almost 30 million Indians perished in epidemics that swept the sub-continent in the second half of the century. The evidence from China illustrates what could happen when man-made disasters coincided with natural catastrophes. One of the few IOW regions in this era initially characterised by very fast demographic growth, China's population leapt from about 300 million to 420 million between 1800 and 1850. However, a combination of epidemics, experienced in 36 of the 61 years from 1811 to 1872, and almost constant warfare between 1850 and 1878, left vast tracts of central and northern China depopulated. In the T'ai-p'ing (1850–64) and Nien (1851–64) rebellions alone, some 25 million people died. In the famine of 1877 to 1879, a further 10 million perished in northern China. By 1900, the Chinese population stood at only 450 million.

IOA in the Long Nineteenth Century

Environment

IOA experienced its most arid cool period of the last 200 years in the first 45 years of the nineteenth century. This reflected in part the cooling effect of volcanic eruptions such as that of Tambora (1815). Northern IOA, southern Africa, and most of central and western (but not northwestern) Madagascar, remained arid until about 1870. Major drought afflicted southern Africa from 1864 to 1868 – in which year the Nile flood recorded its second lowest level since 1700. From 1880 until the start of the twentieth century, IOA generally experienced another two remarkably arid decades. There were, however, significant exceptions: Equatorial East Africa experienced a dramatically increased warmer, wetter period between 1845 and 1880, as did southwest Madagascar between 1870 and 1900, and southeastern Africa in the years around 1890.

Commercial Networks

Northeast Africa

Egypt was early affected by industrialisation in Western Europe which, from the mid-1700s, supplied it with finished goods in return for primary and semi-processed products. For example, from 1750 to 1780, the quantity of cloth imports almost doubled to comprise 50 per cent of Egypt's imports from Europe. Other European imports included dye, paper, metals, glass, amber, spices, and weapons. In return, Egypt exported to Europe – which by 1780 absorbed 60.4 per cent of its total exports – rice, flax, wool, cotton thread, leather, senna, saffron, and salammoniac. European imports hurt Egypt's domestic industrial sector, but it picked up again during from 1789 to 1815, when Western Europe was embroiled in the turmoil of the French Revolution and Napoleonic Wars. Thus from 1790 the Egyptian linen and cotton industries and exports showed signs of recovery and, by the early 1800s, a small cotton manufacturing industry had also developed at Dongola, in the Sudan. However, other factors dampened the economy: extended drought and famine, and a major epizootic, afflicted Egypt in the first half of the 1790s, leading to economic dislocation that was further accentuated from 1798 to 1802 by the French occupation, famine, plague, and further epizootics. Again, a particularly severe winter in 1813 caused high human and animal mortality.

The conventional view is that from the 1810s, European cloth imports, initially chiefly from southern France but after 1815 from Manchester, again undermined Egyptian cloth production. More generally, greater volumes of European manufactured exports disrupted the traditional trading nexus joining Upper Egypt, Ethiopia, Arabia, and India over which Cairo formerly had considerable control, and hit Egyptian artisans hard. Moreover, Egyptian grain exports to Europe, which boomed during the periods of European conflict, started to fall from around 1820. Subsequently, Egyptian exports became increasingly dependent on raw sugar, sent chiefly to France which shipped back refined sugar. In consequence, large areas of Upper Egypt formerly dedicated to grain were converted to sugar cane.

However, Egypt continued to play a vibrant role in commercial exchange with the wider IOW. The Napoleonic invasion caused a dip in this trade, but it revived during the European wars. Indian cloth, spices, and coffee flowed along Red Sea routes, as did Somali commodities (see below), while ostrich plumes, ivory, gold dust, gum, and skins were shipped down the Nile from Sudan – much for reexport. Egypt exported leather work, wheat to Arabia – a market supplemented by rice from Bengal – and, to Sudan, cottons, linens, woollens, Egyptian and Syrian silks, metalwork, hardware, writing paper, and provisions. Exports expanded again from 1818, when it was noted that Sudanese (Sennar) merchants travelled regularly to India.

The staple exports from northeast Africa were coffee, gum Arabic, frankincense, myrrh, ivory, ghee (clarified butter), ostrich feathers, ambergris, hides, antelope horns, horned cattle, and slaves. These were shipped from Berbera and other ports, chiefly by Somali traders in their own dhows, to Mocha and Aden. The trade was well organised and profitable. Indeed, it has been estimated that as late as 1848 Aden derived over 80 per cent of its revenue from duties charged on imports from Berbera – a clear indication that Aden's economy was then dependent largely on its trade with Somalia and Ethiopia. In Mocha and Aden this commerce operated through Indian Banian traders although IOA traders were the dominant partners. Somali and Ethiopian merchants placed their orders with Indian traders a year in advance. It is worth underlining that the exchange was conducted according to a centuries-old seasonal rhythm, the Berbera market operating only during the northeast monsoon. In October, at the onset of the monsoon, caravans started to arrive in Berbera laden with commodities from the Somali interior and Ethiopian highlands. In the early 1800s, most exports were shipped initially to Mocha from where the greater part was carried up the Red Sea to Egypt, while small quantities were re-exported to Arabia, Iran, and (via Bombay) to Europe. At the same time, vessels arrived from Mocha and increasingly from Aden, with cloth, brass and copper wire, zinc and beads from India, dates and grain from Arabia, and some European cloth. In 1848, Charles Cruttenden, an English naval officer, described the seasonal closure of the Berbera market:

> By the end of March the fair is nearly at a close, and craft of all kinds, deeply laden, and sailing generally in parties of three or four, commence their homeward journey ... and by the first week in April Berbera is again deserted, nothing being left to mark the site of a town lately containing 20,000 inhabitants, beyond bones of slaughtered camels and sheep, and the framework of a few huts carefully piled on the beach in readiness for the ensuing year. Beasts of prey now take the opportunity to approach

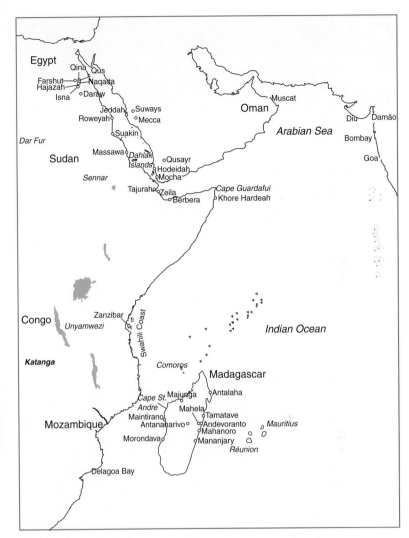

MAP 9.1 Indian Ocean Africa: Hubs of Production and Trade
Note: Produced by Carl Hughes, IOWC.

the sea. Lions are commonly seen at the town-well during the hot weather; and in April last year, but a week had ended, I observed three
ostriches quietly walking on the beach.[1]

---

[1] Charles J. Cruttenden, "Memoir on the Western or Edoor Tribes, Inhabiting the
Somali Coast of N.-E. Africa, with the Southern Branches of the Family of Darrood,
Resident on the Banks of the Webbe Shebeyli, Commonly Called the River Webbe"
(Aden, 12 May 1848) *Journal of the Royal Geographical Society of London* 19, (1849): 55.

FIGURE 9.1 The Suez Canal

Note: NASA Suez Canal Image, 2011 – www.strangerplanets.com – in the public domain.

The opening of the Suez Canal in 1869 coincided with the start of the great age of steamships, facilitating not only Europe-IOW and considerable Africa-IOW trade, but also trans-IOW pilgrimages: One steamship in 1880 carried almost 1,000 pilgrims from Southeast Asia to Aden. However, steam complemented rather than replaced sail in intra-regional trade, while even on long-distance runs, only the traffic to Europe fully converted to steam, American merchants continuing to use sailing ships until the 1890s.

East Africa and Madagascar

Conventional histories emphasise the "opening up" of the IOA hinterland by external Arab and later European agents who subsequently came to dominate commerce in the interior. However, it is increasingly clear that these agents largely depended on, and forged alliances with, African traders experienced in collecting and organising the coastwise transport of ivory and other staple exports, and the interior distribution of cloth and other imports through domestic trading networks. Such groups included the Nyamwezi of the Lake Tanganyika region, the Yao and Bisa to the east and west respectively of Lake Nyassa and, in Madagascar, the Merina. We here briefly examine the cases of the Nyamwezi and Merina.

The Nyamwezi ("people of the moon") are a Bantu-speaking people who probably migrated eastwards and settled in what became known as Unyamwezi (west central Tanzania) in the seventeenth century. High agricultural productivity, in part due to the adoption of rice cultivation, and use of slave labour in the fields, enabled many Nyamwezi men to specialise in trade. They early became engaged in inter-regional commerce involving commodities such as salt, iron, iron goods (hoes, spears), cattle, and hides and, by the start of the nineteenth century, were sending ivory, Katanga copper, wax, salt, and slaves, to the coast. Their ability to take full advantage of the growth in IOW commerce as the international economy took shape was restricted by a major drought that afflicted East Africa from the mid-1700s to the 1840s that provoked famine, disease, significant animal and human mortality, mass migration and depopulation. However, from 1845 to 1880 the onset of a dramatically warmer wetter climate brought economic stability, and Nyamwezi traders flourished. They possessed an advantage in the valuable ivory trade as some Nyamwezi were specialist elephant hunters, organised into a guild, who ranged as far west as the Congo for prey. Nyamwezi porters carried ivory to the coast for export, and returned with imported goods, predominantly cloth. Major Nyamwezi traders hired young Nyamwezi men as porters, but the latter took advantage of the system to trade in small items on their own account and thus, over time, increase their wealth and status. It is estimated

FIGURE 9.2 Mirambo (d. 1884) – Nyamwezi Leader

Note: From Rob Wilson, "Mirambo: The Man Who Changed the Face of Nineteenth-Century Tanzania" Think Africa Press 2 September 2012 – http://thinkafricapress.com/tanzania/mirambo-political-transformation-nineteenth-century-tanzania (accessed 02/09/12) – open access.

FIGURE 9.3 Rainilaiarivony (1828–1896), Merina Prime Minister

Note: USC Digital Library. Published in 1896 in "Two campaigns: Madagascar and Ashantee" by Bennet Burleigh, see plate facing page 13.

that, during the dry "trading" season, as many as 200,000 Nyamwezi males were engaged in porterage and trade. The traffic in ivory was so significant that from 1873 to 1874 internal conflict erupted in which Mirambo (d. 1884), a Nyamwezi leader, asserted such control over the trade routes that the price of East African ivory soared. However, another extended drought in the 1880s and 1890s, accompanied by epizootics, caused major instability in East Africa, as did the imposition of German colonial rule in Unyamwezi in the 1890s. Nevertheless, the Nyamwezi continued to dominate regional long-distance trading caravans into the early twentieth century.

In Madagascar, two distinct trading networks had developed by the 1820s. One, which fell outside the sway of the Merina regime which claimed suzerainty over Madagascar, embraced the west and south of the island. To the north of Cape St. André, Indian and Swahili traders, whose centre of operations was Majunga, dominated trade. During the course of the nineteenth century, the Indian-Swahili network expanded to integrate the region south of Cape St. André where, until the 1870s, commercial exchange was largely unorganised, foreign traders negotiating directly with local chiefs.

The second trading network incorporated the Merina Empire, comprising the central and eastern provinces of Madagascar. Here, the Merina army played a crucial commercial role. From the 1820s, the Merina crown declared monopolies over all valuable commodities and moulded the imperial army into a commercial rather than a military institution, and used armed expeditions as primarily commercial ventures. Military service was unremunerated, but officers were encouraged to both trade and plunder. Moreover, between 1822 and 1840, a network of Merina garrisons was erected along most major trade routes, simultaneously establishing a Merina military presence and control over long-distance commerce. Some garrisons, such as Mahabo and Malaimbandy, on the route between Antananarivo, in the central highlands, and Morondava, the major port on the mid-west coast, maintained Merina commercial influence well beyond Merina military sway. The Merina elite vied for control of the commercially most important garrisons with, by mid-century, members of the powerful Tsimiamboholahy and Tsimahafotsy clans gaining governorships of all east coast ports as well as of Majunga, the chief entrepôt in northwest Madagascar. The governor of every Merina-controlled port shared its customs revenue with the imperial treasury and his patron at court.

Rank and file soldiers for the imperial army were recruited directly through village-level conscription, and aides-de-camp, called *deka*, via the mission schools. The number of *deka* permitted each rank of officer rose steadily under Ranavalona I (r. 1828–61); by 1857, Raharo, one of the court elite, possessed 800, and his father, commander of the army, 1,500. This changed in the 1860s when effective government passed from the crown to the Merina Prime Minister, Rainilaiarivony (1828–96). In the mid-1860s, in a measure intended to undermine his political rivals, Rainilaiarivony limited *deka* numbers to between one for an officer of 9 honours and 30 for an officer of 16 honours. Through their *deka*, court officials speculated in commercial ventures, purloined crown booty, and exploited both common soldiers and subjugated provinces. The system ensured that each member of the court oligarchy commanded a military company that he used to further his private commercial and other interests.

Garrison soldiers also traded on their own account. Indeed, after military expansion was curtailed in the early 1850s, most *deka* – who comprised a majority in most Merina forts – became virtually full-time traders. In 1869, for instance, 500 of the 800-strong Andevoranto garrison, on Antananarivo-Tamatave route, were *deka*. Moreover, garrison *deka* were frequently absent on trading ventures: in 1877, 96 per cent (114 men) of the personnel of the Ihosy garrison were so missing. They travelled from one fort to the next, using slaves as colporteurs, bartering primarily cloth and trinkets for gold dust and cattle. They were regulated by passport inspections in all garrisons through which they passed. The *deka* system excluded non-Merina from the most valuable aspects of trade in areas under Merina domination. On the east coast, for example, court *deka* obliged local Betsimisaraka to sell export commodities to them at low prices.

The Merina court also granted some commercial monopolies to select foreigners. Thus, in 1837, in exchange for an annual payment of $6,000 to the Merina crown, Napoléon Delastelle (1802–56), a Breton trader, gained a monopoly over east coast exports of beeswax, gum copal, ebony, and hides, and in 1843 granted his associate, de Rontaunay, control of the foreign trade of Mahela, Mananjary and Mahanoro. However, in 1845, foreigners were banned from Merina-controlled ports in reprisal for a Franco-British naval attack upon Tamatave, and even after the ports re-opened in 1853 the majority of foreign traders on the east coast were small-scale Mascarene Creoles or "British" Indians from Madras. A handful of larger British and

American firms handled the bulk of the most lucrative commodities, exporting notably hides, wax, and gums, and importing cloth. In the 1880s, to compete more effectively with foreign merchants, primarily in the import and distribution of cottons and the collection and export of hides, the Merina court established the "Ambohimalaza" cartel, a "civilian" middlemen group comprising five Antananarivo-based "houses" dominated by leading traders Raoelina and Andriampatra (or Andriampatsa). Much to the chagrin of foreign dealers, the cartel established control in the interior over the price and distribution of major legitimate commodities and, unlike foreign traders, enjoyed privileged access to cheap porterage.

The Expansion of the Indian IOA Commercial Network

Studies of eastern IOA from 1750 have focussed extensively on the slave trade. The predominant view is that, from the mid-eighteenth to late nineteenth century, external agents, notably "Arabs" and Europeans, exercised a growing demand for slaves, and often financed slave raids that penetrated ever deeper into the East African interior, violently robbing Africa of its manpower. They thus eroded the economic and social basis of African communities over which European imperial powers subsequently imposed political domination. However, this viewpoint largely ignores the fact that, in addition to a vigorous traffic in slaves, the IOA also experienced an immense expansion of "legitimate" commerce from which significant benefits accrued to IOW and IOA agents. One of the greatest beneficiaries was Indians, most of whom by the early nineteenth century were British subjects. Indeed, "British" trade in the western IOW in this period was largely Indian, and the expansion of the Indian financial and commercial frontier laid the economic basis for British colonial intervention in much of IOA.

The Indian commercial nexus was stimulated when, following France's defeat in the Napoleonic Wars, the British Navy established unparalleled security in western IOW waters. By the early 1820s, in alliance with Omani authorities on Zanzibar, and Portuguese authorities on Mozambique Island – both under British informal dominance – it had largely suppressed piracy off northern and eastern Madagascar, the Mascarenes, and along the Swahili and Mozambique coasts. By the 1830s, it had also largely eliminated piracy in Arabian and Persian Gulf waters. Thereafter, there existed a maritime *Pax*

Britannica in the western IOW. Moreover, in 1813, the EIC monopoly was restricted to tea and commerce with China, and in 1833
was abolished altogether – to the benefit of smaller companies and
individual traders, including those indigenous to the IOW.

As noted in earlier chapters, Indians had a long history of involvement in IOA-IOW exchange. Indian trade with Red Sea Africa
dated to well before the BCE/CE changeover, and by the early 1800s
small colonies of Indian traders, chiefly from the west coast of the
sub-continent, had developed in all important regional ports, notably Mocha, Jeddah, and Aden, from where they dominated the foreign trade of northeast Africa and the Red Sea. For example, Indian
merchants in Mocha (over 200 in 1778; 250 in 1811) and Aden largely
financed Indian trade with the Horn of Africa and Ethiopia, notably
via the ports of Berbera, Zeila, Tajurah, and Massawa. Letters of credit
issued by leading Indian traders enjoyed currency along the coast and
for a considerable distance into the interior on both sides of the Red
Sea. To northeast African ports, Indian traders shipped Indian timber,
textiles (cotton and silk), rice, sugar, spices, and tobacco chiefly from
(in order of importance) Bengal, Surat, Bombay, Java, Malaya, and
Indochina, as well as European goods. In exchange, they shipped
out African ivory, gold, musk, myrrh, gum, coffee, slaves, livestock
(camels, horses, mules and asses), and Red Sea pearls from the Dahlak
Islands. The Indian presence in the region was boosted in 1839 by the
British takeover of Aden where a garrison of 2,000 Indian troops was
established, the rupee made the official currency and, in 1855, a fort-
nightly steamer service to Bombay inaugurated.

Taking full advantage of maritime security, liberty of trade, and
their status as subjects of the English crown, Indian traders expanded
their commercial frontiers in northern IOA. This development was
facilitated by improved climatic conditions in IOA from the mid-
nineteenth century, and technological innovations, notably the
opening of the Suez Canal and extension of the steamship network.
From 1882, the British seizure of Egypt and its Red Sea colonies
offered Indian traders even greater opportunities. Indian merchant
houses in Jeddah, Aden, and Bombay increased their presence in
ports such as Massawa, where their number increased fourfold from
about 12 in the early 1800s to 50 or more by the mid-1880s. They also
established agencies in Suakin, which the British made their primary
Red Sea port, and Aqiq, chiefly to supply markets in the Red Sea Hills
with durra (Indian millet).

Further, Indians expanded their long-standing trade with the
Swahili coast, Mozambique, and Madagascar. This expansion
occurred initially under the auspices of Oman, where they held dominant positions as financiers, and which in 1823 fell under informal
British domination. Oman had since 1698 claimed control of Zanzibar,
where in the 1830s it invested in clove plantations, and to which in
1840 Seyyid Said, the sultan, moved his headquarters (from Muscat).
Subsequently, British Indians dominated the Zanzibari economy as
capitalists, wholesalers, and retailers. Although the Swahili coast, notably Zanzibar, remained the centre of Indian trade and investment in
southern IOA, Indian commercial influence spread rapidly south of
Zanzibar from the 1840s, to Mozambique, the Comoros, and northwest Madagascar where they supplemented long-established Indian
groups. Throughout the 1880s, a fleet of Indian-owned dhows, of
from 60 to 100 tons each, sailed annually from Bombay and other
western India shipping centres directly to ports, notably Maintirano
and Manambolo, on the independent west coast of Madagascar before
crossing to East Africa. There, they joined the established Indian community which, in Delagoa Bay, largely comprised merchants from
Portuguese India (Goa, Diu, and Damão).

Indians dominated the foreign trade of IOA, the staple exports of
which were ivory and slaves from continental Africa, and precious
woods, gum, and slaves from Madagascar. Ivory, the most valuable
export, had traditionally been transhipped via India to Europe, but
from the mid-1800s was increasingly shipped direct. Indians also
dominated the trade in cotton cloth, by far the major import into
IOA, despite the growing influx of cheap cotton textiles from British
and, notably from the 1870s, New England factories. Indeed, Jeremy
Prestholdt has demonstrated that in the 1880s, at the time of general depression and the European scramble for colonies, the value of
imports into Zanzibar of goods produced in India more than doubled
between 1885 and 1890 when Zanzibar, which in 1890 became a
British protectorate, was the destination of almost half of Bombay's
exports of unbleached cotton cloth.

In Madagascar too, Indians eventually surpassed American and
European traders in the cotton cloth import trade. Western commercial agents discovered the sophisticated local tastes for cloth from the
1820s, leading American cloth merchants to have material designed
specifically for the imperial Merina market. Unbleached cotton
sheeting, chiefly in six-yard (5.5 metre) pieces, and seldom retailed in

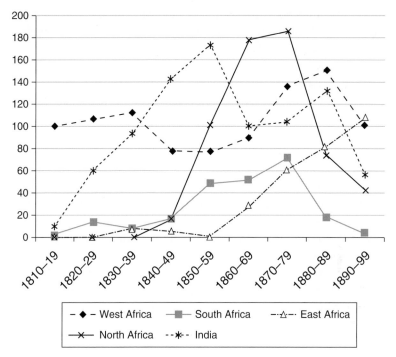

FIGURE 9.4 Britain: Ivory Imports, 1810 to 1899 (ten-year averages in tons)

Note: Gwyn Campbell, *An Economic History of Imperial Madagascar, 1750–1895. The Rise and Fall of an Island Empire* (Cambridge: Cambridge University Press, 2005), 309.

less than one-yard (0.9 metre) lengths, found ready sale, notably from April to May when the plateau population lined their *lamba* (a kind of Malagasy toga) with cotton for protection against the cold. Also popular were brown and white shirting and printed cotton pieces, used to make clothes. Moreover, until the 1880s, imports augmented rather than undermined indigenous production of silk, vegetable fibre, and cotton cloth for the domestic market. Imported cloth failed to affect Malagasy cloth exports which comprised chiefly coarse materials made of cotton mixed mostly with other fibres which, cheap and durable, were valued on the Mascarenes where they were used to clothe plantation workers.

The 1880s depression heralded renewed competition in the cotton trade. The near monopoly that Americans enjoyed of cotton imports into east Madagascar was broken in 1879–80 by German and British firms whose challenge was consolidated by a dramatic increase in the import of European cloth fraudulently carrying American trademarks. Similarly, American domination of cotton cloth imports into western Madagascar ended about 1880 when Indians captured most of the cotton import trade by marketing as "standard", i.e. 30-yard long (27.4 metre) cloth that was 25 to 26 yards (22.9–24.0 metres) in length.

Moreover, like the Omani authorities, European commercial agents in Zanzibar, including representatives of major concerns such as William O'Swald of Hamburg, often ran short of money and turned to Indian financiers for credit. In a very real sense, therefore, the Indian mercantile empire in the western IOW and its IOA (Swahili, mainland African, Malagasy, and Indian) trading partners formed the basis for British economic influence in IOA. For their trade to Europe, Indian merchants increasingly took advantage of steamship services. However, for their western IOW trade, they hired Swahili dhow owners who offered low freight rates, and possessed captains with an intimate knowledge of regional winds and currents who could, unlike the captains of larger European vessels, sail their craft into shallow waters. As Eric Gilbert has underlined, indigenous craft and ship captains competed advantageously against steamships in inter-regional maritime trade well into the twentieth century.

In sum, the rise of the international economy did not automatically result in European dominance of the IOW economy. Rather, it led to enormously enhanced commercial opportunities that IOW traders and financiers seized, notably from mid-century when climatic conditions improved. IOA witnessed a spectacular expansion of the long-standing Indian trading frontier. Indians largely financed the burgeoning international trade of IOA, offering credit even to "respectable" European merchant houses. Moreover, they forged alliances with local groups who similarly seized expanding trade opportunities. Such groups included the Swahili who dominated commercial shipping in IOA waters, and the Nyamwezi of present-day Tanzania. The Merina in Madagascar were less closely associated with the Indian trading structure, but similarly displayed entrepreneurial spirit in profiting from expanding international commerce. Another generally underestimated reflection of indigenous entrepreneurship was attempts by some IOA powers to resist imperial European pretensions by modernising their economies – a theme to which the next chapter is devoted.

10

Indigenous Modernisation in Indian Ocean Africa: Egypt, Imerina, and Ethiopia

The nineteenth century witnessed the emergence of a truly international economy and a new European imperialism. The conventional view is that by 1914, the forces of modern capitalism had drawn all but the most remote communities into its orbit while, with few exceptions, IOW societies crumbled under the economic and political domination of the West. However, a number of indigenous IOW polities attempted to modernise their economies in order to resist domination by European countries and to rival them as regional imperial powers. This chapter examines three cases from Indian Ocean Africa (IOA), Egypt, Imerina (in the central highlands of Madagascar), and Ethiopia. The conventional view is Muhammad Ali (r. 1811–49) of Egypt, Radama I (r. 1810–28) of Imerina, and Tewodros II (r. 1855–68) and Menilek II (r. 1889–1913) of Ethiopia, laid the foundations of, respectively, the modern Egyptian, Malagasy, and Ethiopian nation states. This chapter focuses on attempts in all three countries, the first two contemporaneous with early industrialisation in Western Europe and North America, to adopt and adapt Western technology in order to promote economic development and self-sufficiency, and build modern armies capable of keeping European powers at bay.

Education

A primary goal of the Egyptian and Merina regimes was to foster education, and access the technical training required for modernisation.

Basic literacy and numeracy play key roles in economic growth as they enhance the value of human capital, and facilitate the ease and speed of worker adaptation to industrial employment. Indeed, a sufficiently high correlation exists between literacy and industrial development to make literacy an accepted precondition of industrial "takeoff". Egypt in 1811 and Imerina in 1822 founded school systems based on European syllabi. In Imerina, it was initially largely supervised by British missionaries, and in Egypt by secular European instructors. Between 1835 and 1840 in Egypt, and between 1820 and 1835 in Imerina, up to 8,500 and 15,000 scholars, respectively, passed through these local educational systems. Literacy was facilitated by printing presses, established in Egypt in 1822, and Imerina in 1828, and informal instruction, notably in Imerina. Consequently, Imerina probably attained a literacy rate of over 7 per cent by 1835, while adult literacy in Egypt increased from 1 to 3 per cent (possibly reaching 33 per cent in Cairo) between 1830 and 1850 – by which year some 5 per cent of Egyptian children were literate. Both countries could by mid-century envisage attaining the 30 per cent literacy threshold generally considered necessary for industrialisation. In both Egypt and Imerina, many scholars subsequently entered the administration and army in which literacy greatly improved efficiency and communications. Thus it was noted in Madagascar in 1853: "Had no schools been established in IMERINA, no important business or affair could have been transmitted to the Garrisons."[1]

The Ethiopian case was different. There, the educational impact of Europeans was limited. The Swedish Lutheran Evangelical Mission, first established in Massawa in 1866, taught both sexes to read and write and set up a mission press. However, by 1900 only about 100 pupils attended its schools. Again, French Lazarists founded an educational system in 1872, but their schools were thinly spread and had little impact. Consequently, formal education in Ethiopia remained largely in the hands of the indigenous *Tewhado* (Orthodox) Christian church which accepted a small number of boys, destined for the clergy, who from the age of five were taught to read Ethiopic Ge'ez characters. A few scholars continued beyond this basic level to study traditional religious writing, art, and medicine. However, it took at least 30 years for them to graduate, following which they joined an elite group of

---

[1] Raombana, "Histoires" (1853), 134 – Archives of the Académie Malgache, Tsimbazaza, Antananarivo.

scholars, artists, religious leaders, teachers, and state officials, or became merchants. Richard Pankhurst estimated that, in the Amharic regions, possibly 20 per cent of the male population could read, a proportion that Edouard Blondeel van Cuelebroeck (1809–1872), a visiting Belgian consul, considered similar to that for Western Europe at the time. However, far fewer people could write. Full literacy was restricted to a tiny elite, chiefly the aristocracy and clergy.

The Merina and Egyptian regimes also placed high priority on scientific, technical and military education. They hired foreign personnel to give such instruction locally, and sent select indigenous youth to train in Europe, with the intention of quickly replacing foreign with indigenous expertise. From 1809 to 1818, Muhammad Ali sent a total of 28 students to Italy, France, and Britain for instruction in, variously, naval construction, military training, engineering, and printing; and from 1826 to 1848 despatched 319 students to an Egyptian School in Paris to study military and practical subjects, sciences, and medicine. In its turn, the Merina court sent 27 youths abroad between 1816 and 1830: nine to Britain to be trained in armaments and gunpowder-manufacturing, cotton production and dyeing, silver-work, and the liberal arts, and the remainder to Mauritius to study military music, gold, silver and iron-working, carpentry, shoe mending, and painting. A further 50 were placed aboard British ships for naval training. Later, specialist schools were established, in Egypt to teach military matters, mining, agriculture, medicine, languages, translation, music, and administration; and in Imerina chiefly to offer a liberal arts education.

By contrast, only from the 1890s were the first Ethiopian youth sent abroad for advanced studies, to Western Europe, Russia, and the Sudan, while the first modern school in Ethiopia, following a basically European-style syllabus, was founded in Addis Ababa in 1908 for about 100 noble children. Others followed in Harar and Dire Dawa. These taught literacy in Amharic and some European languages, as well as mathematics and science.

The Industrial Experiment

Industrialisation was a key objective of the modernisation programmes in Egypt and Imerina. As contemporaneously in Europe, textile production played a central role. Both countries lacked capital, but possessed considerable resources in the form of land, raw materials, and labour, as well as a long tradition of growing plants such as cotton, hemp, and silk, used locally for cloth production. The Egyptian and Merina regimes implemented plans for cotton production on an industrial scale in 1817 and 1822 respectively, prompted in Egypt by the wish to reverse the increasing trend of exporting raw cotton to Europe and importing European finished cloth; and in Imerina by loss of revenue entailed by the 1820 ban on slave exports. Muhammad Ali pursued with greater rigour, and on a wider scale, measures implemented by his Mamluk predecessors to divert agricultural surpluses into state hands. He confiscated Mamluk landholdings, comprising approximately 75 per cent of Egypt's cultivable land, in 1811, and other private domains and *waqf* (religious endowments), amounting to about 20 per cent of the total land area, in 1814. These he parcelled out to tenant farmers, thereby enormously increasing state revenue from land taxes. Between 1812 and 1816 he also imposed state monopolies over traditional cash crops including short-staple cotton, hemp, and indigo (used to make dyes). By 1821, Egypt had developed the long-staple *Jumel* cotton which produced soft, lustrous, yet strong and durable, silk-like yarn, and in 1825 imported Sea Island cotton that was cross-bred with *Jumel*, resulting by around 1860 in the high-quality *Ashmouni* variety.

In 1816, the first state textile factory opened in Old Cairo and by 1823, when Ali banned cottage textile production, state factories were producing cotton textiles on a large scale. By the early 1830s, Egypt possessed probably the world's fifth largest domestic cotton spinning industry, with between 15,000 and 20,000 workers, up to 400,000 spindles, and over 2,000 looms (400 were steam-driven), that annually produced up to 2.7 million kg of yarn and possibly 10 million m^2 of cloth. State factories also manufactured woollen and linen cloth, leather goods, processed foods (ground maize, hulled rice, roasted coffee, and refined sugar), ink, paper, and indigo.

In Imerina by the late 1700s, the crown had geographically concentrated peasant populations in specific locations and directed their labour in canal, dyke and other water-control projects in order to promote hydraulic riziculture. Textile production remained a predominantly ubiquitous cottage and part-time female occupation. However, in 1817, Radama I introduced Indian breeds of mulberry silkworm (*Bombyx mori or Sericaria mori lin*), from 1820 encouraged widespread cultivation of new mulberry-bush cuttings, and in 1825 created mulberry plantations at Mahela and Andevoranto on the

FIGURE 10.1 Mohammad Ali (r. 1805–48)

Note: By Auguste Couder, from the Bibliotheca Alexandrina's Memory of Modern Egypt Digital Archive – in the public domain.

east coast. Ranavalona I, who succeeded Radam in 1828, adopted new species of silkworm and created further plantations. Again, in 1821–2, the Merina government established workshops to produce calico and other cottons, and sent a Merina to Manchester to learn modern techniques of production. However, Malagasy spinners, who worked on a seasonal basis, could not provide state workshops with regular yarn supplies. Moreover, workshop output could not compete locally in price or quality with cloth produced by independent part-time weavers who had far fewer overheads, and failed to establish a niche in foreign markets because of prohibitively high transport costs. Finally, in 1829, Ranavalona scrapped plans laid by Radama in 1827 for a large-scale cotton factory. Thus neither silk nor cotton cloth were produced on an industrial scale, although from 1829 government weavers worked imported textile machinery on a small scale to produce *lamba* for the domestic market.

Self-sufficiency in armaments was a prime goal of the Egyptian and Merina regimes. Ali established arsenals in Cairo (the Citadel),

FIGURE 10.2 Ismail Pasha (r. 1863–79)
Note: NNDB. In the public domain.

Būlāk, Rosetta, and Alexandria in 1815, and a gunpowder factory at Aswan in 1821. Further, the state constructed military barracks, dockyards, hospitals, administrative buildings, and schools that together absorbed some 20 per cent of domestic cotton goods output. In 1821, Ali also initiated a naval programme. He first purchased old ships from European powers, but in 1824 commissioned the building of four new warships from Italian and French shipyards. However, in October 1827, British, French and Russian warships almost completely destroyed the Egyptian navy at the battle of Navarino, during the Greek War of Independence (1821–32). Consequently, in 1829, Ali established a shipyard at Alexandria, complete with foundry and rope-making factory, supervised by French, Italian, and Maltese artisan-shipbuilders. In 1831, Egypt launched its first modern (110-gun) warship; and for a campaign against Syria in 1832 employed 16 warships and 17 transport vessels. By 1840, Alexandria naval base had a 5,000-strong workforce and Egypt possessed the largest and

FIGURE 10.3 Radama I (r. 1810–28)

Note: By André Coppalle (1825–26) in Regis Rajemisa-Raolison, *Dictionnaire historique et géographique de Madagascar* (Fianarantsoa: Librairie Ambozontany, 1966), 276.

best-equipped navy, comprising both imported and locally built vessels, of any Muslim power.

By 1837, Egypt possessed 14 armaments factories, an iron foundry with eight furnaces, an arsenal, three sugar refineries and rum distilleries, a fez factory, paper mill, press, copper mill, and chemical factory. In 1838, state expenditure on industrial production amounted to £12 million. The government also assumed control of hitherto independent domestic industrial establishments, including rice mills, oil presses, and flour mills. Steam engines, navigational instruments, irrigation pumps, dyes, soap, glass, and acids were all produced locally. Indeed, by the 1830s, the capital stock of Egyptian industry amounted to some £6–7 million – half that of the British cotton industry.

The Merina regime, which unlike Egypt possessed high-quality iron ore, excellent ironworkers and, on its eastern borders, plentiful wood for fuel, also established large-scale armaments production.

FIGURE 10.4 Ranavalona I (r. 1828–61)

Note: Photograph of the original work on display at the Lapan' Andafiavaratra (Antananarivo). In the public domain.

FIGURE 10.5 Tewodros II (r. 1855–68)

Note: www.wemezekir.blogspot.com. In the public domain.

Traditionally, specialist ironsmith villages produced bayonets and spear heads, and from the early 1820s the crown constructed artisanal workshops to manufacture articles, such as boots and spears, for the military. Further, following an abortive French invasion in 1829, it constructed four factories near Antananarivo that produced gunpowder, swords, bayonets, muskets, and cannon, as well as three tanneries for military boot, belt, saddle, and pouch manufacture, and a special chemistry class at the capital, instructed by Scottish missionary artisan James Cameron (1799–1875), for select mission-educated youth. In late 1834, after several hundred Merina youth had completed apprenticeships under foreign artisans, the crown declared self-sufficiency in the manufacture of bayonets, swords, and military leather ware. By then, possibly 48,000 quality bayonets and swords were being produced annually, and two factories supervised by European master craftsmen were manufacturing large quantities of gunpowder, muskets, cannon, and bullets – all from local resources. In 1835, British artisans left Madagascar, but indigenous personnel ensured continued production, while from 1837 French master craftsman Jean Laborde (1805–78) constructed at Mantasoa, 40 km east of Antananarivo, a major industrial complex. By 1850, Mantasoa comprised five factories with blast furnaces that

FIGURE 10.6 Menilek II (r. 1889–1913)
Note: www.lisapoyakama.org. In the public domain.

specialised in musket and cannon manufacture, but also produced
swords, gunpowder, grapeshot, copper, steel, lightening conductors,
glass, pottery, bricks, tiles, silk, candles, lime, dye, refined white
soap, paper, potassium, sweets, alcohol, tanned leather, and a variety of cloths.

Attempts at industrial production came much later in Ethiopia.
In this respect, it is noteworthy that while water was a prerequisite
for early industrialisation, all central Ethiopian towns were situated
on elevations distant from rivers. Initial manufacturing experiments
were artisanal. By the 1840s, some gunpowder and cannon were made
locally, but production was small-scale and irregular. In the 1880s,
the Ethiopian court hired Luigi Capucci (1857–1920), an Italian
engineer, to produce gunpowder, but he had limited success. Indeed,
throughout the nineteenth century Ethiopia depended chiefly on
imported armaments. By 1894, Menilek allegedly possessed 82,000
imported rifles and 5.2 million cartridges. These proved decisive in his
victory over the Italians at Adwa in March 1896, and thus to resisting
colonial conquest. However, as late as 1900 it was reported that

FIGURE 10.7 Cairo Citadel, Nineteenth Century

Note: Library of Congress – http://hdl.loc.gov/loc.pnp/cph.3c04856. In the public domain.

"There is practically no industry throughout Abyssinia, except for the manufacture of swords and knives, and of a cloth of silk and cotton."[2]

Transport and Communication

Communications play a critical role in economic development and military deployment. For Egypt, linkages between the Mediterranean, Red Sea, and the Nile were of primary importance. From early times, a canal network connected the three, and from 1819 to 1821 the Mahmūdiyya, an 80 km-long canal linking the Nile to Alexandria, and thence to the Mediterranean, was constructed. Many canals built primarily for irrigation also facilitated transport, and by 1879 Egypt had a canal network of over 13,900 km. In 1830, a mail steamship service linked Egypt to Calcutta and Bombay. This made the "overland" (Suez Isthmus) route between India and Europe slightly quicker

---

[2] Report based on that of Lagarde, French agent in Ethiopia, in "Geographical Notes" *Scottish Geographical Magazine* 16.3 (1900): 180.

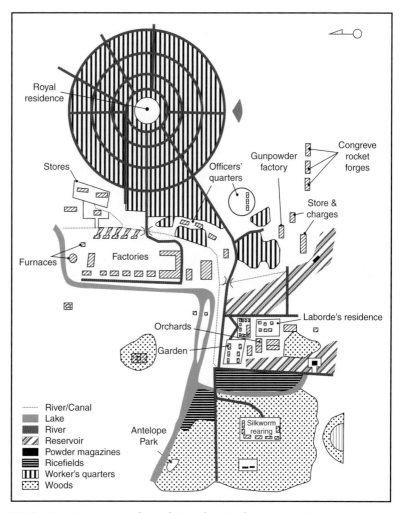

MAP 10.1 Mantasoa Industrial Complex, Madagascar ca 1850

Note: Source: Gwyn Campbell, "An Industrial Experiment in Pre-colonial Madagascar, 1825–1861" *Journal of Southern African Studies* 17. 3 (1991): 550.

than the voyage around the Cape, although steamships were initially hindered by the lack of coaling stations. Under Abbas (r. 1848–54), roads were improved, some with paving, notably between Cairo and Suez. Also, in 1854, Alexandria and Cairo were linked by a British-built telegraph, and in 1856 by a standard gauge railway – the first in the western IOW after that constructed in India in 1837.

Along the Malagasy coast, except in the northeast during the cyclone season from January to March, communication was easiest by boat, as it was up major west coast rivers such the Onilahy and Ikopa, respectively 400 km and 300 km long. However, the east coast possessed few natural harbours or rivers that were navigable for any length, and was separated from the high central plateau by a steep escarpment. Moreover, most overland transport was restricted to the dry winter season between April and October. The Merina defence policy of *hazo* (wood) and *tazo* (malaria) accentuated natural difficulties. *Hazo* referred to the dense tropical rainforest of the eastern escarpment up which any European military advance was expected to come while, before the widespread adoption of quinine, malaria proved life threatening to Westerners. The Merina court made some transport improvements. For instance, from 1817 to 1827, roads were built in Antananarivo and Foulepointe, bridges erected over the rivers Ivondrona, near the chief east coast port of Tamatave, and Ikopa, in Imerina, and canals constructed to link a natural series of east coast lagoons. Subsequently, however, concern that such developments might facilitate a foreign invasion resulted in a general ban on transport improvements, which meant that, until the French conquest, the carriage of mail, freight, and people relied almost exclusively upon slave porters, who received wages for their work. Consequently, transport costs remained very high,

In Ethiopia, few transport improvements occurred until the end of the nineteenth century. During the reigns of Tewodros II and Menilek, forced labour was used to enlarge the road system to serve strategic military rather than commercial purposes. Capucci and Alfred Ilg (1854–1916), a Swiss engineer, built the first bridge over the river Awash in about 1887. However, carriage remained traditional. Most goods were, in the highlands, transported by mules, and in the lowlands by camels. Many merchants also used human (slave and hired) porters. This ensured that freight costs remained very high, which imposed considerable restraints on trade. Only from 1897, following the victory of Ethiopian forces over the Italians, and British recognition of Ethiopia as a sovereign state, did the emperor prove capable of attracting sufficient foreign investment to build more bridges, a railway, and establish a telephone and telegraph line, and a regular postal service linking the main port of Djibouti to the imperial capital of Addis Ababa.

Secondary Imperialism

The creation of "secondary" (i.e. non-European) empires, and the exploitation of their human and natural resources, was intrinsic to nineteenth-century Egyptian, Merina, and Ethiopian state programmes. By 1800, Egyptian forces already controlled much of the Sudan, and portions of the southern Red Sea coast. From 1811 to 1813, they also captured the Hijaz, by 1818 dominated central Arabia, and from 1820 to 1822 established complete control over Sudan. At the same time, the Egyptian navy expanded to dominate the Red Sea. Egypt henceforth controlled the region's Red Sea trade and gold deposits passing through Sennar, in the Sudan. Further, it moved to exploit Sudan's trade in "tropical" products, especially ivory, and its population (through enslavement and conscription). Egyptian forces occupied the Ottoman territories of Crete in 1830, Palestine, and Syria, which possessed vital sources of construction timber and coal, in 1831, and advanced towards Yemen in 1833 with the aim of conquering the Arabian Peninsula and thus establishing control over the entire northern Red Sea coast and a presence on the Persian Gulf.

By the close of 1839, after it had also occupied eastern Anatolia, Egypt was the strongest military power in the Middle East, ruling an empire of some 10 million people, 50 per cent of whom lived in the Nile Valley. However, in 1840, European powers, notably Britain and Austria, fearful that Egyptian expansion might destabilise the balance of power in Europe, forced Egypt to retreat from Syria, and in 1841 supported the Ottoman *ferman* (edict), recognising Ali as hereditary governor of Egypt on condition that the size of his army be limited, all Ottoman legislation and treaties apply to Egypt, and Egyptian foreign relations be subject to Ottoman approval. Conventional accounts consider that European powers thus critically undermined Egypt's imperial ambitions. However, Ali applied a liberal interpretation to the 1841 *ferman* and concentrated on expanding his IOA empire. By 1840, Egyptians had broken through the Sudd, the world's largest fresh-water swamp, following which almost incessant military expeditions were launched to exploit the resources of tropical zones to the south. Indeed, the first major surge of the ivory frontier into the African interior was less from the Swahili coast than from Egypt into the southern savannah where a trading station was established at Gondokoro, on the east bank of the White Nile, 1,200 km south of Khartoum. For ten years, the government monopolised

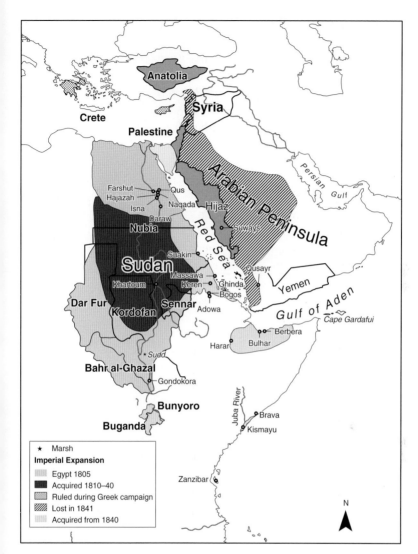

MAP 10.2 The Nineteenth-Century Egyptian Empire

Note: Adapted from http://commons.wikimedia.org/wiki/File:Egypt_under_
Muhammad_Ali_Dynasty_map_en.svg (accessed 15/04/12) – GNU Free
Documentation License

trade, exchanging primarily beads for ivory, and organising raids to
the south to capture cattle to meet regional demand, slaves for the
Egyptian market, and ivory that was shipped both to Egypt and, in a
contraband trade stimulated by high prices, to Red Sea ports, Arabia,

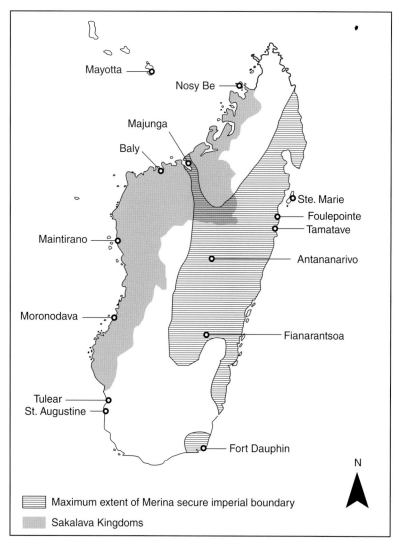

MAP 10.3 The Nineteenth-Century Merina Empire

Note: Adapted from Campbell, *Economic History of Imperial Madagascar*, 220.

and the Yemen. From 1851, the government lifted its trade monopoly and Egyptian merchants advanced to establish informal Egyptian rule in present-day northeastern Zaire and northern Uganda where they raided and traded chiefly for ivory and slaves. By the 1870s, when expeditions from Khartoum were penetrating as far south as Bunyoro and Buganda, where they encountered Zanzibari expeditions from the east coast, the Egyptian government attempted to incorporate the northern Great Lakes region into its empire.

Egypt also advanced along the African Red Sea coast, capturing successively Suakin and Massawa in 1865, Bogos in 1872, and Harar in 1875 – thereby gaining control of the main trade route inland from the Gulf of Aden. However, expeditions in 1876 against highland Ethiopia failed. Egypt forces also advanced in the Horn of Africa. In 1870, they occupied Bulhar and Berbera and extended control to Cape Guardafui, and in 1875 captured the Zanzibari garrisons at Brava and Kismayu on the Indian Ocean coast of Somalia. Only a British naval presence prevented the capture of Swahili posts south of the Juba River.

Contemporaneously, the Merina regime in Madagascar also attempted to create a secondary empire. In 1810, Imerina was a small landlocked country some 7,252 km^2 in area, in the central highlands of the world's fourth largest island, 587,040 km^2 in size. With the aim of conquering the rest of the island and exploiting its human and natural resources, the Merina launched military expeditions in all directions. To the east, from 1808 to 1810, they conquered the Ankay Bezanozano, a powerful middleman entity on Antananarivo-Tamatave route, in 1817 overran the chief port Tamatave, and in 1822 expelled the French from Foulepointe, the second most important east coast port. In 1824–5, they launched expeditions against southeast Madagascar where they expelled the French from Fort Dauphin, and in 1829–30 repelled French forces that invaded Tamatave and Foulepointe. From 1840 to 1845, ironsmiths on the captured eastern littoral manufactured pickaxes, axes, and shovels for export to Réunion, and a shipyard was established at Mahela where 150 Malagasy carpenters, ironsmiths, and coopers were employed building and maintaining boats for use on the coasts, rivers, and lakes.

By 1822, Merina forces had also subdued Betsileo and in 1823 captured Antsihanaka – highland provinces respectively to the south and north of Imerina. From 1823, they invaded Iboina, the Sakalava kingdom of northwest Madagascar, securing the main trade route to the chief west coast port of Majunga which they captured in 1824; and in 1831 finally defeated the Sakalava Boina army. This victory secured for the Merina crown vast herds of Sakalava cattle which it used to develop large-scale production of raw and salted hides for export. By 1840, Merina garrisons straddled key trade routes into Ibara in the south, and the Sakalava kingdoms of Menabe, Ambongo, and Iboina to the west. They also rebuffed a Franco-British attack on Tamatave in 1845, and in 1855 expelled French agents from Ambavatobe in north-west Madagascar.

By contrast with Egypt and Madagascar, imperial expansion in Ethiopia occurred chiefly from the mid-nineteenth century. From about 1769 to 1855, Ethiopia was plagued by internecine conflict between rival warlords. In the 1830s and 1840s, under Sahle Sellasie (r. 1813–47), Shoans conquered the Tulema Oromo and parts of the northern Gurage to the south of the Awash River. They thus controlled Oromia, a well-watered zone stretching across the centre and south of the Horn of Africa that was the main regional source of ivory, coffee, gold, civet, skins, and slaves. Amharic-speaking highlanders considered that most members of groups such as the Oromo, who lived between the periphery and the imperial centre, and all Shankilla, meaning blacks from the lowland peripheries, as uncivilised and thus appropriate for enslavement.

Further expansion occurred after Kassai, who emerged victorious over rival warlords, assumed the title Emperor Tewodros II and, like Ali and Radama I, concentrated power in the crown, created a hand-picked bureaucracy, and built a standing army trained by foreigners (Europeans and Turks). Subsequently, Menilek hired French and Russian military advisors, and used the standing army and irregular draftees to expand territorially. His imperial aims, similar to those of Egyptian and Merina rulers, were to capture the chief sources of export staples, main trade routes between the interior and the coast, new lands to colonise, and also to ruthlessly exploit the human and natural resources of vanquished regions. The conquest of Gojjam in 1882 enabled the Shoan army to overrun a number of hitherto autonomous Oromo polities. When, in 1885, Mahdist forces compelled Egyptian soldiers to evacuate garrisons close to Ethiopia, this opened the way for Ethiopia to conquer Harar in 1887, and by 1889 secure the main east-west trade route leading to Zeila and Berbera on the Somali coast. In 1886, in order to govern Oromia, the Shoans constructed a new military and administrative centre at Finfinne that, renamed Addis Ababa, became the imperial capital in 1892. Much of it was built by captive slaves from the southern provinces. Menilek's imperial incursions into Somalia in 1894 were promoted by a severe famine at home from 1888 to 1892, and by the desire to seize provisions and agriculturally productive lands. A further bloody campaign resulted in the conquest of Kaffa in 1897. The same year, encouraged by the collapse of the Mahdist movement and defeat of the Italians at Adwa in 1896, Ethiopia expanded into the Wallaga region, thus establishing control of the state of Jaffa and city state of Jimma, and their trade in ivory and slaves over which the Ethiopian crown declared a monopoly.

By the early twentieth century, Shoans had conquered the Tigray of modern-day northern Ethiopia, the Oromo of central, eastern, western, and southern Ethiopia, the Somali of the Ogaden region, and the Cushitic-speaking Sidama of southeastern Ethiopia. Subsequently, Ethiopian imperial domains comprised an empire 2 million km² in area, with a population of 12–13 million people.

Consequences

By the late 1870s it was clear that the Egyptian and Merina state modernisation programmes had foundered. Conventional accounts ascribe these failures to European political and military influence. Thus, in the case of Egypt, the 1838 Britanno-Ottoman treaty and 1840 Convention of London, between major European powers and the Ottoman Empire, undermined Egyptian foreign trade, and radically reduced the size of its empire and army. When the American Civil War (1861–5) disrupted American cotton supplies to the world market, Egyptian cotton filled the gap and the Egyptian economy recovered. This encouraged Ismail (r. 1863–79) to embark on major government investment, notably in transport and shipbuilding and, after American cotton supplies resumed in the late 1860s, large-scale sugar refining and associated transport facilities. For this, however, he borrowed increasingly from foreign financiers. During his reign, government debt to the British and French grew from £3 million to almost £100 million. This formed the pretext for British intervention in 1882. Likewise, European aggression, notably the 1883–5 Franco-Merina War, followed by French-imposed indemnities, takeover of customs, and concessions, precipitated the bankruptcy of the Merina regime, and established the basis for the French takeover of Madagascar in 1895.

However, the failure of modernisation programmes in Egypt and Imerina was primarily due to a combination of the impact of domestic policies of forced labour and military expansion, and adverse climatic factors.

Forced Labour

Egypt and Imerina lacked financial resources. However, they did possess substantial populations: that of Egypt increased from about 3.5 million to 5.6 million between 1800 and 1850, while in the 1820s that of Imerina increased probably fivefold to 500,000. Given this, the Egypt and Merina regimes invested in heavily labour-intensive production. Each had access to two types of labour: slaves and peasants. As most slaves were in the hands of private slave-owners, the state resorted predominantly to corvée (forced) peasant labour.

For Egypt, Alan Mikhail has argued convincingly that from 1780 a series of adverse climatic events and diseases decimated the domesticated animal population, comprising chiefly water buffalo, oxen, cows, donkeys, and camels, on which its economy depended. This resulted in a realignment of wealth in rural areas in which, in the late 1700s, land became concentrated in the hands of a small elite who made up for the lack of draft animals by imposing corvées on the peasantry on a hitherto unparalleled scale. Mohamed Ali took this further by enforcing centralised control over all labour resources which he used systematically for state projects even after draft animal numbers had recovered. Following state monopolisation of land, all *fellahin* (small tenant farmers) performed state corvée in agriculture and associated projects. Forced labour was, for example, used to expand the canal system from about 827 km in 1805 to 1,931 km by 1847. In the early nineteenth century, an average of 400,000 men, comprising possibly 8 to 9 per cent of Egypt's population were, often through military pressure, forced to contribute each year about 60 days of corvée labour – excluding the time taken for them to travel to and from the location to which they were drafted.

The mortality rate amongst forced labourers, who were also often obliged to supply their own provisions and tools, and were sometimes accompanied by their families, was high. For example, some 100,000 men and women, comprising about one-third of the total workforce forcibly employed building the Mahmūdiyya canal in 1819 to 1821, died due to the exploitative nature of the labour. Moreover, when from 1838 Muhammad Ali started allocating large estates to members of his family and the ruling elite, he granted them corvée rights over local *fellahin*. Egypt's industrial workforce also comprised chiefly forced labour, mainly *fellahin*, supplemented by spinners and

FIGURE 10.8 Fellahin Field Workers, 1882
Note: Acknowledgement to Brooklyn Museum.

FIGURE 10.9 Ironworkers, Imerina, Early Nineteenth Century
Note: From William Ellis, *History of Madagascar*, vol. 1 (London: Fisher, 1838), 308.

weavers whose guild Ali abolished in 1816. Overall, by the 1830s, the
state industrial sector employed from 30,000 to 40,000 workers, some
12,000 in Cairo alone, including women and children. For most of
those drafted into state factories, pay was so low and irregular that
many fell into debt.

As in Egypt, the Merina regime in Madagascar had ample slave
sources. From 1820 to 1853, during the height of economic modernisation and military expansionism, possibly one million provincial captives
were transferred to Imerina as slaves: from 1820 to 1830 the slave
population of Antananarivo alone rose fourfold from about 7,500 to
30,000. Most originated from the relatively densely populated Betsileo
and southeastern provinces. However, as these captives were almost
exclusively women and children who served primarily as domestic and
agricultural slaves of the elite, the Merina court conscripted predominantly "free" subjects for *fanompoana* (unremunerated forced labour)
in industrial and public works. Thus most workers drafted into industrial workshops and factories were Merina, while the carriage of raw
materials to industrial centres was generally allocated to *fanompoana*
units comprising conquered provincial peoples. Other *fanompoana*
workers included vagabonds, and *gadralava*, a term for people of free
status convicted for crime, debt, sorcery, and sedition – including
adherents of Christianity when it was prohibited from 1835 to 1861.

Muhammad Ali initially relied on the traditional Mamluk army.
However, in 1811–12, fearful of their power, he had over 2,000
Mamluks massacred and replaced them with Albanians. They in
turn proved so difficult to control that Ali deliberately sacrificed
them in his Hijaz campaign. From 1820, he drafted into the army
enslaved Sudanese under the command of loyal Mamluk officers.
However, mortality among the Sudanese was high: of the 20,000
forcibly enlisted from 1820 only 3,000 were still alive in 1824.
Moreover, the Sudanese carried guinea worm disease (*dracunculiasis*)
which spread to non-slave soldiers. Consequently, Ali increasingly
replaced Sudanese soldiers with forcibly drafted *fellahin*: 4,000 in
1822, rising by 1840 to 160,000 regulars, supplemented by 90,000
auxiliaries. Conscription was applied largely irrespective of age and
physical fitness. Troops were also used for non-military purposes.
For example, in 1838, Ali commanded 20,000 soldiers to work on
a canal to supply Cairo with water. From 1841, European-Ottoman
pressure caused the size of Egyptian army to fall, to a low of 3,000
soldiers by 1863. However, in 1864, Ismail boosted army numbers to

18,000 – the maximum allowed by international treaty – and in 1866
the Porte permitted numbers to rise to 30,000. Additionally, Ismail
introduced short-term military service. In 1872, all constraints were
removed, and thereafter the number of soldiers fluctuated between
60,000 and 120,000.

   In Imerina, a British-trained standing army of 13,000 men was
formed in 1822. The number of soldiers increased to 30,000 by 1830,
and 100,000 by 1852 – after which campaigns slackened dramatically
and numbers dropped to around 25,000. Conscription, almost entirely
Merina, was initially drawn chiefly from the mission schools. Although
Radama I imposed a 5 per cent tax on wealth and a 10 per cent tax on
rice harvests ostensibly to support soldiers, the latter in fact received
no remuneration. Moreover, court officers not only monopolised campaign booty, but commonly stocked up with provisions which they sold
at exorbitant prices to soldiers. For example, on the 1828 Ambongo
expedition, Rainijohary sold cattle to his troops at 70 times the normal
market price, while on the 1845 Manerinerina campaign, Rainihiaro
and Rainijohary held back provisions until rice prices were 6,400 per
cent above those operating in Imerina. On both occasions, many poor
soldiers and camp followers, unable to afford famine prices, starved
to death. Others were forced to borrow money, at extortionate rates
of interest, from the very officers to whom they immediately returned
the loan in payment for rice and meat. If, upon their return, soldiers
failed to raise the money to cancel their debts, they were sold as slaves,
often alongside their wives and children, in order that the creditor
might be repaid.

   Conscripts from the traditionally malaria-free highlands also
proved highly susceptible to disease (malaria) and starvation (due to
both their opponents' raze and burn guerrilla tactics and inadequate
army provisioning). In 1821, from 25,000 to 30,000 Merina troops
(an estimated 69 per cent of the total), and in 1828, 9,800 troops (98
per cent of the total) perished of malaria and starvation in campaigns
against the Sakalava. Altogether, an estimated 50 per cent of Merina
army recruits died each year. Thus large numbers were annually
conscripted simply to maintain army numbers. The pace of military
campaigning fell off radically from the early 1850s but overall, during
the nineteenth century, an estimated 235,000 Merina soldiers died,
mostly from malaria and famine.

   In Ethiopia, a standing army was first formed in the 1850s, and by
the 1880s numbered some 200,000 men, backed by 600,000 irregular

riflemen and an almost unlimited number of traditional warriors. Recruitment was largely compulsory, and most soldiers had to equip and feed themselves and their camp followers. A minority received irregular pay, even after October 1892 when Menilek imposed a special tax to support the military. Soldiers also experienced high mortality on military campaigns. Nevertheless, surviving soldiers and their families gained substantially from plunder, and received significant land grants: some two-thirds of conquered lands were apportioned to military officers, the Church, and Shoan nobles and settlers – who in addition had access to local labour, both forced and enslaved.

Resistance

Unsurprisingly, there was widespread resistance to Egyptian, Merina, and Ethiopian state policies, both from subjects on whom forced labour was imposed, and from conquered and exploited peoples. In Egypt, traditional peasant usufruct rights to state and *waqf* lands, and protection of peasant land, that had developed gradually from the 1600s, were abruptly removed under Muhammed Ali who claimed state monopoly of all land and human resources. Many peasants objected profoundly to such changes. From the outset, male draftees into state factories engaged in industrial sabotage, and so many fled the factories that the authorities conscripted also females and children. Resistance to the military draft was as widespread. For instance, in 1823, of the 1,960 peasants conscripted in the Middle Provinces, nearly one-third went missing. In 1829, in response to worker resistance, the authorities imposed passes to control peasant mobility, and employed physical coercion to enforce conscription. The 1830 *Qanuin al-Filaha* (Law of Agriculture) enacted punishments, including execution, for *fellahin* who attempted to evade conscription or desert, and those who abetted them. The state also established a spy network to capture deserters, and tattooed captured runaways from naval stations. In 1831, some 15,000 military deserters were tracked down in Alexandria alone. One of the pretexts for the Syrian campaign of 1831 to 1841 was that 'Abdallah Pasha of Acre had given refuge to 6,000 refugee *fellahin*. By the late 1830s, police surveillance was so successful that the number of public executions declined dramatically. However, rural migrancy and theft grew to such an extent that in 1863 and 1866 anti-vagrancy laws were extended to rural areas.

Increasingly, *fellahin* practised self-mutilation to avoid conscription, generally by cutting off an index finger, pulling out front teeth, or using rat poison to induce at least temporary blindness in one eye. Many mothers, when they and their children were drafted for forced labour, blinded themselves and their offspring. The state responded by incarcerating such "culprits" for life and conscripting their relatives in their place. In one case, the wives and mothers who reportedly aided potential army conscripts to maim themselves were publicly hanged. Merchants who sold rat poison were sent to death camps such as Liman, the arsenal works in Alexandria, where in 1843 the Pasha authorised Russian researchers to dress prisoners in the clothes of plague victims.

In Imerina, *fanompoana* was similarly resisted. There was immediate and popular opposition to state schools which supplied draftees for the army and workshops. Again, workers engaged in industrial sabotage. One of the first violent anti-*fanompoana* protests was the firing in 1825–6 of the workshop of Louis Le Gros, a French carpenter, by two of his *fanompoana* "apprentices". They were burnt alive by Radama I, and thereafter direct protest in Antananarivo was somewhat muted – although the 1853 explosion of the Isoraka powder mills might have been an act of sabotage. Parents commonly bribed army officers to exclude their sons from military conscription: in mid-1840, following the draft of 20,000 men, the state arrested some 500 army officers for allegedly accepting such bribes. So worried was Ranavalona I at the possibility of revolt within the army that she created a military secret police.

Some draftees feigned physical disability or mutilated themselves, despite the death penalty if caught. Military *fanompoana* had become so onerous by the late 1830s that civilian *fanompoana* units formerly 100 strong had been reduced to between 10 and 15 men because of desertion. In 1841, about 1,000 soldiers deserted, some 10 per cent of whom were caught and executed. Many *fanompoana* and army deserters fled to the *efitra* – a no-man's land straddling the border zones of Merina controlled regions of the central highlands. From the 1820s, as Merina exploitation of the conquered eastern littoral increased, growing numbers of local Betsimisaraka abandoned the land and took to banditry. In 1828, government troops captured and executed 60 such "rebels" in the eastern forest, and a further 200 in 1835. Other refugees fled to the western *efitra*. Thus many Vonizongo joined the brigand Bemihimpa in Sakalava country, and in 1852–3 many soldiers deserted to join similar bandit communities. Refugee republics were established in some parts of the *efitra*. The most notable was Ikongo, southeast of Betsileo, which survived numerous Merina assaults. In 1853 the Ikongo rebels allied with Sakalava forces to attack Fianarantsoa, the main Merina garrison in Betsileo. They were so redoubtable that, from the time of Radama II (r. 1861–3), the Merina government granted Home Rule to Ikongo.

Ultimately, the cost of creating empires was great for both Egypt and Imerina. For example, despite its superior weaponry and military training, Egypt lost its 1873 war with Ethiopia which cost it, in money terms alone, an estimated £3 million. The Merina launched several military expeditions each dry season from the early 1820s until 1853 by which time they had secured firm control over only one-third of the island. Most of the south and west of Madagascar, and rebel enclaves in the east such as Ikongo, remained largely independent.

In Ethiopia, Shoan avoidance of military and civilian corvées was less widespread, although a number of army deserters fled to the Lake Turkana region, which was relatively free of Ethiopian domination and surveillance, and to the ill-defined border with the Sudan, a no-man's land that was a refuge for people fleeing from both the Ethiopian and Egyptian authorities. Such protest was limited due to the benefits accruing to Shoan soldiers through plunder, land grants, and access to the forced labour of conquered peoples. Provincial peoples, such as the Oromo of the Jimma region, in modern-day southwestern Ethiopia, who submitted without conflict and collaborated with the Shoans, were sometimes permitted to live in relative autonomy. Others were placed under Shoan military rule and subjected to enslavement or forced labour. For example, for six days a week the Sidama of the Sidamo region of modern-day south-central Ethiopia were forced to provide food and services to Shoan garrisons, settlers, and institutions. Also, conquered peoples were subject to taxes and tribute in the form of luxuries such as honey, and slaves who were sold in regional and foreign markets.

However, the relationship between conqueror and conquered changed over time, particularly as the Shoan settlement frontier advanced. Military campaigns often eradicated or displaced subjugated communities whose land and villages were frequently distributed to conquering soldiers and colonists. Shoan settlers in the colonies, many of whom were originally farmers, became part of the administrative class, enslaved conquered peoples, or forced them to work their farms. In some cases, Shoan males demanded sexual access to local women. Where imperial land grabs, forced labour, and enslavement were substantial, subjugated people often abandoned cultivation.

Ethiopian colonial rule was sometimes met with major resistance. In 1896, after conquest and two years of Shoan exploitation, the population of Bako, in southern Ethiopia, rebelled. From 1898, the Berta of Bela Shangul, on the present-day Ethiopian Sudanese border, opposed both exaction of tribute and imperial authority in general. The Oromo of the Arsi, Bale, and Sidamo regions also resisted imperial Ethiopian expansion. In all cases, Shoan repression was brutal. Shoan forces, like the Merina, generally killed all male opponents and enslaved captive women and children. Overall, this reduced the Oromo population by an estimated 50 per cent. To punish fierce resistance by the Arsi Oromo, Shoan commanders systematically ordered that when captured, Arsi men have their right hands and Arsi women their right breasts severed. Some people fled Ethiopian rule. Thus many Gojjamis, of modern-day northwestern Ethiopia, migrated to remoter low-lying regions. Others fled to Sudan even at the risk of attack and enslavement by Egyptian soldiers.

The Economic Fallout

One of the first signs of the economic fallout from Egyptian and Merina policies was rebellion against schools. Rising literacy improved efficiency in the army and administration, into which most school graduates were channelled, but not in industry which remained heavily dependent on an illiterate peasant workforce. Moreover, leaders of the dominant indigenous belief systems, Islam in Egypt and ancestral beliefs in Madagascar, attacked European education, in Egypt secular and in Imerina Christian. For example, Egyptian *ulama* publicly criticised the medical school's practice of dissection as contrary to Islamic tenets. More importantly, the state drafted children into the schools, and conscripted scholars into the army. The result was extensive absenteeism. Indeed, some parents in Egypt mutilated their children and many in Imerina sent slave substitutes, in order to avoid their offspring entering school. In Imerina the majority of schools collapsed in 1835 following the exodus of foreign missionaries. From 1861, missionaries were re-admitted to Imerina and a school system recommenced, but always under the control of the Merina state which used it increasingly to recruit *fanompoana* for state ends. Popular opposition to schools thus continued. In Egypt most secondary schools closed following the retreat of the Egyptian army from Syria in 1841, and by 1848 only some specialist educational institutions and a few primary schools remained open.

As modern education failed, so did the industrial experiment. As early as the 1820s, state-run sectors of the Egyptian economy experienced chronic labour shortages due primarily to peasant conscription into the army, and peasant evasion of military and industrial forced labour. The flight of young males was such that, by the 1840s, the state increasingly conscripted boys and older men. Falling village populations and resistance to conscription resulted in inadequate manpower to maintain the irrigation system required to tap the low (summer) and flood (winter) Nile waters needed to provide all-year-round irrigation for the cotton and other cash crop plantations. Such problems were exacerbated by adverse environmental factors, notably severe drought in Egypt in the 1820s and 1830s. By 1850, the military complex was also foundering due to shortages of raw materials and manpower. From 1848 to 1854, Abbas sought to revive the armaments industry, but was plagued by persistent shortages of human and material resources. Moreover, while the opening of the Suez Canal in 1869 permitted for the first time direct maritime communications between the Mediterranean and India, and attracted much of the traffic that formerly passed via the Cape, it deprived the Egyptian government of much of the valuable Isthmus transit traffic, and contributed significantly to Egyptian indebtedness to Europeans.

Rural self-sufficiency was similarly undermined by government conscription of young male fellahin for military training (short term), the army (often for life), and industrial projects or public works (often long term). Because their wives and children followed most conscripted men, fields were abandoned, harvests ruined, and famine often ensued. When exploitation reached unacceptable levels, remaining villagers often burnt their crops, or fled into the hills of Middle and Upper Egypt – leading to depopulation of considerable tracts. As early as 1831, an estimated 25 per cent of farmland in Upper Egypt lay deserted and uncultivated. Agricultural production was further eroded by low Nile floods in the late 1830s and by disease, notably the 1834–5 cholera epidemic which killed an estimated one-third of the Egyptian population, and rinderpest which from 1841 to 1846 killed over one million cattle (see Table 11.1). Such were manpower deficiencies that, when the state imposed unpaid corvée on 20,000 *fellahin* to construct the Suez Canal, Ismail was forced to reduce the draft to 6,000 in order to avoid completely undermining agricultural production. When the American Civil War ended in 1865, cotton prices collapsed and Egypt proved unable to generate sufficient export earnings to service the growing foreign debt and, by 1875, was bankrupt. In 1882, after the local landed elite and army officers protested at the British financial controller's decision to raise taxes on land and reduce funding for the army, the British government, concerned about risks to their investment in Egypt and thus control over the Suez Canal and Red Sea route to India, intervened militarily.

In Imerina, despite the government announcement in 1834 that it had become self-sufficient in arms manufacture, local production proved insufficient and the regime continued to depend on imported armaments. Moreover, due to high troop mortality and mounting provincial opposition, imperial campaigns halted in the early 1850s leaving most of the island unconquered, and its resources largely untapped. In November 1853, the Isoraka gunpowder mills exploded and, following the 1859 expulsion of foreign specialists for political intrigue, production at Mantasoa ended. Subsequently arms manufacture was limited to a small factory near Ambohimanga. Of the foreign industrial techniques introduced into Imerina only soap making succeeded, but on a handicraft rather than factory basis.

More importantly, as in Egypt, the state's forced labour policies undermined the agricultural sector as peasants were either forced into public works, factories, and the military, or fled to avoid conscription. With up to four military campaigns each year between 1822 and 1852, the founding of garrisons, and military training, a considerable proportion of the male workforce was diverted from agriculture, and self-sufficiency was endangered. Adverse environmental factors and disease added to peasant woes, notably excessive rain and epidemics in the 1830s (see Table 11.3). By making unremunerated forced labour the principle of the imperial economy, the Merina regime alienated the vast bulk of its subjects. Artisans, often drafted into permanent *fanompoana*, relinquished their crafts. From the early 1820s, civilian and military corvées diverted a considerable proportion of the male workforce from agriculture. In consequence, self-sufficiency was endangered, and the cost of living rose sharply, the price of rice in Imerina increasing by 180 per cent between 1828 and 1853. The highland economy improved in the 1860s, when there was a general improvement in the standard of living, but thereafter more intensive *fanompoana*, increased French military aggression and raids on the plateau by Sakalava and Bara war bands, combined with an unparalleled upsurge in disease, further impoverished the ordinary peasant.

Ethiopia did not attempt to modernise its economy before the twentieth century. However, there was considerable economic fallout from its system of imperial expansion and exploitation. First, from 1868 to 1896, the Ethiopian army fought 11 major battles against foreign foes, one against the British in 1868, two against the Egyptians in 1875 and 1876, four against the Mahdists in 1885, 1887, 1888, and 1889, and six against the Italians, in 1887, 1895 (4 times) and 1896 (twice). These and continual military expansion against other peoples, both in the Ethiopian highlands and in surrounding regions, caused major direct and, through encouraging the growth of banditry, indirect damage to agriculture and trade.

Moreover, Ethiopian soldier-settlers generally exploited captured land, people, and other resources for maximum short-term profit. They extracted possibly 30 per cent of the agricultural production of conquered regions. Governors also vied for the most lucrative non-agricultural commodities, notably slaves and ivory. In addition, imperial officials imposed arbitrary taxes, and Shoan soldiers and settlers impressed subjected people into forced labour, often to the degree that it undermined local self-sufficiency in agriculture and forced peasants into debt. When, as often happened, peasants fled the land, agriculture collapsed, and only tributary trade in slaves and ivory persisted. Peasant suffering was exacerbated from 1888 to 1892 due to epidemics and cattle disease (see Table 11.2). This reduced tribute payments to imperial authorities who reacted by imposing additional taxes. The exaction of tribute expanded systems of trade, chiefly in ivory, gold, and slaves, often well beyond the effective frontiers of Ethiopian control, but these constituted commercial networks based on the use of firearms and pillage rather than on reciprocal exchange relationships.

In sum, the conventional view that no indigenous IOA society attempted to modernise its economy prior to colonial takeover needs revision. Contemporaneously with attempts at economic modernisation in Western Europe, Egypt, and Imerina attempted to forge domestic industrialisation through armaments and textile production. Such attempts failed, primarily due not to European political, military, commercial, and financial pressure, but to domestic factors, notably state policies of forced labour and military expansion. Such factors also had major repercussions in terms of the loss of political sovereignty to European countries.

Ethiopia is often portrayed as the sole example of an African state which modernised sufficiently to militarily defeat an Italian invasion force, and create a modern unified state whose independence was accepted by Britain and France. This interpretation is far too sanguine. Imported armaments certainly assisted Ethiopian forces in defeating the Italians at Adowa in 1896. However, the Ethiopian state never amassed sufficient finance or skills to attempt an industrial revolution, as occurred in Egypt and Imerina. It rather adopted age-old warlord tactics based on military expansion, conquest, and exploitation of the human and other resources of neighbouring peoples. Its ability to retain political independence was a reflection of other factors – an issue discussed in the next chapter.

Some scholars have also focussed on modernisation in Buganda and Zanzibar. However, as in nineteenth-century Ethiopia, the modernising impulse in Buganda and Zanzibar was limited. Like Egypt and Madagascar, the kingdom of Buganda expanded greatly in the early nineteenth century to create a small empire in the Great Lakes region. The crown constructed a large army, a navy of outrigger canoes on Lake Victoria, and constructed a wide network of roads, passage along which was assisted by bridges and viaducts. The sovereign, Muteesa I (r. 1856–84) seized on the burgeoning commerce of the region as the Swahili commercial frontier swept deep into interior East Africa from mid-century in search primarily of ivory and slaves, exchanged for cloth and arms, to consolidate his rule. He concentrated commercial exchange in his capital (present-day Kampala), brought surrounding chiefs under his control, and imposed major corvée on his Ganda subjects. He also welcomed European Protestant and Catholic missionaries who, like Muslim clerics, made many converts and created intense religious rivalry and conflict. However, that represented the limits of modernisation. Mwanga II (r. 1884–8, 1889–97) attempted to expel the missionaries and persecuted indigenous Christians, thus invoking the ire of British authorities who removed him from power. He was restored, however, after agreeing to cede some of his authority to the British East Africa Company, and in 1894 Buganda became a British protectorate.

Zanzibar experienced a different but similarly limited experiment in modernisation. Following his move from Oman to Zanzibar in 1840, Seyyid Said (1791–1856) built a state apparatus to which he subjected local rulers and a commercial empire that extended along the Swahili littoral. Profits from the trade in slaves and ivory, and slave-produced cloves, underwrote the modernisation projects inaugurated by his sons. Majid (r. 1856–70) built a harbour at Dar es Salaam and Barghash

(r. 1870–88) established postal and telegraph services to Aden, a fleet of steam ships, and a European-style army. He also provided his capital with electricity and fresh-water supplies. However, neither Zanzibar nor Zanzibari domains were more than superficially touched by modernisation. Zanzibari rulers never sanctioned modern secular education, as occurred in Egypt, competition from other suppliers made the price of cloves unstable, in 1869 cholera killed an estimated 70,000 people – most of its slave workforce – and in 1872 a cyclone devastated Zanzibar's commercial fleet and plantations. In 1873 the British forced a ban on the slave trade, and in 1888 Britain and Germany carved up Zanzibari-claimed territory on the continent. British informal rule, which became progressively more imposing as the nineteenth century wore on, climaxed in the imposition of a protectorate and the extinction of the remaining vestiges of Zanzibari independence in 1890.

11

The Scramble for Indian Ocean Africa

This chapter explores the reasons behind the Scramble for Indian Ocean Africa (IOA). In the space of 23 years, between 1882 and 1905, four European powers, Britain, France, Italy, and Germany, imposed political rule over most of IOA. Portugal already possessed a long-standing colony in Mozambique. France, which had laid claim to the Mascarenes in 1649, and Britain, which seized the Cape in 1806, imposed rule over other IOA areas in the early and mid-nineteenth century (see Table 9.2). However, the late nineteenth-century imperialist surge was unprecedented in speed and scale, and by 1905 Ethiopia was the only remaining independent IOA territory. With few exceptions, such as the Franco-British confrontation at Fashoda in 1898, the division of IOA proceeded with remarkably little friction between the colonising powers as they followed a protocol established at the Berlin Conference of 1884–5. Most recent interpretations of the late nineteenth-century Scramble for Africa focus on the interplay of three factors: developments in Europe, Europeans in Africa, and indigenous African forces. However, whereas most scholars consider that Europeans created the preconditions for the imposition of colonial rule, it is here suggested that in IOA, environmental and indigenous human factors were as significant.

Developments in Europe

A number of interlocking developments in Europe helped spur the rush for colonies from the 1870s. One was the collapse of the post-1815

Concert of Europe, in which Britain, Austria, Russia, Prussia, and France had been recognised as the dominant powers. The breakdown of the traditional order was due notably to the rise of Germany in the wake of the 1870–1 Prussian military defeat of France and seizure of Alsace and Lorraine. This underpinned much of the pro-imperialist movement in France and Germany. In France the imperialist surge was driven by humiliation that followed its military and territorial losses to Germany, and the desire to reassert national prestige on the world stage. In its turn, the newly unified and economically burgeoning Germany, unable to greatly extend its political frontiers within Europe, sought colonies overseas to reflect its new great power status. Such aims required military backing. France and Germany promoted a rapid buildup of their armies and navies to the extent that Britain, long used to almost total dominance of the seas, felt its navy, and thus its empire, to be under threat. Economic factors, notably the 1880s depression, accentuated imperialist aspirations and rivalry. In the late nineteenth century, Britain, the established superpower, found Germany and the United States surpassing it in technological progress. Moreover, German and American manufactures proved competitive even in the domestic British market. Britain's economic vulnerability was greater because, whereas most of its rivals reacted to the economic downturn by passing protectionist measures to safeguard their domestic industries, it continued to adhere to free trade. Faced with a growing willingness by France and Germany to intervene politically outside Europe, Britain moved reluctantly to secure its own overseas interests.

Britain was acutely aware of French imperial rivalry in IOA. French humiliation at its economic and military losses to Germany in 1871 overlay long-simmering resentment against the British dating to the Seven Years (1756–63) and Napoleonic (1803–15) wars when Britain deprived France of the bulk of its empire. In the western IOW, this included Mauritius, and most French posts in India and Madagascar. In 1882, Britain rubbed salt into the wound of French pride by occupying Egypt where France held significant long-term financial and other interests. Indeed, Ronald Robinson and John Gallagher argued that Britain's intervention in Egypt ignited and drove the late nineteenth-century scramble for colonies. It certainly helped provoke a French forward movement in Madagascar although, when analysed closely, the 1883–5 Franco-Merina War represented a rare moment when the French navy, rather than its government, dictated French imperial policy. In July 1882, the French parliament rejected a government proposal to join Britain in offering military protection of the Suez Canal, and the ministry resigned. Unilateral British intervention in Egypt in August 1882 undermined previous Franco-British cooperation and created an Anglophobic atmosphere in France. This Jean-Bernard Jauréguiberry used, when he moved from the Ministry of the Marine to temporarily assume the premiership, to adopt an aggressively anti-British line in Madagascar. A shooting incident on the island's northwest coast formed the pretext for François de Mahy, a Réunion deputy and Minister of Commerce, who in early 1883 temporarily filled the post of Minister of the Marine, to order an attack on Madagascar. The French navy and Réunionnais interests effectively hijacked the French government into war with the Merina.

British intervention in Egypt also convinced France that the northern sea route to its Indochina colony and Madagascar were threatened, and in 1884 it seized Djibouti to counter Aden's threatened monopoly control over the Indian Ocean approach to the Red Sea. The French navy further secured bases at Obock in present-day Djibouti in 1885, and Diego Suarez in northern Madagascar in 1886. In addition, Egypt provided the context for the Franco-German *entente* against British interests in Africa that manifested itself, amongst other things, in the 1884–5 Berlin Conference.

Some historians have also revived the theory of John A. Hobson that late nineteenth-century finance capitalism promoted imperialism through seeking investments overseas more profitable than could be found in Europe. Hobson's theory was based on his analysis of South Africa, where he regarded British military and political expansion to be a direct consequence of the British desire to control the output of diamonds and gold – discovered in 1866–7 and 1886 respectively. Certainly British capital investment in South Africa was considerable, standing at over £370 million in 1914 when it represented almost 21 per cent of total British investment in its overseas empire, just behind Australia and New Zealand combined at 23 per cent and Canada at 29 per cent. A case for financial imperialism can also be made for Egypt which became heavily indebted – to the tune of almost £100 million by 1879 – to Europeans, due chiefly to borrowing by Ismail to finance his attempts at economic modernisation. In 1878, British and French representatives stepped in to govern Egyptian finances, provoking an Egyptian army revolt in 1879 that toppled the local regime and thus threatened foreign, predominantly British, investment in the country. In consequence, Britain invaded.

Historians have generally dismissed finance capitalism as a contributory factor to the scramble for colonies in the rest of IOA, with the exception of Madagascar where, some claim, a combination of the cost of the 1883–5 war, French-imposed indemnities and takeover of imperial Merina customs, and concessions to French investors provoked the bankruptcy of the Merina government. However, while there was some French investment, notably in sugar plantations, the Suberbie gold mines, and in a loan enabling the Merina government to pay the indemnity imposed by France following the 1883–5 hostilities, it was insufficient to back claims that it rendered the Merina regime subservient to French financiers. Indeed, little French capital was exported to the tropics. From 1882 to 1902, one-quarter of French foreign investment flowed to Russia and a further 13 per cent to Latin America. Far less capital was attracted to Africa where it was invested chiefly in Algeria, which France occupied in 1830, or the South African diamond and gold mines where substantial French financial interest in the 1870s and 1880s failed to stimulate calls for French political intervention.

Robinson and Gallagher's argument about Egypt is that Britain was propelled into extending formal control over the rest of IOA in order to protect the Route to India, the "jewel" of its empire. Britain felt unable to hold its own from the time of the Franco-German entente in the early 1880s, when Germany entertained proposals for a Germano-Boer link from South West Africa via the Caprivi Strip and Transvaal to Delagoa Bay on the Mozambique Channel, Karl Peters was busy signing treaties in hinterland East Africa for his *Company for German Colonisation* (*Gesellschaft für deutsche Kolonisation*), and the French attacked Madagascar. Hence, George Granville, Secretary of State for Foreign Affairs, asserted that Britain should immediately move to consolidate its position in IOA in order to safeguard the routes to India. In 1885, Britain declared a protectorate in Bechuanaland (present-day Botswana), tightened informal control over Portugal in an attempt to neutralise the threat of a link between German East Africa and the Transvaal – although the project remained alive until the Britanno-German treaty of 1898 when Britain gained full access to Delagoa Bay and Maputo – and urged the Sultan of Zanzibar, over whom Britain also claimed informal control, to make good his claims to sovereignty on the African continent as far inland as Kilimanjaro.

Eventually, unable to constrain rivals on all fronts, the Foreign Office decided to establish a new status quo in IOA that would preserve British dominance in areas deemed of vital strategic and economic importance. The Marquess of Salisbury, Prime Minister for most of the period from mid-1885 to mid-1892, considered France and Russia to be Britain's chief imperial rivals. However, he condoned the Italian occupation of Massawa on the Red Sea, and, in return for Bismarck's acceptance of British action in Egypt, acknowledged a formal German presence in East Africa. He considered the Italians to be under British informal influence, and German territory in East Africa to be of little commercial value and of no real threat to Britain's strategic interests in the region. Two Germano-British treaties were signed. The first, in December 1885, recognised a German protectorate over Dar es Salaam and the adjacent portion of coast; the second, in October 1886, defined a frontier running east from Lake Victoria that divided German and British areas of influence, and limited the sultan's sovereignty to the island of Zanzibar and a 10-mile coastal corridor on the mainland.

Further treaties with Portugal in 1890 and 1891 defined respective frontiers, reiterated the right to free trade, navigation, and settlement in Mozambique, and negated Portugal's claim to the gold-producing hinterland. Also, in return for German and French recognition of British predominance in Zanzibar, Britain ceded Heligoland, in the North Sea, to Germany, agreed to partition German and British spheres of influence in Africa, and recognised French hegemony in Madagascar. Madagascar was a small price to pay. Although British subjects were the island's most important commercial partners, Britain's trade with continental East Africa was of a far greater magnitude than that with Madagascar. With the 1891 Italian agreement over boundaries between Egyptian Sudan and Ethiopia, international recognition for British paramountcy in IOA was complete.

Crisis of Indigenous Aristocracy

Antony Hopkins has indicated that, for West Africa, indigenous elements contributed to the implantation of colonial rule. He points to a crisis of the "indigenous aristocracy" from the end of the 1870s. This was related to four main factors: the loss of slave export earnings that followed the progressive closure of the Atlantic slave trade; subsequent

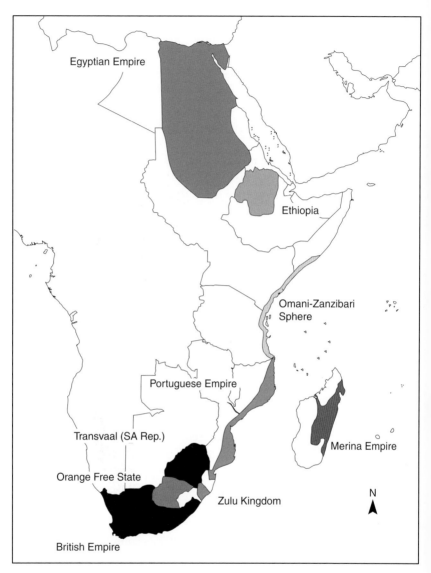

MAP 11.1 Indian Ocean Africa, ca 1850

Note: Produced by Carl Hughes, IOWC.

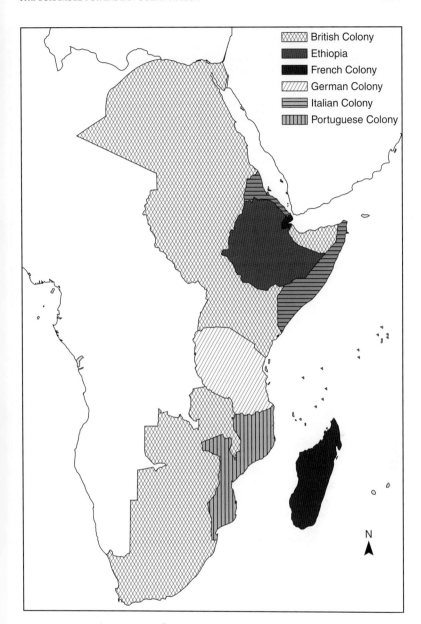

MAP 11.2 Indian Ocean Africa, 1914

TABLE 11.1 *The Scramble for Indian Ocean Africa*

Year	Region	Colonising Power	Year	Region	Colonising Power
1806	Cape	Dutch > British	1886	Anjouan	French
1810	Mauritius	French > British	1886	Grande Comore	French
1810	Seychelles	French > British	1886	Moheli	French
1841	Mayotte	French	1889	Eritrea	Italian
1843	Natal	British	1890–5	Rhodesia (Zimbabwe-Zambia)	British
1854–8; 1900	Orange Free State	Afrikaner > British	1890	Buganda (Uganda)	British
1868	Basutoland (Lesotho)	British	1890	Zanzibar	British
1877–81; 1902	Transvaal	Afrikaner > British	1891	Nyasaland (Malawi)	British
1882	Egypt	British	1895	British East Africa (Kenya)	British
1882–7	British Somaliland	British	1895	Madagascar	French
1883–7	French Somaliland	France	1899	Sudan	British
1885	Bechuanaland (Botswana)	British	1902	Swaziland	British
1885–90	German East Africa (Tanganyika-Burundi-Rwanda)	German	1905	Italian Somaliland	Italian

efforts by indigenous leaders to control and tax the trade in "legitimate products"; the international depression in the 1880s characterised by falling prices on both the African and European sides of the commercial frontier; and competition from peasant producers of cash crops who enjoyed substantially lower overheads than the African elite, and the ability to retreat into subsistence agriculture. In IOA, however, slave exports remained vibrant up to the end of the nineteenth century, and in some regions into the twentieth century. British anti-slave trade squadrons largely ignored the western Indian Ocean until the 1840s. In 1839, Britain claimed the right to search suspect Portuguese ships, and in 1842 established a naval patrol in the Mozambique Channel. In consequence, some 4,000 Prize Negroes were landed at Cape Town by 1846, and a further 2,532 in the Seychelles between 1861 and 1872. Nevertheless, rarely as many as three cruisers were employed at any one time, and the captains of slavers became adept at avoiding them. Anti-slave trade treaties with local powers also initially had limited effect.

Possibly the strongest case for abolitionist pressure undermining an IOA leader was in Zanzibar, where in 1870 the British forced Sultan Barghash to close the local slave market, the largest in IOA, and prohibit slave-trading in his sultanate. However, this measure was a reflection of a long-standing weakness of the sultanate which was ridden by internal faction-fighting, had failed to recover economically from a decline in clove prices in the mid-nineteenth century, had its slave workforce decimated in a cholera epidemic in 1869–70, and its plantations and shipping devastated by a cyclone in 1872. Moreover, the sultanate had failed to establish firm rule on the mainland, Indians largely dominated its economy, and like the Portuguese in Mozambique was under British informal political influence. Again, in Madagascar, the Merina regime in 1877 "freed" an estimated 150,000 slaves, but did so less in response to Western abolitionist pressure than to "free" the slaves from private ownership, without compensation to their owners, and drive them into state-run forced labour camps.

Also, the price of IOA "legitimate" export staples remained generally buoyant on the international market whereas those of Western manufactures fell, with the result that the terms of trade for the IOA as a whole improved. Zanzibar's clove, copra, and sesame production was unstable, but in 1859 accounted for less than half the value of ivory, cowry, and gum copal exports. The price of ivory, which alone constituted about 40 per cent by value of total Zanzibari exports, and of rubber, an IOA export of growing importance, remained buoyant. The price for ivory in Britain rose from £34.6 per cwt in 1870–4 to £46.1 in 1875–9, dipped slightly to £45.8 in 1880–4, only to rise again in the latter part of the depression years to £47 in 1885–9 and £47.1 in 1890–4. However, in contrast to West African "hard" ivory, IOA ivory varieties, "Egyptian", "Abyssinian", "Zanzibari", "Mozambican", and "Natal", were classified as "soft", i.e. more malleable and hence more suitable for carving. They therefore commanded significantly higher prices. For example, the price of Natal ivory increased from £32.9 per cwt in 1870–4, to £38.5 in 1880–4, to £77.7 in 1890–4.

In Egypt, ivory was surpassed in export value by cotton, for which the terms of trade (1880=100 – using British export prices as a proxy) improved steadily from 52 (1820–2) to 71 (1850–2), 107 (1870–2), 100 (1890–2) to 136 (1908–12). In Madagascar, which possessed no elephants and thus no ivory, the evidence points in the same direction. The 1883–5 war damaged French and official east coast commerce, but there remained a brisk clandestine and unofficial foreign trade with non-French merchants via unauthorised ports. Moreover, during the 1880s, the price of "legitimate" Malagasy export staples, not-ably hides, rubber, beeswax, and hemp, remained generally buoyant. Analysis of direct visible trade between Madagascar and Britain, its major trading partner, suggests that the terms of trade were unfavour-able to Britain for much of the period from 1875 to 1895, and that the trade balance was in Madagascar's favour from 1882 to 1885, in 1887, 1890, and from 1892 to 1895.

In addition, the argument that foreign cloth, probably by far the most important import into IOA, undermined local textile industries, critically fails to distinguish between types of fabric, both imported and manufactured locally, or to analyse their uses. Indeed, the evi-dence indicates large and sophisticated indigenous IOA demand for cloth which served a large number of purposes, and that imported cloths supplemented, rather than replaced, local cloth production.

Moreover, Europeans did not possess enormous military super-iority as is often assumed. The rapid fire Gatling gun developed in 1861, and the Maxim gun invented in 1884, were huge advances on flintlock muskets which Africans continued to use. However, the rapid fire guns were bulky and ill-adapted for use in much of the difficult terrain and forests of tropical and semi-tropical regions, especially during inclement weather. Also, European troops suffered from a lack of knowledge of local geography, and often from inadequate provisions, and disease – all of which often severely reduced their ability to use advanced military technology to their advantage. In South Africa, the British Army, the world's foremost, took four years (1899–1902) to defeat a relatively small force of Boer commandos. Again, the 1895 French military expedition to Madagascar was characterised by poor planning, inadequate medical and other supplies, and incompetent management. It lacked the means to quickly transport troops and supplies over the difficult terrain from the coast to the central plateau, and the quinine vital to the survival of their troops in a malarial environment. Thus of the 6,725 fatalities during the campaign, only 25 were due to battle wounds; the remainder were caused by malaria (72 per cent) and typhoid (12 per cent). The invasion succeeded due only to the use of Senegalese colonial troops in a rapid push to the plateau interior. Even then, had any real resistance been offered by imperial Merina forces, the likelihood is that the expedition, a costly and therefore increasingly unpopular affair in France, would have collapsed and troops been withdrawn. The British-trained Merina army comprised 13,000 soldiers equipped with modern rifles and Armstrong cannons. Given the extensive logistical mistakes made by the French commanders, and the impact of disease on their troops, the Merina government would in all likelihood have been able to repulse the French advance of 1895 had its own men not deserted en masse.

The indigenous IOA aristocracy did experience crisis, but it had less to do with anti-slave trade measures, commodity prices, or superior European military technology, than a combination of misguided domestic policies and environmental factors. As in the previous chapter, we here examine the case studies of Egypt, Madagascar, and Ethiopia. There is clear evidence that the economic and expansionist policies adopted by the Egyptian and Merina regimes backfired to the extent that they undermined their economies and caused widespread domestic hostility to the ruling regime. First, their attempts to industrialise failed. Had they succeeded and a modern industrial sector been created based on free wage labour, the story could have been very different. However, both states relied on the unfree labour of mostly unpaid peasant farmers for their factories and workshops, infrastructural improvements, and cash crop production. Growing peasant animosity to the state-run forced labour regime (called *fanompoana* in Madagascar) was one of the chief reasons for the failure of the industrial experiment in Egypt and Madagascar. Also economically damaging was the erosion of the traditionally strong artisan class due chiefly to state-imposed, sometimes permanent, corvée labour. This crushed individual enterprise and pushed artisans into abandoning their trades. Most serious of all, a deepening crisis developed in the agricultural sector as peasants were coerced into the army, factories, or other state enterprises, or fled the land to avoid forced labour and other taxes.

In Egypt, *fellahin* (peasant) resistance to impositions by state authorities had a long tradition, so opposition to state-imposed forced labour and other forms of taxation under Muhammad Ali was immediate and sustained. There was widespread falsification of cultivation declarations and burning of crops in order to avoid tax; and self-mutilation, bribery, and trickery to escape conscription. When exploitation reached unacceptable levels the *fellahin* fled with the result that considerable tracts of fertile land were left uncultivated. This inevitably impacted on the production less of cotton, the staple export, than of subsistence crops. The story was similar in the central highlands of Madagascar where *fanompoana* peaked during periods of industrial exploitation from 1825 to 1861 and 1883 to 1895. As highland riziculture, in contrast to that practised on the coast, required a constant and heavy labour input, the forcible transfer, or flight, of peasant labour, led to abandoned villages, fields, and dykes. Consequently, in many areas, the complex infrastructure required to sustain irrigated riziculture, the basis of the local economy, was irreparably damaged.

When pushed to the extreme, the peasants revolted. In Egypt in 1823–4, following the introduction of conscription, five major popular revolts erupted, one in Lower and four in Upper Egypt. These the Egyptian army eventually suppressed with the loss of over 4,000 rebel lives. In Madagascar in 1888 there occurred a revolt of former slaves that the state "liberated" in 1877 and then forced to work in the Maevatanana gold mines. In 1889, "brigands" disrupted the mine railway and launched raids on the neighbouring Andranomiangana and Ambalamamoko gold works. More commonly, peasants fleeing forced labour sought sanctuary among brigand bands living in semi or fully autonomous regions. These outlaws survived by raiding surviving peasant communities, thus accentuating the cycle of impoverishment, flight, and abandonment of land. In Egypt, an upsurge of banditry started in the 1870s and was characterised by gangs of up to 70 members raiding large estates, robbing merchants, and establishing protection rackets. In Madagascar, increased state-imposed forced labour during and after the 1883–5 Franco-Merina War swelled the number of local brigands who the Merina regime termed *fahavalo* ("enemies"). In Imerina, by the early 1890s, brigand bands were virtually unopposed as they preyed off villages, seizing food and cattle, and carrying off local people as slaves.

Egypt and Imerina were also hit hard by the repercussions of state policies of military expansionism. For example, the 1821 Egyptian conquest of the Funj sultanate of Sennar, in the north of Sudan, and the forcible levying of slaves in Sudan in 1822–3, led Sudanese slave-owners to revolt. Again, demands made by Egyptian forces upon nomadic Arabs in the border region with Ethiopia, north of Khartoum, provoked revolt by the nomads. Mek Nimmur, one of the nomad leaders, fled to Ethiopia from where, every dry season, he launched cross-border attacks on Egyptians as, after his death, did his son and namesake. These confrontations led to much of the Ethiopian borderlands in Kordofan-Darfur and Darfur-Wadai becoming depopulated and hence uncultivated. Similarly, Egyptian raids south of Bahr al-Ghazal, in Sudan, for cattle, ivory, and slaves, aroused great local animosity. Indeed, due to imperial expansionism, the Egyptian army found itself increasingly overstretched. Crushing defeats at the hands of the Ethiopians in 1876, and in 1878 of Walad-el-Michael, their Ethiopian nominee in Bogos, undermined Egyptian imperial pretensions in the region and led the Khedive to send General Gordon there to try to negotiate a peace. When in 1881 Mohammed Ahmed, who declared himself Sudan's Mahdi (literally "one who guides in the right way"), started the Mahdist revolt, he gained huge popular support not least for his opposition to Egypt's imperial claims to the Sudan.

In Madagascar, where from 1820 to 1853 an estimated 333,000 provincials were killed in imperial Merina campaigns, an enduring hatred arose for the Merina regime among non-Merina, some of whom counter-attacked. For example, by the 1850s, Sakalava warriors from Baly Bay and Ambongo combined every two to three months to launch raiding parties, 4,000 to 5,000 strong, into Imerina. In one such assault in 1852 that lasted from five to six months, 400 Merina soldiers were killed and 600 cattle seized. The Menabe Sakalava from the Tsiribihina Valley even maintained spies in Imerina to assist in planning attacks. Such forays into the plateau interior slackened from 1853, when Merina military expeditions tapered off, but picked up again in the 1870s, and notably from the early 1880s as the economic and political basis of the Merina regime weakened. By the early 1890s, immediately prior to the French takeover, armed Sakalava and Bara assaults on the highland interior for cattle and slaves were common. Many brigand bands composed of Merina refugees from *fanompoana* cooperated with the Sakalava raiders.

Certainly forced labour was the most important causative factor in the collapse of the imperial Merina economy in the early 1890s. It thus indirectly laid the basis for the French takeover. More directly, desertion from the imperial army – itself a form of *fanompoana* (always unremunerated) – guaranteed the success of the French troops in 1895.

Moreover, when the French declared a protectorate that maintained a highly unpopular Merina regime, a massive revolt erupted in which one of the key rebel targets was not the French, but the Merina state church structure used to implement *fanompoana*.

Ethiopia forms a contrasting case study. Its ability to retain independence during the European scramble for Africa has conventionally been attributed to its remote mountainous terrain. However, this did not prevent major trade routes operating for centuries across highland Ethiopia, or a successful British invasion in 1868. Similarly, the Merina, who believed that natural factors, notably malaria in the lowlands, and a thickly forested and steep eastern escarpment, would deter foreign invasion, were ultimately conquered by the French. Some Western observers underscored Ethiopia's superior (paler skinned) non-African and "Christian" culture as a core element in preserving its independence, but again, the Merina were also considered non-African, and in 1869 converted to Christianity.

The difference between Ethiopia, on the one hand, and Egypt and Madagascar on the other, was twofold. First, the Ethiopian government did not face sufficient opposition to its policies from within the region to pose any significant political or economic threat. This in turn was due to the absence of any meaningful attempt at economic modernisation, and to a more effective and ruthless policy of imperial expansion. The lack of any significant effort to establish large-scale cash crop cultivation, industrialise, expand artisanal production, or implement improvements in communications, meant that the military constituted the only sector in which the Ethiopian state applied forced labour to a major extent. It thus avoided the risk, which both Egypt and Imerina incurred, of serious dissent from its own subjects. Ethiopia established a large standing army, which was irregularly paid at best. However, the Ethiopian court granted soldiers the right to pillage and settle the territories they overran, and to claim conquered peoples as either forced labour, or slaves that they might profitably sell. Therefore, unlike Egypt and Imerina, where soldiers increasingly sought to evade military conscription, or even rebel, Ethiopian soldiers, for the most part, remained loyal to the imperial regime. Moreover, they used their military superiority to ruthlessly suppress dissent from colonised peoples such as the Oromo. Indeed, anti-imperial revolt in Ethiopia manifested itself only from the 1960s.

Second, whereas Britain, the global superpower, occupied Egypt, and abandoned the Merina to the French, it decided to shore up the Shoan regime in the Ethiopian highlands. The successful British expedition of 1868 against Tewedros II opened the way for the ascension to the imperial throne of Yohannes IV (r. 1871–89), formerly known as Lij Kassay Mercha, a warlord who had both aided the British and benefitted militarily from them. Thus, from 1871, the British considered Ethiopia to be firmly under their influence. Informal domination of the Ottomans and direct control of Egypt increased the British desire to limit expansion in the region of its European rivals lest they gain significant control over a portion of the Red Sea and hence potentially imperil British control of the Suez route to India. Britain was particularly concerned about the imperial pretension of France and Italy. From 1883, France signed a series of treaties with Somali chiefs that led to the French occupation of Djibouti in 1894 and creation of French Somaliland in 1896. Again, from 1889 Italy started to advance into territories claimed by Ethiopia, and through signing a series of protectorates over small sultanates, and leases with the Sultan of Zanzibar for the towns of Brava, Merka, Mogadishu, and Warsheikh, on the Benadir coast, formed the basis of what in 1905 became Italian Somaliland. However, victories by the Ethiopian army over the Italians at Adawa in 1896, and the British over the Mahdist army at Omdurman in 1898, and the retreat of French forces at Fashoda that secured the Sudan for the British, assuaged the fears of the latter. Subsequently, they negotiated the Tripartite Agreement of December 1906, signed with France and Italy, that secured Britain's aim of nominal independence for Ethiopia – the political demise of which it nevertheless saw as ultimately inevitable. At the same time, Britain pushed to eliminate Ethiopian influence, recognised by France in 1897, along its borders with Kenya, Sudan, and Egypt. Italian support for the allies in the First World War led Britain to concede Jaghbub in Libya and Jubaland in Somalia to Italy, but it rejected Italian proposals to partition Ethiopia.

Climate and Natural Disasters

Most histories of nineteenth-century European imperialism overlook environmental forces, yet the period witnessed the end of the Little Ice Age and, in its closing decades, dramatic climatic turbulence. These changes inevitably influenced the scramble for IOA and indigenous reactions to it. Equatorial East Africa experienced a dramatically increased warmer, wetter period from 1845 to 1880, but major drought during the last two decades of the nineteenth century. By contrast, regions to the north and south of equatorial East Africa, namely northern IOA, southern Africa, and most of central and western Madagascar, experienced relatively arid conditions until about 1870, and thereafter heightened rainfall, except for a major El Niño-associated drought in 1877. Another drought hit eastern and central Madagascar around 1890 when, however, southeastern Africa experienced its wettest period in 200 years.

While droughts, abnormal rains, or armed conflict could reduce harvests, political authorities often accentuated the problem, as in the cases of Egypt and Madagascar, by preventing adequate production, stockpiling, or distribution of provisions. Droughts could also force people to migrate. A prime example was the *Mfecane*, a massive dislocation of people in Zululand, in southern Africa, in large part due to a major drought that hit the region during the first decade of the nineteenth century. One major consequence was, from 1835, the migration north of the Ngoni who spread destruction as they moved.

The incidence of disease also increased during the nineteenth century. This was due in part to two decades of drought and diminished harvests experienced by most of IOA from about 1820 to 1840. Ethiopia, for example, suffered an exceptionally severe drought from 1835 to 1836. Drought was frequently followed by famine which significantly weakened the physiological defences of those affected, making them more vulnerable to disease. The dramatically warmer and wetter period from 1845 to 1880 created an environment more conducive to disease vectors, while the expansion of irrigation and construction projects in the tropics created pools of stagnant water (ideal breeding ground for disease vectors of, for example, bilharzia and malaria). At the same time, large troop, population, and cattle movements, assisted by improved and more extensive transport facilities, resulted in increased diffusion of diseases across the IOW. These included malaria, the greatest killer disease overall, the plague, smallpox, and cholera which broke out of the Ganges Delta in 1817 in epidemic form and in 1834–5 killed an estimated one-third of the Egyptian population. Human diseases took a particularly heavy toll on forced labour, and malnourished and displaced peoples, who all possessed lower physiological resistance.

Epizootics, epidemic disease amongst animals, also caused significant socio-economic damage. For example, an estimated 700,000 draft animals died in the 1863–4 rinderpest outbreak in Egypt, forcing the

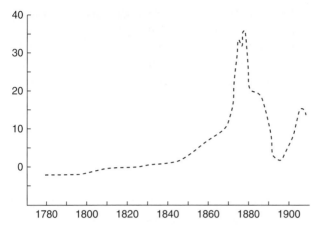

FIGURE 11.1 Lake Tanganyika: Estimated Surface Levels 1780 to 1900 (metres)

Note: Adapted from Sharon E. Nicolson, "Historical and Modern Fluctuations of Lakes Tanganyika and Rukwa and their Relationship to Rainfall Variability" *Climatic Change* 41 (1999): 57.

government to import steam-driven ploughs. The greatest rinderpest plague to hit IOA erupted in 1889 in Somaliland, and spread rapidly south to reach Uganda in 1890 and Zambia (formerly Northern Rhodesia) by late 1892. The Zambezi temporarily checked its progress, but the disease reached Zimbabwe (Southern Rhodesia) in 1896, and Cape Town in November 1897, decimating cattle stocks. Overall, rinderpest caused 85 per cent mortality among unprotected cattle, although the toll could be higher. In 1896–7, for example, it killed an estimated 90 to 95 per cent of cattle in Mafeking and the Transkei.

A strong argument can be made that rinderpest critically undermined members of the African elite for whom cattle represented their chief capital asset. However, rinderpest was but one of many diseases to seriously affect cattle in IOA in the mid to late nineteenth century. For example, southern Africa was hit in the 1850s by lungsickness (bovine pleuropneumonia), initially in Zululand, and during the following few decades in neighbouring regions, and redwater (*Babesiosis*) from 1870 to 1871. By 1890, redwater affected all regions of South Africa, causing initially high mortality until some stock developed resistance to it and effective prophylactics emerged in the early twentieth century. Gallsickness (*Anaplasmosis*) also accounted for many cattle deaths, as in South Africa did an outbreak of fluke disease (*Fasciola hepatica*) in 1889.

TABLE 11.2 *Egypt and the Sudan: Natural Catastrophes and Disease, 1800 to 1900*

Year	Event
1800–1	Egypt: plague epidemic – 2,937 deaths out of Cairo's population of 250,000 in Apr. 1801 alone
1800–44	plague outbreaks in 21 of these years
1803	Egypt: Nile floods insufficient – drought, great shortages, and suffering
1808	Egypt: plague
1811–13	Sudan: smallpox epidemic
1813	Lower Egypt: plague (severe)
1814	Sudan: smallpox (from Suakin) – 2/3 of cases died
1814–15	Egypt: plague
1816	Lower Egypt: plague (severe)
1818	Lower Egypt: floods adversely affect crops
1819	Lower Egypt: floods adversely affect crops
1820	Lower Egypt: floods adversely affect crops
1822–5	Egypt and Sudan: drought and famine – cotton exports decline by about 12%
1829	Egypt: murrain – Nile Delta canals choked with dead bullocks
early 1830s	Egypt: drought
1830–2	Egypt: cholera pandemic – in 1831 150,000 died (almost 6% of the population) incl. in Cairo 36,000 civilians and 5,000 soldiers
1833–7	N. Sudan: droughts and famine
1834	Egypt: cholera – similar impact to 1831 pandemic; plague
1834–5	Egypt: plague epidemic – est. 34.000 deaths in Cairo April–June 1835; Worse than in 1783–4. Total deaths over 150,000 (incl. 15,000 African slaves). In Upper Egypt many villages depopulated
1834–40	Plague
1835	Egypt: an estimated 33% of the population die of cholera and 200,000 of famine
1839	Sudan: violent storm (31 Aug.) – severe flooding & many houses destroyed in Khartoum, 11 vessels sunk on the White Nile
1839–40	Sudan: smallpox epidemic
1841	Egypt: plague; Sudan: violent storm (27 Jul.) – severe flooding in Khartoum
early 1840s	Egypt: bad harvests, cholera
1841–3	Egypt: rinderpest – from infected cattle offloaded at Alexandria from a Russian ship. Killed total of 665,000 cattle
1843	Egypt: locust plague – caused depopulation of entire villages [probably due to crop destruction and consequent famine]

TABLE 11.2 (*cont.*)

Year	Event
1843–4	Egypt: plague
1843–6	Egypt: rinderpest – re-erupted among Nubian cattle imported to replace decimated stock – 350,000 cattle died (90% of total stock)
1844–5	Northern Sudan: low Nile and famine
1848	Egypt: cholera
1850	Egypt: cholera
1855	Egypt & Nilotic Sudan: cholera – 116,020 deaths
1857	Egypt and Sudan: major flooding along Nile
1861	Egypt: rinderpest – killed large numbers of camels – becomes enzootic
1863–4	Egypt: rinderpest – est. 700,000 animals die forcing government to import steam-driven ploughs
1864	Egypt: famine
1863–5	Sudan: drought (major) accompanied by devastating plague afflicting cattle and camels
1865	Egypt: cholera epidemic – 60,000 deaths (mortality rate almost 100 per 1000 in Rosetta; 42 per 1000 in Dalmietta; 22 per 1000 in Cairo and Alexandria)
1865–6	Sudan: smallpox epidemic
1870	Alexandria: tsunami (Jun.)
1879	Gulf of Suez: tsunami (Jul.); Mosul: famine
1886	Egypt: smallpox –264 deaths
1887	Egypt: smallpox –271 deaths
1888	Egypt: smallpox – 181 deaths; Sudan: famine
1889	Egypt: smallpox – 861 deaths; Sudan: famine
1890	Egypt: cholera; smallpox – 498 deaths
1891	Egypt: smallpox – 202 deaths
1892	Egypt: smallpox – 544 deaths
1893	Egypt: smallpox – 313 deaths
1894	Egypt: smallpox – 155 deaths
1895	Egypt: smallpox – 358 deaths
1896	Egypt: smallpox – 945 deaths
1897	Egypt: smallpox – 846 deaths
1898	Egypt: smallpox – 467 deaths
1899	Egypt: smallpox – 431 deaths
1900	Egypt: smallpox – 485 deaths

TABLE 11.3 *Ethiopia: Natural Catastrophes and Disease, 1800 to 1900*

Year	Event
1800	Highlands: famine
1811–12	Highlands: smallpox epidemic, locust plague – high mortality
1816	Locust plague, famine
1825	Shoa: famine, cholera
1828–9	Shoa: famine
1830–1	Cholera epidemic – killed an estimated ⅔ of Sahla Sellasés' slaves
1831	Locust plague – great damage to crops
1834–5	Shewa: drought, famine, cholera epidemic – high mortality in Shoa
1836–7	Drought, famine, cholera epidemic – high mortality (e.g. kills half the population of Ankobar)
1838	Locust plague
1838–9	Smallpox epidemic
1839	Influenza epidemic
1840	Gondar: famine (due to plundering troops)
1842	Ankober: earthquake – between 100 and 1,000 deaths
1845	Drought and famine; earthquake (Feb.) – 51–100 deaths
1854	Smallpox epidemic
1856	Cholera epidemic – high mortality (e.g. killed 300 at Massowa)
1858	Drought and famine
1861	Dubbi: earthquake (May)
1864–8	Locust plague – great damage to crops
1865–6	Cholera epidemic
1866	Famine; typhoid epidemic – high mortality (e.g. ⅔ of population of Adowa)
1867	Famine
1875	Drought and famine; Eritrea: earthquake (Nov.) – 51–100 deaths
1876	Plague; locust plague
1878	Smallpox epidemic – high mortality (e.g. kills 500 at Adowa out of total population of 7,000)
1879	Adal: cattle plague, famine
1880	Adala to Begemder: famine
1881	Famine
1886–9	Smallpox epidemic
1887	Massawa: rinderpest
1888	Drought, famine, rinderpest, cholera
1889	Drought, famine, rinderpest (overall kills 90% of all cattle), typhoid epidemic, cholera epidemic – high mortality
1890	Famine, cholera epidemic, smallpox epidemic, typhoid epidemic
1891	Cholera epidemic, typhoid epidemic, locust plague

TABLE 11.3 *(cont.)*

Year	Event
1892	Drought, locust and rat plagues devastate crops, famine, cholera epidemic, smallpox, typhoid
1893	Locust plague
1899	Drought and famine
1900	Volcanic eruption (Tulle Moje)

TABLE 11.4 *Madagascar: Natural Catastrophes and Disease, 1800 to 1900*

Year	Event
1807	NE coast: cyclone – severe damage, many boats lost; smallpox
1808	NE coast: cyclones – severe damage to shipping
1811	NE coast: cyclone – severe damage to shipping (Mar.)
1815	NE coast: [cyclone?] – shipwreck (13 Feb.)
1816	NE coast: cyclone (Nov.), crop failure & famine (Dec.)
1817	NE coast; E. forest; Ankay: famine (Sep.) follows Merina military march on Tamatave. High mortality
1817–18	Imerina: smallpox epidemic (starts Nov. 1817)
1818	NE coast: cyclone – destroys harvest (28 Feb.–1 Mar.)
1818–19	[NE coast]: cyclone – destroys harvest (Dec.–Mar.?)
1819–20	[NE coast]: cyclone (Jan.–Mar.?); Madagascar: cholera outbreak (brought from Bombay, India via the Mascarenes) (Nov.–Jan.)
1820	'Marmandia' [Maromby?]: smallpox outbreak (Sep.)
1822	Imerina: outbreak of malaria (starts Jan.)
1822–3	Imerina: measles outbreak. Several children die
1825–53	On imperial Merina army expeditions to lowlands 50% die of malaria
1826	Imerina: starts in west – extensive disease with high mortality [malaria?] (starts in May)
1827	[NE coast]: cyclone (30 Mar.–2 Apr.)
1829	NE coast: cyclone (before end of Apr.) – many ships lost; Majunga: destroyed by fire (before mid-July)
1831	Imerina: malaria outbreak in north and west
1833	N. Madagascar & Imerina: smallpox epidemic (peak in Nov.)
1833–4	Imerina: rainfall highest in living memory – rice harvest spoiled (Nov.–Feb.); outbreak of malaria (dry season, May–Sep.)
1834	Imerina: smallpox – causes great turmoil; NE. coast (Tamatave, Foulepointe) & Imerina: severe famine (Jul.–Sep.)
1835	Imerina: smallpox – causes great turmoil (Jan.–Feb.); Antananarivo: great storm (7 Mar.) destroys many houses
1841	NE coast: cyclone (before April) – damaged shipping

(continued)

TABLE 11.4 (*cont.*)

Year	Event
1845	NE coast: famine [follows 1835 Merina ban on swidden cultivation?]
1846	NE coast: cyclone (16–17 Dec.) – some ships lost, 250 deaths
1847	NE coast: famine
1854	Disease [cholera?]
1857	E coast: cyclone [Jan.–Mar.?] destroys boats and littoral
1859	Cholera
1860	Tuberculosis
1862	N Imerina (Ambohimanga): drought; crops fail; famine anticipated; Imerina: tubercular leprosy
1863	Imerina: malaria; smallpox epidemic; choreomania (*ramanenjana*) (Feb.–Apr.) started "west or south west of Imerina" and by March, common in Antananarivo
1864	Imerina: malaria
1866	Imerina: smallpox "raging"
1867	Imerina: smallpox
1870	Majunga: cholera epidemic – 2,000 deaths (Oct.–Dec.); smallpox
1873	Betsileo: smallpox
1874	Nosy Be: smallpox; Imerina (Vonizongo): severe malaria outbreak
1875–7	E coast and highlands: smallpox epidemic
1876	E coast: cyclone (Feb.)
1878–9	Highlands: malaria – kills many; Betsileo: smallpox
1879	Highlands: malaria
1880	E coast: cyclone hits crops; Highlands: malaria
1880–1	Smallpox epidemic
1881	Rabies
1882	E coast: typhoid; Imerina: drought
1882–3	Imerina: typhoid and malaria – severe
1884	Smallpox epidemic; measles; severe outbreak of malaria; choreomania
1885	E coast: cyclone (Feb.)
1885–8	Smallpox epidemic; typhoid
1887	Highlands: excessive rainfall
1888	E coast: cyclone (Feb.)
1889	Smallpox epidemic; plague; Imerina: excessive rainfall damages crops
1890	Highlands: excessive rainfall, harvest shortfall, influenza; Betsileo: malaria epidemic (May)
1891	Highlands: drought, famine, malaria, smallpox
1892	NE coast: floods destroy rice crop; Imerina: drought; Betsileo: smallpox epidemic
1893	Imerina: heavy rainfall; influenza epidemic; NE coast: cyclone (Feb.)

TABLE 11.4 (*cont.*)

Year	Event
1894	Imerina: influenza epidemic and typhoid; NE coast: cyclone destroys rice harvest, smallpox, famine
1895	Tamatave: smallpox, typhoid; Highlands: malaria epidemic
1896	Highlands: malaria
1898–1900	Tamatave: bubonic plague
1898	[E coast]: tidal wave (Aug.)
1899	Antananarivo: cyclone (Nov.)

Drought and locust plagues accentuated cattle losses by depleting harvests and thus forage. Calamitous droughts hit southern Africa in 1877 (possibly the result of a major El Niño), 1890, and 1894–5. The result was a drastic reduction in crop production, the death of stock – in the 1890 drought 100,000 cattle died in the Transkei alone – widespread malnutrition, and disease. Severe droughts created particularly favourable conditions for the hatching of locust eggs; southern and eastern Africa experienced a series of red locust plagues culminating in 1896 with the wholesale destruction of crops and animal and human starvation throughout much of region. Human and cattle disease thus eroded the capital assets (labour and cattle) of affected indigenous elites at various times and places throughout the nineteenth century.

In sum, a variety of factors contributed to the late nineteenth-century European scramble for IOA. The French, humiliated by Prussia in the war of 1871 and unilateral British intervention in Egypt in 1882, seized bases in Somaliland and insisted on ancient claims to Madagascar. Germany in the 1880s floated the idea of a Germano-Boer corridor linking their colony in South West Africa to Mozambique, and in 1888 backed Carl Peters in local treaties that created the basis for German East Africa (present-day Tanzania). Britain, fearful that its rivals might impinge upon its direct investments in IOA, notably in Egypt and South Africa, that would endanger its control of the route to India, moved to consolidate and expand its direct and informal control in IOA. The ability of Ethiopia to retain independence was due less to its military prowess in defeating an Italian army, than to Britain's desire to prop up an Ethiopian regime that it considered to fall within its sphere of informal rule.

For Africans in IOA, the price of staple exports remained high and the terms of trade generally favourable. Nevertheless, indigenous leaders experienced crises of various natures and at different times. Some were due primarily to European pressure, as with

British anti-slave trade measures applied to Zanzibar. In other cases, indigenous IOA regimes, such as those of Egypt and Imerina (Madagascar), adopted ambitious economic and military policies that backfired chiefly because of their ruthless exploitation of forced labour. Faced with military and industrial conscription, young men, the chief victims, opted massively to evade the draft. Increasingly they did so through flight, which undermined not only state modernisa-tion and expansionist policies but also subsistence agriculture upon which the economy ultimately rested. Again, natural disasters, notably drought and disease, provoked crises by eroding the capital assets of indigenous elites in the form of human labour and cattle. All these factors undermined the ability of local leaders to resist the European imperial advance.

Overall, however, the IOA economy remained remarkably buoyant, to the extent that it largely sustained, for example, Bombay textile exports. Indian financiers and merchants, almost all of whom were British subjects, steadily expanded their trading frontier along the coasts and into interior IOA. In most of IOA they provided the credit essential to the commercial relations not only of their Indian agents and African and Malagasy partners, but often also European traders, large and small. It could be argued that they, and the significant waves of Indian indentured workers to island and continental IOA, underwrote British colonialism in IOA. Certainly Indian commercial networks, and in many cases those of indigenous traders and sailors, survived the vicissitudes of environmental change, the end of the slave trade, and the imposition of colonial rule, and remained vibrant well into the twentieth century.

12

Africa and Slavery in the Indian Ocean World

Most slavery studies focus on the Atlantic slave trade and New World slavery. These project a remarkable consensus as to slave identity, the structure of the slave trade, and the nature of bondage. IOW slavery studies has, since the 1980s, received growing attention from scholars who have generally carried New World paradigms of slavery to the IOW where, as this chapter sets out to demonstrate, those exemplars are largely inappropriate.

The Context: Slavery Studies

Slavery scholars generally follow Moses Finley's distinction between "societies with slaves", which applied to all human communities, and "slave societies" in which slaves formed at least 20 per cent of the population, were the principal source of economic production, and shaped all social relationships. Finley observed that there have existed only five "slave societies": classical Greece and Rome, and the slave plantation economies of the West Indies, Brazil, and the American South, although Martin Klein has added to that list the Hausa emirates and Jula states of West Africa, and nineteenth-century Zanzibar. Most slave studies have concentrated on the transatlantic slave trade model that lasted from about 1500 to 1888. In this period, some 12 million slaves, chiefly West and Central African males aged from 15 to 30, were shipped to European-owned plantations or mines in the Caribbean, Brazil, and the American South. There, slaves formed concentrated communities of chattel labour, deprived in perpetuity of civil rights. Masters owned the slave and any "property" the slave accumulated, including children. Owners could legally move or sell any slave, even if this entailed separating slave couples or children from their parents. They could also assert sexual access to female slaves, irrespective of the partnership status or will of the slave.

The Atlantic slave trade was undermined in part by European humanitarians inspired by a mixture of Enlightenment thinking, and the evangelical awakening that recognised that all human beings possessed individual rights and souls. Of arguably greater importance was the onset of modern capitalism which rejected slavery in favour of wage labour and free market forces. Britain led the way, banning the slave trade in 1807, abolishing slavery throughout its empire in 1834, and mounting an increasingly successful international anti-slavery campaign that culminated in the abolition of slavery in Brazil in 1888.

This Atlantic slave model has formed the backdrop for studies of IOW slavery which most scholars have approached with the assumption that black Africans formed the bulk of slaves traded. For them, the export of African slaves to IOW markets experienced three major upswings: in the ninth century due to Middle Eastern Muslim demand; from 1500 due to combined European and Muslim demand; and in the nineteenth century when it was fuelled by Muslim demand, chiefly in the Middle East and South Asia, and increasingly clandestine European demand, notably from the Mascarenes and New World. As with Atlantic slavery studies, scholars of the IOW slave trade have focussed predominantly on African males, who performed a range of menial tasks from labouring on date, clove, and sugar plantations, to mining, pearl diving, and soldiery. As in the Atlantic system, slaves were property who could be bought and sold, and masters enjoyed sexual access to slave women.

IOW Bondage Reassessed

Slavery first emerged as a significant social institution in the centralised hierarchical polities at the core of the Neolithic Revolution: the Middle East, South Asia, and China. However, it developed in tandem with other forms of servile labour. The innovations associated with the Neolithic Revolution, notably the domestication of plants and animals, and techniques of water control and distribution, required large, permanent, inputs of manual labour. The religio-political elites of hierarchical IOW polities secured this through imposing physical and ideological constraints on their subject populations, restricting their geographical mobility, and directing their labour. Thus Alexander the Great found that Egyptian pharaohs had forcibly concentrated their peasant subjects on the fertile cultivated lands along the Nile, and that the core of the Persian Empire comprised large landed estates worked by bonded peasants. These servile workforces produced agricultural surpluses sufficient to maintain the ruling elite, and eventually also a specialised artisanal sector and merchant class. They also supported the formation of standing armies that the elite used to expand state frontiers. When they defeated peoples who opposed them, these armies generally enslaved captive women and children, who were thus indebted for their lives to their captors. By contrast, they executed male captives who were more difficult to subdue, required far greater surveillance, and were less likely to adapt to conditions of enslavement than women and children. Generally, only in the wake of epidemics which ravaged the subject population, and created an urgent need for replacement manpower, were adult male captives enslaved. Over time, slave-raiding became a major motive of military campaigns, and a class of specialist slave-raiders emerged. However, when victorious armies overran peasant settlements unopposed, they generally maintained those communities *in situ* in a form of bondage that tied them to the land. This might well be the origins, in the first millennium BCE, of praedial (agrestic) servitude in India wherein servile peasants could only be sold with the land they worked.

Enslaved captives were sent back to the imperial centre as prizes for court members and army generals, to be distributed as gifts or sold. As the bulk of productive labour was already provided by servile subjects, most of the enslaved were absorbed by elite households as objects of conspicuous consumption, used to reflect their owner's wealth and power. Male and female slaves became servants, and attendants, females also served as concubines and wet nurses, and boys as eunuchs, artisan assistants, and agents for merchants.

Captives formed the core of the first regular local market in bonded people. The first extant evidence of the slave trade in the IOW dates back 4,300 years to Mesopotamia and refers to the sale of females. However, a specialised long-distance slave trade developed that catered for a different category of servile labour. These were invariably of foreign origin and thus "exotic". In addition, for them to bear

the cost of long-distance travel and still produce a handsome profit for
the merchant, they had to possess exceptional beauty, or special skills
such as juggling, dancing, and singing. Most such slaves were females
and children, although eunuchs, who alone were trusted by male elites
to supervise their harems, were also in high demand.

Supply and demand thus played significant but different roles in
the IOW slave trade. Supply, which generally peaked during the long
economic downturns, from 300 to 800 CE, and 1300 to 1830, notably
at times of natural disaster and warfare, was the predominant influence on local and regional slave trades. Demand, the paramount influence on the long-distance slave trade, largely shaped the slave traffic in
the major economic upturns from about 200 BCE to 200 CE, the ninth
to thirteenth centuries, and again from about 1830.

Nature of Bondage

The IOW had a wide variety of forms of unfree labour. Critical here is
the issue of language. In the Euro-Atlantic world, almost all terms for
"slave" derive from a common term, "slav", with the connotation of
chattel slave. However, indigenous IOW terms for servile labour, that
Western scholars commonly but mistakenly assume to mean "slave"
in the Western sense, vary in meaning according to time and location.
For instance, in nineteenth-century Somalia different terms employed
to denote slaves included *Jareer, Bantu, Mjikenda, Adoon, Habash,
Bidde, Sankadhuudhe, Boon, Meddo*, and *Oogi*. As with similar ranges
of words in other IOW cultures, each of these terms had different
meanings, depending on context. Certainly in most IOW societies
there existed little correspondence with the conventional Atlantic
image of a chattel slave, assigned to field and mining labour. An exception was the Mascarenes which possessed no indigenous population
prior to European settlement, and formed an enclave characterised by
a plantation economy, a white master class, and chattel slavery.

The definition of "slavery" is best sought by defining its opposite,
"freedom". However, freedom in the modern sense of individual liberty did not exist in any pre-modern society. Rather, each person
had an allotted status that carried with it a multiplicity of rights and
obligations. For example, in Sharia-governed Muslim societies, slaves
who bore their master's child could not be sold, and the child was
automatically granted free status, as was the mother should she outlive

her master – a common occurrence given that most concubines were much younger than their masters. Also, it was deemed spiritually meritorious for Muslim slave-owners to manumit their slaves. Moreover, there existed an overlap in status between slaves and other forms of labour. For instance, in late eighteenth- and early nineteenth-century Sulu, the dominant Taosug ethnicity permitted bonded *banyaga* to marry, own property, and to perform a wide range of functions each with the same rights and privileges as those accorded to non-slaves. Overlapping statuses in the IOW render it difficult to forge hard and fast distinctions between types of servitude, or to contrast "slave" with "free" for, as Anthony Reid underlines, the concept of personal freedom only becomes meaningful as a tool of analysis when all forms of servitude are subsumed into a clearly defined category of "slavery".[1]

The meaning of bondage in the IOW becomes clearer if Western notions of a division of society into free and slave, and of slaves as property, are replaced by a vision of society as a hierarchy of dependency in which "slaves", in the Atlantic sense, constituted one of a number of unfree groups. IOW societies were overwhelmingly characterised by reciprocity, in which obligation implied servitude to an individual with superior status, a kinship group, or the crown, in return for protection. Generally, the highest status was accorded in acephalous societies to a group of elders and in centralised societies to the sovereign who theoretically "owned" all of inferior status – as was possibly most visible with corvée labour which in most IOW countries was considered crown "property". Moreover, in the world-view of pre-industrial societies, there was no division between the temporal and the supernatural. Rather, the living and the dead were incorporated into a giant hierarchy of overlapping statuses, each with associated rights and obligations, in which the concept of bondage transcended the here and now. Even kings imbued with sacred power were in turn governed by ancestors or gods. In Islam, for example, all Muslims were "slaves" of Allah.

Cycles of human-environment interaction played a pivotal role in enslavement. During human (e.g. war) or natural (e.g. harvest failure, epidemic disease) disasters, people often entered slavery as a survival strategy, either voluntarily or propelled by kin. Thus in famine

---

[1] Anthony Reid, "Introduction" to idem (ed.), *Slavery, Bondage and Dependency in Southeast Asia* (St Lucia: University of Queensland Press, 1983), 21.

years, communities in densely populated monocrop regions, such as Makassar in Indonesia and areas of South India, exported their surplus population as slaves. Those deemed expendable were chiefly children, especially girls, who were often sold outright or as "pawns". Such slaves/pawns could be redeemed, but seldom were. Or the child could be sold for adoption, widely viewed in India and China as a charitable system. Others were enslaved for crime or debt, both of which were frequently a reflection of hard times. There also existed a strong connection between natural catastrophes, gambling – ubiquitous in Southeast and East Asian communities – and debt. Indeed, over the long term, more people entered slavery due to indebtedness than to warfare, raiding, or natural disasters *per se*. Although adult males formed the majority of criminals and debtors, most of those enslaved in consequence of their actions were women and children – the most vulnerable household members and the most in demand as bonded labour.

In such contexts, concepts of "slave" and "free" are of limited analytical utility. For most of the IOW population, security, food, and shelter, rather than an abstract concept of liberty, were the primary aims. "Liberty" in the sense of individual freedom from inherited status and responsibilities undermined the web of obligations that offered protection from man-made and natural dangers. This helps explain the remarkable absence of revolt and class-consciousness amongst IOW slaves who generally sought to integrate themselves into the slave-holding society that provided them with basic sustenance and sometimes the chance of an enhanced lifestyle.

Race in IOW Slavery

In the Atlantic slave model, the victims were black Africans and their masters white. This fundamental cleavage pervades slavery studies and public discourse on slavery and its aftermath. Growing awareness of the enslavement of indigenous Indian communities in the Americas has left the basic thesis untouched. Moreover, the dominance of the Atlantic paradigm has ensured that race has become similarly significant in the history of bondage in the IOW, where most slavery scholars, and UNESCO's slave routes project, focus on African slaves.

However, bondage in the IOW reflected, in the main, fluctuations in the IOW global economy, human and natural disasters, and structures of indebtedness. The major centres of demand for slaves were centralised polities and major ports, while slaves overwhelmingly originated locally or from within the region. Thus, in China most bonded labour was Chinese or from neighbouring regions. Local slave supplies were easier to locate than long-distance ones, cheaper to transport, and suffered fewer losses en-route. Hence, African slaves were a rare luxury outside the western IOW. By the second century CE, some skilled African sailors and entertainers – such as Alexandrian jugglers – may have been exported as slaves to China. There, by the fourth century, a regular market existed for *Kunlun*, a term some scholars have interpreted as meaning inhabitants of Pemba, in East Africa, or more generally Africans. However, *Kunlun* also applied to dark-skinned Himalayan communities, Annamite islanders, or darker-skinned peoples of the Malay Peninsula, Indonesian Archipelago, and Melanesia. Certainly by the late 800s, East African slaves were valued in China as divers and sailors. However, they were seldom employed inland, where the arrival of a Negro slave at the Tang court caused much excitement in 976. Thereafter, there are increased references to African slaves in the eastern IOW. In the 1400s, Malagasy and East African slaves were imported into Aceh by Bengali traders, and by Banten merchants into Malacca, from where some were transshipped to China. During the Mongol era (1260–1368), elite Chinese households vied to possess Negro menservants, and shortly after, in 1382, the Javanese court sent 101 African slaves as tribute to the imperial Chinese court. After 1500, African slaves were also exported to European enclaves in the eastern IOW, notably to Portuguese settlements in Macao and Japan, and VOC forts and plantations in Indonesia. However, the slaves suffered high mortality on the long voyages to the East. For example, 61 per cent of its cargo of Malagasy slaves died aboard a ship to Batavia in 1684. Africans thus always formed a tiny minority of bondspeople in the East.

Even in the western IOW, Africans rarely constituted a majority of slaves outside the African continent. By the first centuries CE, a few were probably imported into India from northeast Africa, and by the third century, Arab merchants were shipping African slaves to the Konkan Indian forts of Sopara, Kalyan, Chaul, and Pal. With the expansion of Islam, demand for African slaves increased, and from the tenth century significant numbers of Berbers, Ethiopians and Sub-Saharan Africans – eyewitnesses from Ibn-Batuta (in 1342–9) to Tomé Pires (in 1512–15) emphasise "Abyssinians" – were shipped to South Asia. From 1500, Portuguese, Dutch, and British posts in South Asia imported East African and Malagasy slaves. Meanwhile, traditional African slave imports into South Asia, via Zebid, Aden, and the Persian Gulf, continued. However, most slaves imported by sea into India in the early era were from the "West", implying the Persian Gulf and Mediterranean regions. In the medieval era, Africans formed possibly the majority of imported slaves in Sind (present-day Pakistan), Bengal, and South India, but Turks and Slavs comprised most slave imports into South Asia generally. Moreover, from 1500, Indian slaves were shipped to Mauritius and Cape Town in IOA, as well as to Macao, Japan, and Indonesia.

Africans periodically formed a majority of slave imports only in parts of the Middle East and the western Indian Ocean islands. The Middle East, the greatest overall IOW market for African slaves, imported slaves from Nubia from Pharaonic times and from Ethiopia, Sudan, and Somalia by the early centuries CE. By the seventh century, Axum exported slaves from its southern frontiers to Egypt, Arabia, and the Persian Gulf. Arab and Persian traders also obtained slaves directly from Somalia. Under the Islamic regimes that arose from the seventh century it was illegal to enslave fellow-Muslims, so they sought slaves primarily from the *Dar al-Kufr* or *Dar al-Harb* ("territory of war", the regions bordering Muslim territory) – lands not governed by the Sharia. By the ninth century, the Middle East had become a significant and durable market for African slaves. Their numbers there increased from the tenth to thirteenth centuries, during the second great boom in the IOW global economy, when they probably equalled, or at times surpassed, the number of slaves of Georgian (Circassian) and Central Asian origin. African slave imports dipped in the fourteenth century, but grew again from the late fifteenth century, mostly via Ethiopia and the Nile Valley but also by sea from East Africa and Madagascar. Cairo, the African Red Sea ports of Zeila and Berbera, and the Arabian markets of Zebid and Aden, served as major redistribution points.

IOA and the Slave Trade

We here examine three major issues in the history of the IOA slave trade and slavery: the Zanj Revolt in the ninth century, the question

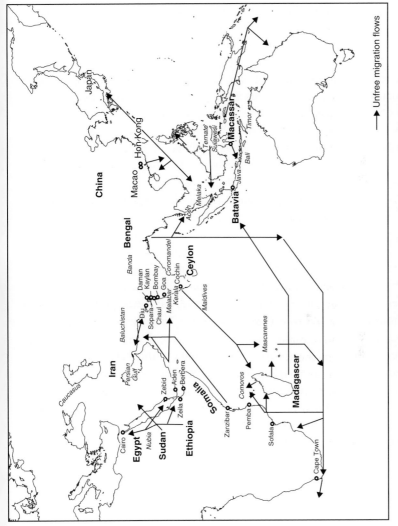

MAP 12.1 Trans-Oceanic Flows of Unfree Labour in the Indian Ocean World, 1500 to 1830

Note: Produced by Carl Hughes, IOWC.

263

of the Malagasy contribution to the Swahili slave trade from 1500 to 1750, and the nature of nineteenth-century bondage.

The Zanj Revolt

From 869 to 883, the "Zanj" in Iraq rose in what James de Vere Allen termed "perhaps the most successful slave rebellion of all times"[2] and Thomas Ricks, "the only mass slave uprising known in the Arab world".[3] The dominant view, following Alexandre Popovic, is that the rebels were adult male slaves from "Zanj", the Swahili coast of East Africa. Under the Abbasids (750–1258), slavery became central to the economies of the Middle East which imported massive numbers of Zanj slaves because they were cheaper and reputedly physically stronger than other slaves and, as sickle-cell carriers, immune to malaria. They were thus a prime choice as labourers when in 833 a project was inaugurated to convert the mosquito-ridden Basra marshes into cultivable land. The conventional view is that, in consequence, the trade in Zanj slaves boomed. Mark Horton claims that, by the mid-eighth century, Basra (Kharijite) merchants and their Omani (Ibadi) collaborators had established a major slave-trading centre on the island of Pemba, and probably also on Zanzibar. From 800 to 870, they shipped possibly 270,000 slaves, an average of about 4,000 per annum, to the Persian Gulf where, Alan Fisher claims, "tens of thousands" of Zanj worked in southern Iraq where they comprised some 75 per cent of the total slave workforce. By 869, possibly 50,000 newly imported Zanj slaves were working in the Basra marshlands in gangs 500 to 15,000 strong. The work was so arduous, and the Zanj so denigrated, that they rose in revolt. The rebels captured 1,900 boats from imperial forces, by 871 controlled much of lower Iraq, and near Basra built a large city called Mukhtara. The rebels were eventually crushed with great loss of life, and from 883 CE massive imports of Zanj slaves into Iraq ceased.

However, there are a number of reasons for questioning the conventional version of the Zanj uprising. First, the term "Zanj" is of

---

[2] James de Vere Allen, *Swahili Origins. Swahili Culture and the Shungwaya Phenomenon* (London: James Currey, 1993), 73.
[3] T.M. Ricks, "Slave Trade: Islamic World" in P. Finkelman and J.C. Miller (eds.) *Macmillan Encyclopedia of World Slavery*, vol. 2 (London: Simon & Schuster and Prentice Hall International, 1998), 833.

disputed origin and application. In Arabic it meant "Land of the blacks or Negroes", but probably derived from the Indian "Zanzbar" or the Persian Pahlevi "zangik", meaning respectively "country of the black man" and "Egyptian, Ethiopian, Moor, Negro; a savage". The term "Zanj" was only sometimes applied to the modern-day Swahili coast or its black population. Muslims often applied it pejoratively to all those of dark skin considered uncivilised "Kaffirs" or unbelievers. Al-Ṭabarī, the chief source for the "Zanj" revolt, indiscriminately conflates the terms "black" and "Zanj". There was similar confusion over the terms "Ethiopian", which could refer to Abyssinian highlanders, eastern Africans (including the Zanj), black Africans generally, or sometimes Indians; and *Kunlun* (see reference to *Kunlun* above).

Indeed, many "Zanj" rebels were not East African. The rebel leader, ʿAlī b. Muḥammad al-Zanjī, was neither African nor a slave. Born near Tehran, in Iran, he was well educated, and became a panegyric poet at the court of caliph al-Muntaṣir (r. 861–2) before rebelling against the Abbasid authorities. ʿAlī rallied local people, desert tribesmen, and *mawlā* – military personnel, usually former slaves, many of Central Asian origin – to his cause, and in 868 moved to the Basra marshlands where he forcibly enlisted "Zanj" gangs who comprised slaves, emancipated slaves, and probably conscripted peasants. Other rebel recruits included slave fugitives, renegade caliphate soldiers, and captive Arabs. Humphrey Fisher and John Hunwick consider most rebels of African origin to have been Ethiopians and Sudanese, and secondarily East Africans, Nubians, and probably West and Central Africans. Other "Zanj" rebels included gang supervisors, Bedouin horsemen, Abbasid officials, Abbasid soldiers (including Turks and Central Asians), and at least one Jew. By 882, the rebels numbered about 50,000, comprising chiefly local Arabs. Most African infantry in the Abbasid army stayed loyal to the regime, while some rebels, including "slaves", joined the imperial cause and in 883 helped to crush the uprising.

Also, while East Africans were sicklers and thus immune to the malaria in the Basra marshes, the inferred timeline for a significant eastern African Bantu-speaking genetic inflow into the Gulf countries is from 980, more than a century after the "Zanj" revolt. Moreover, studies of chromosomal haplotypes indicate different geographical origins for the sickle-cell trait in the Middle East. The "Arab-Indian", the dominant haplotype in Iraq, derived from the Indus Valley "Harappa" and Sasanian eras, and spread to Saudi Arabia, Bahrain, Kuwait, and Oman. The other four haplotypes are of sub-Saharan African origin: West African "Senegal" (Atlantic West Africa), Benin (central West Africa), Cameroon, and Bantu (central, east, and southern Africa). The predominant haplogroups amongst Marsh Arabs of Iraq are of autochthonous Middle Eastern origin. Southwest Asian and African contributions are weaker and are more evident in mtDNA, inherited solely from the mother, indicating a greater female than male African input into the local DNA pool. In addition, the greatest African affinity for the Y-chromosome haplogroups of the Basra marshlands are northwest Africa, the Sudan, Ethiopia, and Somalia, not the Swahili coast or its East African hinterland.

Through trade, tribute, and capture, the Abbasids obtained thousands of Indian, Turkic, European, and African slaves, most via overland networks. The indications are that from the seventh to fifteenth centuries most African slaves were shipped from Ethiopia and Somalia. By contrast, the trade in Zanj slaves was spasmodic and relatively small-scale because the Swahili coast was distant, trade with it comparatively risky, and slave supplies uncertain. As Arab geographer Ibn Ḥawqal noted in the ninth century, the Zanj littoral was "miserable and sparsely populated. It was hardly cultivated, with the exception of the outskirts of the king's residence".[4] Some scholars cite the work of Arab literary figure Al-Jāḥeẓ (776–869) as evidence of a large export trade in Zanj slaves, but he specifies that they originated not from the mainland, or Zanzibar, but from Pemba Island alone – which could not have supplied significant numbers.[5] Buzurg ibn Shahriyar in ca 950 is the first source to indicate that slaves were obtained from the East African mainland, while Al-Idrisi (1099–1165/6) noted that the ruler of Kish, an island at the entrance to the Persian Gulf, raided East Africa for slaves. However, these isolated references are insufficient to support the proposition of a large, regular trade in Zanj slaves in either the ninth century, or any time before 1600.

The chief potential East African slave source would have been the relatively populous agricultural communities in the interior, notably the intralacustrine region, for which archaeologist Peter Schmidt provides evidence of depopulation in the period from 500 to 700 CE.

---

[4] Quoted in Talhami, "The Zanj Rebellion Reconsidered", 446.
[5] Al-Jāḥeẓ. *Al-Fakhar al-Sudan min al-Abadh*. Trans. Pieter Derideaux. http://realhistoryww.com/world_history/ancient/Misc/Arab_texts/Arab_texts_2.htm (accessed 07/05/14).

However, Schmidt concludes that depopulation was predominantly due, not to the slave trade, but to the human impact on the environment, notably intensive iron production that resulted in deforestation and soil erosion. There is other evidence of depopulation associated with climate change. Population density in Africa is generally closely related to climate, specifically to rainfall. Following a wet period from around 500 CE, interior East Africa and the Great Lakes region including Lake Malawi experienced an extended arid period in the eighth century, while major droughts affected the Lake Tanganyika region from 700 to 850 and Mozambique from about 800 to 900. These droughts probably propelled significant human migration from equatorial East Africa to southern Africa which, by contrast, experienced an almost continuously wetter climate for the first five centuries CE and again from about 900 to 1300.

Additionally, large-scale, long-term slave-raiding and shipping would have incurred considerable costs. Slave-raiding parties needed to be recruited, armed, provisioned, and paid; and interpreters hired. Also, maritime trade was seasonal. Vessels could sail from Zanj to the Persian Gulf only in April to early May or September, before and after the stormiest period (mid-May to mid-August) of the southwest monsoon. Should contrary currents prevent boats from sailing north in March or April, they were obliged to "winter" in East Africa. The optimum departure point for ocean-going vessels returning to the Gulf from East Africa was from Zanzibar and points farther north, although they could sail from as far south as Kilwa, some 300 km south of Zanzibar. Thus a large-scale slave export trade would have involved significant numbers of well-guarded adult male captives being marched to the coast, shipped to coastal entrepôts, and there held, fed, and surveyed in stockades pending the arrival of the sailing season and the availability of sufficiently capacious, sea-worthy, and well-equipped boats.

The coastal archaeological evidence Horton cites in support of his argument for massive East African slave exports indicates East Africa-Persian Gulf commercial links but not specifically the slave trade. He asserts that a few chain links found in East Africa dating to the period from about 750 to 850 could "possibly" be interpreted as slave chains and indicate a trade notably in adult male slaves. However, they were unearthed in the Lamu not Zanzibar archipelago, and slave irons were a rarity in the Indian Ocean even at the height of the dhow slave trade in the nineteenth century. The transport of very large numbers of bonded males would have entailed large costs and risks in terms of surveillance and the possibility of revolt. Additionally, maritime transport of slaves in large quantities over long distances would have accentuated problems of space, sanitation, and provisions aboard ship. For example, ships' holds suffered from rat and cockroach infestation and, during storms, bilges quickly became foul with stagnant water. Starvation and disease were the main causes of death amongst slaves, who, often malnourished and physically weak, were particularly vulnerable to dysentery and infectious diseases. In all, the mortality rate among slaves on the voyage from East Africa to the Persian Gulf was probably a minimum of 20 per cent.

Indeed, commodities other than slaves fuelled the movement of the Muslim trading frontier south down the East African coast, notably gold, ivory, ambergris, tortoise shell, animal skins, dried fish, rock crystal, and high-grade iron ore. The Swahili coast became a significant slave export centre only from the mid-eighteenth century.

Enslavement in Highland Madagascar and the Swahili Slave Trade, 1500 to 1750

In 2003, Thomas Vernet published claims for a hitherto unsuspected Swahili-run slave trade network that existed from about 1500 to 1750.[6] Of particular interest is his assertion that the Swahili shipped chiefly highland Malagasy from ports in northwest Madagascar to Muslim markets throughout the western IOW, a traffic fuelled by population growth and internecine strife in highland Madagascar, and growing Muslim demand for slaves. Vernet estimated that the Swahili exported an annual average of 2,000 Malagasy in the early 1500s, 3,000 by the mid-1600s, 4,000 from 1660, and over 4,000 between 1690 and the 1750s, amounting to around 200,000 for the sixteenth century, 180,000 from 1600 to 1660, and 360,000 from 1660 to 1750, totalling some 740,000 for the entire period between 1500 and 1750. The figure would be yet higher if exports of Malagasy slaves from the Comoro

---

[6] Thomas Vernet, "Le commerce des esclaves sur la cote swahili, 1500–1750" *Azania* 38.1 (2003): 69–97 – republished in English as "Slave trade and slavery on the Swahili coast (1500–1750)" in Paul Lovejoy, Behnaz A. Mirzai, and Ismael M. Montana (eds.), *Slavery, Islam and Diaspora* (Trenton, NJ: Africa World Press 2009), 37–76. Many thanks to Thomas Vernet for his comments on this section.

Islands are included. Only from the mid-1700s, when traders switched to East African sources, did the export of Malagasy slaves to Muslim markets decline. Vernet thereby challenges the traditional view that in the seventeenth century Muslim merchants shipped from Madagascar between 400 and 1,500 slaves annually, and that the height of the slave trade from the Malagasy highlands was from 1770 to 1820 when numbers exported averaged 700 to 1,336 annually and in 1820 reached an exceptional peak of 4,000.

Vernet now acknowledges that his estimates may have been exaggerated, like those of many researchers pressurised by scholars of the Atlantic slave trade to produce comparative figures for the traffic in IOW slaves. However, his claims have gained wide academic acceptance, and he maintains that highland Madagascar was a significant source of slaves for the Swahili. This is highly problematic as he fails to take into account the environmental, economic, and demographic factors affecting highland Madagascar. First, the, period under review was the height of the LIA, when the Malagasy highlands probably experienced a comparatively arid period, notably from the 1790s to 1810s. Moreover, as noted in Chapter 8, oral traditions indicate three severe famines which occurred probably sometime between 1696 and 1716, in ca 1747, and in 1755–6. Of notable comparative significance is famine which from 1748 to 1751 and 1747 hit respectively Mozambique and Cape Colony; sulphur-rich volcanism from 1740 to 1744 and 1752 to 1756; and very strong ENSO effects in 1754 and 1759.

It is against this background that the demographic history of the Malagasy highlands needs to be considered. Madagascar was first permanently settled in the eighth century, but human activity became noticeable in the plateau interior only from the thirteenth century, and significant population growth associated with the adoption of intensive wet-rice cultivation from around 1500. The highest concentration of population – a cluster of eight villages in Ambohimanga – would have held about 2,500 people in the early 1600s, rising to 3,000 by 1700.

The highland economy was dominated by riziculture. Yields were inferior to coastal wet rice and swidden because of inferior soil fertility, low temperatures, wind and hail, and locust attacks. Highland soil needed to be assiduously broken, oxygenised, irrigated, and fertilised before a reasonable yield could be expected: an average family of four to five people, adults and children, working 330 days a year on one hectare of land, produced from 2,000 to 2,500 kg of rice. The manpower demands of both intensive riziculture, and the need to construct defensive settlements, led to an enlargement of *fanompoana* (unremunerated obligatory labour for the crown) from its original ritual and honorific function. Andrianjaka (r. ca 1610–30) first geographically concentrated the manpower of his subjects by restricting clans to certain localities. Subsequently, following the first major famine, Andriamasinavalona (r. ca 1675–1710) extended *fanompoana* to include all "first fruits". He also summoned *hova* – here denoting lower caste "Merina" freemen, but also commonly used outside the plateau to mean all those from present-day Imerina – labour for state infrastructure, notably in draining marshland, constructing dykes, and building grain silos. The silos, which were defended, attracted peasant cultivators seeking both protection and, in times of dearth, provisions. The resulting concentration of population facilitated the imposition by Andrianampoinimerina (r. ca 1787–1810) of further limits on the geographical mobility of his subjects in order to control their labour. He incorporated the territorially restricted communities, or *foko*, into larger regional units called *toko*, six of which formed greater Imerina, and claimed the labour of each male subject for six days each season (a total of 24 days a year) for "public works", notably in agriculture. By the end of the eighteenth century, *fanompoana* permitted the expansion of rice cultivation from one to two crops annually, thereby guaranteeing a regular agricultural surplus for the first time in Imerina's history.

It is in the context of the fragility of the agricultural base of the highland economy during the LIA, and intense all-year-round demand for labour, that the issue of enslavement and the slave trade must be evaluated. The annual efflux of 2,000 to 3,000 *hova* would have critically undermined the local economy, and this is reflected in the structure of slavery. Enslavement through warfare and raiding was common in the highlands. Merina royal traditions indicate that slaves become numerous due chiefly to warfare, but this occurred first under Andramasinavalona (r. ca 1675–1710), well after 1500, the year that a massive and continuous export of highland slaves allegedly started. Also, the inflow of foreign coins and arms, indices of the volume of external exchange, only gained magnitude in the early and late seventeenth century respectively.

Moreover, the Portuguese observation cited by Vernet that victors in war were captured rather than killed cannot be interpreted as indicating a massive investment in the slave export trade. Initially, conquering armies spared passive non-combatants, but killed captured male opponents and enslaved their wives and children. Central highlanders also kidnapped and enslaved "blacks" from the south – possibly Betsileo – and the wives and children of men executed for breaking royal ordinances. Most of the enslaved were retained locally, forming the *andevo*, or third of the three castes of Imerina. Those sold for export were chiefly "unransomable" criminals, rejected by their communities. Forms of enslavement changed in the wars that characterised Imerina from about 1720 to 1790 when fighting was effected largely with the goal of capturing enemy warriors and ransoming them back to their relatives. Only when the family could not afford the ransom was the captive retained or sold as a slave.

Armed conflict and slave-raiding were, like long-distance trade, restricted to the dry season from mid-April to mid-November, as over-land travel in the wet season was often impossible, notably between the interior and lowlands. Moreover, highlanders visiting the lowlands were highly vulnerable to malaria against which, unlike coastal peoples who carried the sickle-cell gene, they possessed no protection: in the early 1800s, some 25 to 50 per cent of Merina soldiers campaigning in the lowlands died each year. Given this, the time-consuming and costly nature of enslavement, and the 600 km overland trail to the northwest Madagascar, it is inconceivable that large highland slave caravans regularly reached the main northwestern ports as early as March and April.

Claude Allibert suggests that highlanders could have been marched to the coast during the dry season, shipped to the Comoros, and there held in camps.[7] However, such slaves would also have experienced high rates of mortality due to endemic malaria on the coast, and other diseases circulating along western IOW trade routes, such as smallpox which caused 40 to 70 per cent mortality amongst concentrated unvac-cinated populations. In 1640, of the 22 Malagasy slaves purchased by the EIC ship the *Francis*, 13 (59 per cent) developed smallpox on the voyage back to Surat where they died shortly after arrival. Had a traffic existed in highland Malagasy slaves of the magnitude and regularity postulated, it might also be expected that smallpox would

---

[7] Claude Allibert, "Une description turque de l'océan Indien au XVIe siècle, l'océan Indien occidental dans le kitab-i Bahrije de Piri Reis (1521)" *Études Océan Indien* 10 (1988): 197–220.

have appeared in the Malagasy highlands during the period under review. However, the evidence is that smallpox affected Imerina only following increased exposure to foreign trade from the late 1700s, major epidemics occurring in 1817, and 1833 to 1835.

A further reason for doubting the report of large annual *hova* slave caravans to the northwest ports is the claim that they were accompanied by 10,000 cattle from the interior. Animal husbandry was widespread in Madagascar, but the main grazing lands were the southern and western plains where cattle-raising was the chief occupation of the pastoral Bara, Mahafaly, Antandroy, and Sakalava, and in the northern highlands occupied by the Tsimihety. By contrast, the *hova* were agriculturalists and possessed few cattle until the Merina imperial expansion at the end of the eighteenth century.

In sum, the highlands could not have supplied the numbers of slaves indicated by Vernet. Only from the mid-eighteenth century, after agricultural surpluses were secured, substantial population growth occurred, and major internecine conflict erupted, did a steady and well-documented slave export trade develop from the highlands. However, it was directed to the burgeoning plantation economy of the French Mascarenes rather than the Swahili network that embraced northwest Madagascar.

It is possible that a significant number of coastal peoples were enslaved during the LIA. Cold, arid conditions affected southern Madagascar from 1690 to 1740 and from the 1790s to 1810s, with extreme drought around 1600 and in ca 1700. Reports of visiting vessels indicate considerable impoverishment of the local population, and of Menabe Sakalava slave raids on the population around Tulear, in the southwest. Northern Madagascar might also have been a source of slaves as, in contrast to areas further south, it experienced increased rainfall during the LIA as a result of a shift in the ITCZ to below 12°S. The northern tip of the island consequently experienced agricultural expansion and population growth, except possibly during markedly arid intervals that occurred in the northeast from 1594 to 1617, 1724 to 1746, and 1785 to 1799, and in the northwest around 1600, 1650, 1700, 1709, and 1770. However, it would have been difficult to obtain the magnitude of slaves indicated from coastal peoples, many of whom were members of decentralised and often highly mobile communities of fishermen, pastoralists, and forest dwellers.

This raises the question of alternative slave sources. Nicholas Buckeridge (ca 1625–1690) noted that Muslim traders found plentiful supplies of cheap slaves in East Africa.[8] This implies that the supply of East African slaves might easily have met demand from the Swahili coastal states, the surplus being shipped to markets in the Red Sea and Persian Gulf. In addition, from at least the early sixteenth century, Muslim traders exported via Massawa, Zeila, and Mocha a significant number of Christian Ethiopian slaves, whom they preferred to neighbouring "pagans". The trade continued vibrant into the nineteenth century. Abdul Sheriff has estimated that between 1827 and 1831, an average of 1,400 to 1,700 African slaves were annually imported into Muscat, some 75 per cent of them from East Africa and the remainder from Ethiopia.[9] Certainly, the transport costs and mortality rates for highland Malagasy slaves would have been significantly higher than for slaves from East Africa who experienced mortality rates of from 10 to 20 per cent aboard ships travelling to Persian Gulf markets which by sail were five to eight days' sail more distant from Madagascar than from the Swahili coast.

Other sources appear to confirm this. In July 1614, William Keeling, an EIC captain who spoke good Arabic, visited the Comoros and upon enquiry, reported that Madagascar's northwest coast provided 400 slaves annually to traders from Mogadishu, Pate, Brava, the Swahili coast, and to the Portuguese. In 1694, a VOC captain stated that by August that year, Muslim traders had already shipped from northwest Madagascar to the Red Sea the 400 slaves held in readiness for export. This suggests Malagasy slaves exports into the Muslim trade network of the western IOW amounted to between 5 and 10 per cent of the figures postulated by Vernet. Moreover, there were certain years, such as in 1710 at the start of a universally cold period, when it appears that few if any slaves were available in northwest Madagascar.

Servitude in Nineteenth-Century Indian Ocean Africa

The international economy that emerged during the nineteenth century had by 1900 drawn all but the most remote regions of the globe

---

[8] Nicholas Buckeridg], *Journal and Letter Book of Nicholas Buckeridge 1651–1654*, ed. John R. Jenson (Minneapolis: University of Minnesota Press, 1973).

[9] Abdul Sheriff, "The Slave Trade and its Fallout in the Persian Gulf" in Gwyn Campbell (ed.), *Abolition and its Aftermath in Indian Ocean Africa and Asia* (London: Routledge, 2005), 104–6.

into its orbit. Driven by the modern capitalist principles of supply and demand, and ever-accelerating technological change, it transformed labour relations. In the West an agricultural revolution underpinned sustained demographic growth, while the Industrial Revolution and liberal economic doctrines promoted the emergence of wage labour. In IOA, limited capital investment and a huge commercial boom heightened demand for labour to service international trade: to hunt, collect, and mine natural resources; grow subsistence crops; cultivate cash crops for IOW and European markets; and to facilitate rapidly expanding transport networks in porterage, and as dockworkers and sailors. However, this placed great structural strain on the IOW labour market as growth on the demand side was not matched by supply for two main reasons: uneven demographic growth and the prevalence of systems of bonded labour.

The population of Britain, Germany, and the United States increased almost fivefold in the hundred years prior to 1914, and that of Europe more than doubled from 190 million to 423 million. However, it took almost 200 years for the Asian population to double: it increased from about 415 million to 970 million between 1700 and 1900. In addition, demographic growth within the IOW was uneven. China's population increased rapidly during the eighteenth century to reach about 300 million in 1795. It climbed further to 420 million by 1850, but the rate of growth then slowed and by 1900 it stood at about 480 million. India's population increased by some 44 million between 1600 and 1800 to reach 161 million, and by 1901 stood at 283.4 million. Mainland Southeast Asia, the Philippines, Java, and South Sumatra also experienced significant population growth rates in the nineteenth century, albeit with periods of demographic crisis. Overall, however, between 1871 and 1921 the IOW population grew at an annual rate of only 0.4 per cent. Indeed, whereas in 1750, Asia possessed 64 per cent of the global population and Europe 21 per cent, by 1900 Asia's share of the world's population had fallen to 57 per cent, Europe had increased its share to 25 per cent, and the Americas to 10 per cent.

It is estimated that between 1750 and 1900, Africa's share of the global population declined from 13 to 8 per cent, population growth rates there expanding significantly only following systematic attempts to improve health from the 1920s. The conventional view is that demographic stagnation in nineteenth-century IOA was due chiefly to the slave trade. Thus Patrick Manning argued that "In the East African region from Mozambique to Kenya, a serious population decline occurred ... from about 1820 to 1890, as slaves were taken both to Muslim areas in Arabia and the Persian Gulf and to European-ruled territories in the Indian Ocean and the New World."[10] This loss, which by mid-century may have bled sub-Saharan Africa of half of its potential population of 100 million, was compounded from the late 1880s, at least in eastern Africa, by the impact of European conquest, human and animal diseases, and drought. However, it is now clear that in Madagascar, demographic stagnation, evident from the early 1830s, resulted from both man-made (warfare, slave-raiding, economic mismanagement, labour exploitation) and natural (disease, cyclones, climatic variations) causes. Such factors similarly affected the African continent, which additionally suffered acutely from rinderpest and other cattle diseases, notably from the 1880s.

The cycle of human-induced and natural disasters, and its demographic impact, forms the backdrop against which to consider IOA systems of unfree labour. Slavery was important: In the eighteenth and early nineteenth centuries, slaves comprised between 20 and 30 per cent of the population of many IOW societies, rising to over 50 per cent in parts of Africa. Indigenous IOW demand for slaves was generated first by traditional canons of conspicuous consumption. However, the nineteenth-century commercial boom also ensured rising demand for slaves for directly economic purposes associated with export commodities, such as pearls, dates, cotton, wool, and opium in the Persian Gulf, and cloves, coconuts, and grain on the Swahili coast. Such was demand that the IOW slave trade peaked in the nineteenth century despite increasing abolitionist scrutiny which induced slavers to adopt indirect routes and other evasionary tactics, and pass slaves off as non-slaves – porters, sailors, domestics, even kin. Large numbers of East Africans were sent to Zanzibar, Pemba, Somalia, Madagascar, and the Mascarenes, and some shipped to Cape Town. They were also exported to India and the Americas, while Indians were sent as slaves to Indonesia, Mauritius, Cape Town, and the Middle East. Most slaves to the Middle East originated initially from the Caucasus, Eastern Europe, and Africa, but the first two sources dried up due to the Russian advance south. Thus in the nineteenth and early twentieth centuries, the Middle East was supplied

[10] Patrick Manning, "The Slave Trade: The Formal Demography of a Global System" *Social Science History* 14.2 (1990): 258.

predominantly from Africa, secondarily from the Makran coast of Iran, but with some slaves arriving from Western India, and even from Indonesia and China. In all of these trades, sources, markets, routes, and slave functions varied considerably.

It is currently impossible to estimate with any precision the number of slaves traded in IOA given the duration of the slave trade there, and the limited nature of extant records. Even in European-dominated enclaves, statistics are patchy. Research is only just beginning into slave-ship journals and records in the region, but in contrast to the Atlantic system, IOW slaves rarely constituted a specialist cargo even on European-captained vessels. Thus attempts by scholars to calculate the number of slaves traded in the IOW are, at best, "guesstimates" that inevitably have considerable range. Because of the conventional focus on black slaves, the only IOW region with concentrated guesstimates for nineteenth-century slave exports is IOA, numbers ranging from 800,000 to over two million for continental East Africa, and 72,000 to double that figure for Madagascar. Ralph Austen considers that possibly 300,000 East Africans were shipped across the Red Sea and Gulf of Aden to meet Middle Eastern demand, and 500,000 from the Swahili coast.

Another major market for African slaves from the mid-eighteenth century were the Omani-run plantations on Zanzibar, growing chiefly cloves, and European plantations on the Mascarenes that increasingly focussed on sugar cane cultivation. Because demand was overwhelmingly for plantation labourers producing cash crops for export, slavery in these markets closely resembled that of the Atlantic system. This was particularly the case for Réunion and Mauritius where, unlike Zanzibar, European rather than Sharia law held sway. A third market developed from the 1820s in Madagascar where Merina law held slaves to be property in much the same way as in the Atlantic system. The major difference was that enslaved Merina, unlike African slaves, could be redeemed, that slaves were more vulnerable to accusations of sorcery for which the penalty was death, and that select slaves were sacrificed to bring their masters good fortune, or to serve them in the afterlife.

However, Africa also proved a market for non-African slaves. For example, from 1658 to 1807, the Cape imported slaves from Bengal, Coromandel, Malabar, Kerala, Cochin, Sri Lanka, Java, Sulawesi, Macassar, Bali, Timor, Ternate, Macao, Madagascar, the Mascarenes, and probably Banda and Iran. Moreover, most enslaved Africans were retained in Africa, including the western Indian Ocean islands, albeit often far from their region of origin. For instance, from the mid-eighteenth century, considerable numbers of East Africans were shipped to Zanzibar, Pemba, Somalia, Madagascar, the Mascarenes, and Cape Town, while significant numbers of enslaved Malagasy were retained in the island, and others exported, many to Réunion and Mauritius, and some to the Swahili coast and the Cape.

Early abolitionist pressure concentrated principally on the Atlantic. It had muted influence in the IOW, except in the Cape where, well before official abolition, the 1826 removal of measures protecting wine diverted investment into the far less labour-intensive wool-producing sector and effectively undermined slavery. Elsewhere, the lack of both capital and a wage labour force rendered academic any arguments that slave workers might be inefficient. Until the abolition of slavery, in British colonies in 1834 and in French colonies in 1848, all European-held territory in IOA initially depended largely on slaves to meet their labour demands. Thus, for example, Robert Farquhar, the first British governor of Mauritius, delayed anti-slave import measures in acknowledgement of requirements of local sugar planters for a cheap servile workforce.

However, slaves also failed to meet the growing demand for labour, and Western powers, notably Britain, applied heavy abolitionist pressure on indigenous IOW authorities with the aim of transforming slaves into free wage labourers. This prompted IOA powers, such as Egypt, Zanzibar, Imerina, and Ethiopia, to announce restrictions on the slave trade and slavery, but such measures proved largely ineffective, or were manipulated by indigenous regimes to divert slaves from private ownership to state-controlled pools of servile labour, as occurred in Madagascar. In some states, including Egypt under Muhammad Ali, and Imperial Madagascar, most productive labour was performed not by slaves but by nominally "free" corvée labour, which was also used to form indigenous armies (see Chapter 10).

Widespread slave ownership, and local elite control of nominally "free" subjects, drove Europeans in the IOW to adopt other forms of bonded labour. Thus indigenous convicts were sent by the Portuguese from Goa to Mozambique and by the Dutch from Batavia to the Cape. The use of penal labour increased in the transition years of abolition as slave labour progressively dwindled. For example, during the early nineteenth century the EIC despatched Indian convicts to Mauritius, ostensibly for public works but sometimes assigned, in return for payment, to private planters who often treated them as slaves. Penal labour was also widely used by indigenous authorities for the harshest types of work. For instance, the Merina regime in Madagascar used convicts in road construction, mining and foundries. Another temporary solution to labour shortages was the placing of "Prize Negroes", "liberated" from slaving ships, under contract to European settlers; those granted to Mauritian planters were leased to the government for four days a year to perform public works.

However, such measures were overshadowed by the indenture system. Indentured labour was an old institution, either formalised by contracts, or practised *ad hoc*, as with Khoi and San boys captured by Dutch farmers in the Cape interior during the eighteenth century. The captives were forced to work until the age of 25, by which time they were often married, with sons who were subject to similar obligations. Many parents refused to abandon their children, and so remained tied to the farm for life. Following abolition of the slave trade in 1807, the Caledon Code of 1809 formalised indenture in the Cape through a "pass" system, which restricted San and Khoi to farms in a system of "virtual slavery". Upon abolition in the Cape and Mauritius, ex-slaves, who received no financial assistance, were declared "apprentices" and obliged to continue working for a fixed period for their old masters. In the Cape, the system ended in 1838, but on Mauritius it continued until mid-century. Many apprentices fell into debt bondage to their old employer or chose to continue working for him in order to remain with their children.

Due to the failure of the 1834 and 1848 abolitionist measures to transform ex-slaves into pliant wage labourers, a new indenture system developed that generally involved five-year contracts. In IOA indentured recruits comprised essentially poverty stricken Indians, Chinese, and, for the French islands, Africans. Contemporary observers, and subsequent historians, have underlined that the recruitment, transport, and living and working conditions of indentured labourers were often similar to those of slaves.

Abolition was central to the "civilizing mission" that formed the pretext for the late nineteenth-century European scramble for colonies. Thus slavery was abolished by the British in Egypt in 1895 and Zanzibar in 1897, and by the French in Madagascar in 1896. For colonial regimes governed by precepts of self-financing, liberated slaves were a potentially vital source of taxation and manpower. A colonial priority was thus to transform the local working population into a free wage labour force. However, as vital was the goodwill of European settlers. In Somalia, the colonial regime initially permitted European settler farmers access to slave labour and even returned fugitive slaves to their owners, while in German East Africa, European planters were permitted to "ransom" slaves who were then obliged to work for them until the ransom had been paid off. Colonial authorities were also highly cautious about offending local slave-owning elites whose cooperation was required to administer the colony. Thus in Africa, the internal slave traffic remained buoyant for some 50 years after the banning of the external slave trade. In the Sudan, effective measures to curtail slavery were taken only in the late 1920s. In the Middle East, drawn into the British informal empire after the First World War, abolitionist pressure remained muted until the post-1945 era.

At the same time, by imposing monetary taxes, promoting commercialisation, and enforcing credit contracts, colonial regimes facilitated a growth in indebtedness. They maintained tight budgetary regimes that avoided funding public welfare programmes. As a result, debt bondage and enslavement through debt expanded considerably. However, colonial powers across the IOW categorised debt bondspeople separately from "true" slaves, considered debt bondage to be a benign form of private welfare, and generally condoned its continuation well into the twentieth century. As they often considered that slaves must be of African origin, and their condition the result of violent enslavement, they also proved reluctant to classify many types of non-African servile labour, notably that of women and children, as "slavery". In this sense, colonial regimes helped perpetuate forms of bondage across the IOW that underlie modern slavery in the region.

References

Abraham, Meera, *Two Medieval Merchant Guilds of South India* (New Delhi: Manohar, 1988).

Abu-Lughod, Janet L., *Before European Hegemony. The World System A.D. 1250–1350* (New York: Oxford University Press, 1989).

Alpers, Edward A., *Ivory and Slaves in East Central Africa: Changing Patterns of International Trade to the Later 19th Century* (Berkeley: University of California Press, 1975).

   The Indian Ocean in World History (Oxford: Oxford University Press, 2014).

Alpers, Edward A., Gwyn Campbell, and Michael Salman (eds.), *Resisting Bondage in Indian Ocean Africa and Asia* (London: Routledge, 2007).

Al-Ṭabarī, *The History of Al-Ṭabarī*. vol. 36. trans. David Waines (New York: State University of New York Press, 1992).

Anon, *The Periplus Maris Erythraei*, trans. & commentary, Lionel Casson (Princeton: Princeton University Press, 1989).

Arnold, David, "The Indian Ocean as a Disease Zone, 1500–1950" *South Asia* 14. 2 (1991): 1–21.

Armstrong, James C., "Madagascar and the Slave Trade in the Seventeenth Century" *Omaly sy Anio* 17–20 (1983–84): 211–232.

Asawi, Charles, *An Economic History of the Middle East and North Africa* (New York: Columbia University Press, 1982).

Ashtor, E., "The Kārimī Merchants" *Journal of the Royal Asiatic Society of Great Britain and Ireland* 1/2 (1956): 45–56.

Atwell, William S., "Volcanism and Short-term Climatic Change in East Asian and World History, c.1200–1699" *Journal of World History* 12. 1 (2001): 29–98.

Austen, Ralph A. and Daniel Headrick, "The Role of Technology in the African Past" *African Studies Review* 26. 3/4 (1983): 163–184.

Bacharach, J.L., "African Military Slaves in the Medieval Middle East: The Cases of Iraq (869–955) and Egypt (868–1171)" *International Journal of Middle East Studies* 13. 4 (1981): 471–495.

Barbosa, Duarte, *An Account of the Countries Bordering on the Indian Ocean and their Inhabitants (c.1518)* I (London, 1918).

Barendse, R.L., *The Arabian Seas. The Indian Ocean World of the Seventeenth Century* (Armonk: New York & London: England, 2002).

Batou, Jean, "Muhammad-'Ali's Egypt: A Command Economy in the 19th Century?" in Jean Batou (ed.), *Between Development and Underdevelopment. The Precocious Attempts at Industrialization of the Periphery (1800–1870)* (Genève: Droz, 1991), 181–218.

Berg, Gerald M., "Riziculture and the Founding of Monarchy in Imerina" *Journal of African History* 22.3 (1981): 289–308.

Blench Roger M. and Kevin MacDonald (eds.), *The Origins and Development of African Livestock: Archaeology, Genetics, Linguistics, and Ethnography* (New York: Routledge, 2000).

Boivin, Nicole, Alison Crowther, Richard Helm, and Dorian Q. Fuller, "East Africa and Madagascar in the Indian Ocean World" *Journal of World Prehistory* 26 (2013): 213–281.

Boomgaard, Peter, *Southeast Asia: An Environmental History* (Santa Barbara, CA: ABC-Clio, 2007).

Bose, Sugata, *A Hundred Horizons. The Indian Ocean in the Age of Global Empire* (Harvard: Harvard University Press, 2006).

Bower, John, "Early Food Production in Africa" *Evolutionary Anthropology* 4. 4 (2005): 130–139.

Brook, George A., Margaret A. Rafter, L. Bruce Railsback, Shaw-Wen Sheen, and Joyce Lundberg, "A High-Resolution Proxy Record of Rainfall and ENSO since AD 1550 from Layering in Stalagmites from Anjohibe Cave, Madagascar" *The Holocene* 9. 6 (1999): 695–705.

Brown, Nathan, "Brigands and State Building: The Invention of Banditry in Modern Egypt" *Comparative Studies in Society and History* 32. 2 (1990): 258–281.

Brummett, Palmira, *Ottoman Seapower and Levantine Diplomacy in the Age of Discovery* (Albany: State University of New York Press, 1994).

Butzer, K.W., "Rise and Fall of Axum, Ethiopia: A Geo-Archaeological Interpretation" *American Antiquity* 46. 3 (1981): 471–495.

Cain, P.J., *Economic Foundations of British Expansion Overseas 1815–1914* (London: Macmillan Press, 1980).

Campbell, Gwyn, "Slavery and Fanompoana: The Structure of Forced Labour in Imerina (Madagascar), 1790–1861" *Journal of African History* 29. 2 (1988): 463–486.

"The Menalamba Revolt and Brigandry in Imperial Madagascar, 1820–1897" *International Journal of African Historical Studies* 24. 2 (1991): 259–291.

The Structure of Slavery in Indian Ocean Africa and Asia (London: Frank Cass, 2004).

An Economic History of Imperial Madagascar, 1750–1895: The Rise and Fall of an Island Empire (Cambridge: Cambridge University Press, 2005).

Early Exchange between Africa and the Wider Indian Ocean World (New York: Palgrave, 2016).

"Servitude and the Changing Face of Demand for Labor in the Indian Ocean World, c.1800–1900" in Bob Harms, Bernard Freamon, and David W. Blight (eds.), *Slavery and the Slave Trades in the Indian Ocean World: Global Connections and Disconnections* (New Haven: Yale University Press, 2017), 23–44.

"Environment and Enslavement in Highland Madagascar, 1500–1750: The Case for the Swahili Slave Export Trade Reassessed" in Gwyn Campbell (ed.), *Bondage and the Environment in the Indian Ocean World* (Cham, Switzerland: Springer International, 2018), 49–78.

Carter, Marina, *Servants, Sidars and Settlers. Indians in Mauritius, 1834–1874* (Delhi: Oxford University Press, 1995).

Casale, Giancarlo, *The Ottoman Age of Exploration* (Oxford: Oxford University Press, 2010).

Chamberlain, M.E., *The Scramble for Africa* (Burnt Mill, Essex: Longman, 1984).

Chami, Felix A., "Roman Beads from the Rufiji Delta, Tanzania: First Incontrovertible Archeological Link with the *Periplus*" *Current Anthropology* 40. 2 (1999): 237–241.

Chami, Felix A., *The Unity of African Ancient History 3000 BC to AD 500* (Dar es Salaam, Tanzania: E & D Ltd, 2006).

Chami, Felix A. and Paul J. Msemwa, "A New Look at Culture and Trade on the Azanian Coast" *Current Anthropology*, 38. 4 (1997): 673–677.

Chatterjee. Indrani and Richard Maxwell Eaton (eds.), *Slavery and South Asian History* (Bloomington: Indiana University Press, 2007).

Chaudhuri, K.N., *Trade and Civilisation in the Indian Ocean. An Economic History from the Rise of Islam to 1750* (Cambridge: Cambridge University Press, 1985).

Asia Before Europe. Economy and Civilisation of the Indian Ocean from the Rise of Islam to 1750 (Cambridge: Cambridge University Press, 1992).

Christie, Jan Wisseman, "Javanese Markets and the Asian Sea Trade Boom of the Tenth to Thirteenth Centuries A.D." *Journal of the Economic and Social History of the Orient* 41. 3 (1998): 344–381.

Clarence-Smith, William Gervase (ed.), *The Economics of the Indian Ocean Slave Trade in the Nineteenth Century* (London: Frank Cass, 1989).

Cockburn, T. Aidan, "Infectious Diseases in Ancient Populations" *Current Anthropology* 12. 1 (1971): 45–62.

Cooper, Frederick, *Plantation Slavery on the East Coast of Africa* (Portsmouth, N.H.: Heinemann, 1997).

Cordell, Dennis D. and Joel W. Gregory (eds.), *African Population and Capitalism: Historical Perspectives* (Boulder: Westview Press, 1987).

Crummey, Donald and Shumet Sishagne, "Land Tenure and the Social Accumulation of Wealth in Eighteenth-Century Ethiopia: Evidence from the Qwesqwam Land Register" *International Journal of African Historical Studies* 24. 2 (1991): 241–258.

Dewar, Robert, "Madagascar: Early Settlement" in John Middleton and J.C. Miller (eds.), *New Encyclopedia of Africa* vol. 3 (Detroit: Thomson/Gale, 2008), 439–441.

Dewar Robert E. and Henry T. Wright, "The Culture History of Madagascar" *Journal of World Prehistory* 7. 4 (1993): 417–466.

Diamond, Jared, *Guns, Germs, and Steel: The Fates of Human Societies* (New York: W.W. Norton, 1997).

Dick-Read, Robert, *The Phantom Voyagers: Evidence of Indonesian Settlement in Africa in Ancient Times* (Winchester: Thurlton Publishing, 2005).

Dols, Michael W., "Plague in Early Islamic History" *Journal of the American Oriental Society* 94. 3 (1974): 371–383.

Donham, Donald and Wendy James (eds.), *The Southern Marches of Imperial Ethiopia* (Oxford: James Currey, 2002).

Ehret, Christopher, *An African Classical Age. Eastern and Southern Africa in World History, 1000 B.C. to A.D. 400* (Charlottesville: University Press of Virginia & James Currey, 1998).

Ekblom, Anneli, "Forest-Savanna Dynamics in the Coastal Lowland of Southern Mozambique since c. AD 1400" *The Holocene* 18. 8 (2008): 1247–1257.

Elkiss, T.H., *The Quest for an African Eldorado: Sofala, Southern Zambezia, and the Portuguese, 1500–1865* (Brandeis University Mass: Crossroads Press, 1981).

Ellenblum, Ronnie, *The Collapse of the Eastern Mediterranean. Climate Change and the Decline of the East, 950–1072* (Cambridge: Cambridge University Press, 2013).

Emile-Geay, Julien, Richard Seager, Mark A. Cane, Edward R. Cook, and Gerald H. Haug, "Volcanoes and ENSO Over the Past Millennium" *Journal of Climate* 21. 13 (2008): 3134–3148.

Fahmy, Khaled, *All the Pasha's Men. Mehmed Ali, his Army and the Making of Modern Egypt* (Cambridge: Cambridge University Press, 1997).

Fernyhough, Timothy, "Slavery and the Slave Trade in Southern Ethiopia in the 19th Century" *Slavery & Abolition* 9: 39 (1988): 103–130.

Finley, Moses, *Ancient Slavery and Modern Ideology* (London: Chatto and Windus, 1980).

Fisher, Alan, "Zanj" in P. Finkelman and J.C. Miller (eds.) *Macmillan Encyclopedia of World Slavery* vol. 2 (New York: Macmillan Reference USA, 1998), 967.

Flecker, Michael, "A Ninth-Century AD Arab or Indian Shipwreck in Indonesia: First Evidence for Direct Trade with China" *World Archaeology* 32. 3 (2001): 335–354.

Forslund, Anna-Lena, *Pottery and East Africa* (Uppsala: Uppsala universitet, 2003).

Frank, André Gunder, *ReORIENT: Global Economy in the Asian Age* (Berkeley: Berkeley University Press, 1998).

Fuller, Dorian Q., George Willcox, and Robin G. Allab, "Early Agricultural Pathways: Moving Outside the 'Core Area' Hypothesis in Southwest Asia" *Journal of Experimental Botany* 63. 2 (2012): 617–633.

Gifford-Gonzalez, Diane and Olivier Hanotte, "Domesticating Animals in Africa: Implications of Genetic and Archaeological Findings" *Journal of World Prehistory* 24 (2011): 1–23.

Gilbert, Erik, *Dhows and the Colonial Economy of Zanzibar, 1860–1970* (Athens, OH: Ohio University Press, 2004).

Gordon, M.S., "Preliminary Remarks on Slaves and Slave Labor in the Third/ Ninth Century 'Abbāsid Empire" in L. Culbertson (ed.) *Slaves and Households in the Near East* (Chicago: Oriental Institute of the University of Chicago 2011), 71–84.

Grove, Richard, "El Nino Chronology and the History of Socio-economic and Agrarian Crisis in South and Southeast Asia 1250–1900" in Y.P. Abrol, Satpal Sangwan, and Mithilesh K. Tiwari (eds.), *Land Use – Historical Perspectives: Focus on Indo-Gangetic Plains* (New Delhi: Allied Publishers, 2002), 147–157.

Le Guennec-Coppens, Françoise, "Social and Cultural Integration: A Case Study of the East African Hadramis" *Africa: Journal of the International African Institute* 59. 2 (1989): 185–195.

Gwynne, M.D., "The Origin and Spread of Some Domestic Food Plants of Eastern Africa" in H.N. Chittick and R.I. Rotberg (eds.), *East Africa and the Orient* (New York: Africana Publishing Company, 1975), 248–271.

Hardyman, J.T., "The Madagascar Slave-Trade to the Americas (1632–1830)" in Association Historique Internationale de l'Ocean Indien Congrès, *Océan Indien et Méditerrannée: Travaux du Sixiéme Colloque International d'Histoire Maritime et du Deuxieme Congrès de l'Association Historique Internationale de l'Ocean Indicen (sesión de Lourenço Marques: 13–18 Août 1962)* (Lisboa: S.E.V.P.E.N. 1964), 501–521.

Hartwell, Robert, "Markets, Technology, and the Structure of Enterprise in the Development of the Eleventh-Century Chinese Iron and Steel Industry" *Journal of Economic History* 26. 1 (1966): 29–58.

Hassen, Mohammed, "Conquest, Tyranny, and Ethnocide against the Oromo: A Historical Assessment of Human Rights Conditions in Ethiopia, ca. 1880s-2002" *Northeast African Studies* 9. 3 (2002): 15–50.

Hastenrath, Stefan, "Variations of East African Climate During the Past Two Centuries" *Climatic Change* 50 (2001): 209–217.

Holcomb Bonnie K. and Sisai Ibssa, *The Invention of Ethiopia. The Making of a Dependent Colonial State in Northeast Africa* (Trenton, NJ: The Red Sea Press, 1990).

Hopkins, A.G., "The Victorians and Africa: A Reconsideration of the Occupation of Egypt, 1882" *The Journal of African History* 27. 2 (1986): 363–391.

Hornell, James, "Indonesian Influence on East African Culture" *Journal of the Royal Anthropological Institute of Great Britain and Ireland* 64 (1934): 305–332.

Horton, Mark, "Early Maritime Trade and Settlement along the Coasts of Eastern Africa" in J. Reade (ed.) *Indian Ocean in Antiquity* (Hoboken, NJ: Taylor and Francis: 2009): 439–459.

Shanga: The Archaeology of a Muslim Trading Community on the Coast of East Africa (London: British Institute in Eastern Africa, 1996).

"EAST AFRICA: Persian Relations with the Lands of the East African Coast, Particularly Somalia, Kenya, and Tanzania" *Encyclopædia Iranica* (1985) – www.iranicaonline.org/articles/east-africa (published online December 2011).

Horton Mark and John Middleton, *The Swahili. The Social Landscape of a Mercantile Society* (Oxford: Blackwell, 1988).

Hourani, George F., *Arab Seafaring in the Indian Ocean in Ancient and Early Medieval Times* (Princeton: Princeton University Press, 1995).

Issar, Arie S. and Mattanyah Zohar, *Climate Change – Environment and Civilization in the Middle East* (Berlin: Springer, 2004).

Jaschok, Maria and Suzanne Miers (eds.) *Women and Chinese Patriarchy: Submission, Servitude and Escape* (Hong Kong: Hong Kong University Press, 1995).

Jiang, Jianmim, Roy Mendelssohn, Franklin Schwing, and Klaus Fraedrich, "Coherency Detection of Multiscale Abrupt Changes in Historic Nile Flood Levels" *Geophysical Research Letters* 29. 8 (2002): 112–114.

Ju-Kua, Chau, *Chau Ju-Kua: His Work on the Chinese and Arab Trade in the Twelfth and Thirteenth Centuries, Entitled Chu-fan-chï*, trans. and edited by Friedrich Hirth and W.W. Rockhill (Taipei: Ch'eng-Wen, 1967).

Kjekshus, Helge, *Ecology Control and Economic Development in East African History* (London: Heinemann, 1977), esp. ch. 1.

Klein, Martin A. (ed.), *Breaking the Chains: Slavery, Bondage, and Emancipation in Modern Africa and Asia* (Madison: University of Wisconsin Press, 1993).

Kusuma, Pradiptajati, Murray P. Cox, Denis Pierron, Harilanto Razafindrazaka, Nicolas Brucato, Laure Tonasso, Helena Loa Suryadi, Thierry Letellier, Herawati Sudoyo, and François-Xavier Ricaut, "Mitochondrial DNA and the Y Chromosome Suggest the Settlement of Madagascar by Indonesian Sea Nomad Populations" *BMC Genomics* 16. 191 (2015) DOI 10.1186/s12864-015-1394-7.

Labib, Subhi Y., "Capitalism in Medieval Islam" *Journal of Economic History* 29. 1 (1969): 79–96.

Lawson, Fred H., "Rural Revolt and Provincial Society in Egypt, 1820–1824" *International Journal of Middle Eastern Studies* 13 (1981): 131–153.

Lejju, B.J., P. Robertshaw, and D. Taylor, "Africa's Earliest Bananas?" *Journal of Archaeological Science* 33 (2006): 102–103.

Liesegang, Gerhard, Helma Pasch, and Adam Jones (eds.) *Figuring African Trade. Proceedings of the Symposium on the Quantification and Structure of the Import and Export and Long Distance Trade in Africa 1800–1913* (Berlin: Dietrich Reimer 1986).

Little Lester K. (ed.), *Plague and the End of Antiquity. The Pandemic of 541–750* (Cambridge: Cambridge University Press, 2007).

Lovejoy, Paul E., *Transformations in Slavery. A History of Slavery in Africa* (Cambridge: Cambridge University Press, 2012).

Low, Pak Sum, *Climate Change and Africa* (Cambridge: Cambridge University Press, 2005).

Lückge, Andreas, H. Doose-Rolinski, A.A. Khan, H. Schulz, and U von Rad, "Monsoonal Variability in the Northeastern Arabian Sea during the Past 5000 Years: Geochemical Evidence from Laminated Sediments" *Palaeography, Palaeoclimatology, Palaeoecology* 167 (2001): 273–286.

Mahdi, Waruno, "Linguistc and Philological Data Towards a Chronology of Austronesian Activity in India and Sri Lanka" in Roger Blench and Matthew Spriggs (eds.), *Archaeology and Language IV: Language Change and Cultural Transformation* (London: Routledge, 1999), 160–242.

Mani, A. and Geoff Wade (eds.), *Early Interactions between South and Southeast Asia. Reflections on Cross-Cultural Exchange* (Singapore: ISEAS, 2011).

Manning, Patrick, *Slavery and African Life. Occidental, Oriental, and African Slave Trades* (Cambridge: Cambridge University Press, 2006).

Martin, B.G., "Migrations from the Hadramawt to East Africa and Indonesia, c.1200 to 1900" *Centre of Arabic Documentation Research Bulletin* 7. 1–2 (1971): 367–390.

Al-Sayyid Marsot and Afaf Lufti, *Egypt in the Reign of Muhammad Ali* (Cambridge: Cambridge University Press, 1990).

McCann, James C., *People of the Plow. An Agricultural History of Ethiopia, 1800–1990* (Oxford: University of Wisconsin Press, 1995).

McCleary, Rachel M., "Salvation, Damnation, and Economic Incentives" *Journal of Contemporary Religion* 22. 1 (2007): 49–74.

McNeill, William, *Plagues and Peoples* (Garden City, NY: Anchor Press, 1976).

McPherson, Kenneth, *The Indian Ocean: A History of People and the Sea* (Delhi: Oxford University Press, 1993).

Metcalf, Thomas, *Imperial Connections: India in the Indian Ocean Arena, 1860–1920* (Berkeley: University of California Press, 2007).

Miers, Suzanne and Igor Kopytoff (eds.), *Slavery in Africa: Historical and Anthropological Perspectives* (Madison: University of Wisconsin Press, 1979).

Miers, Suzanne and Martin A. Klein (eds.), *Slavery in Colonial Africa* (London: Frank Cass, 1998).

Mikhail, Alan, "Unleashing the Beast: Animals, Energy, and the Economy of Labor in Ottoman Egypt" *American Historical Review* 118. 2 (2013): 317–348.

Miller, J. Innes, *The Spice Trade of the Roman Empire 29 B.C. to A.D. 641* (Oxford: Clarendon Press, 1969).

Morton, Fred, "East Africa: Swahili Region" in P. Finkelman and J.C. Miller (eds.) *Macmillan Encyclopedia of World Slavery* vol. 1 (London: Simon & Schuster and Prentice Hall International, 1998), 2.

Munro, J. Forbes, *Africa and the International Economy 1800–1960. An Introduction to the Modern Economic History of Africa South of the Sahara* (London: J.M. Dent, 1976).

Murdock, George Peter, "Staple Subsistence Crops of Africa" *Geographical Review* 50. 4 (1960): 523–540.

Nicholson, Sharon E., "The Nature of Rainfall Variability over Africa on Time Scales of Decades to Millennia" *Global and Planetary Change* 26 (2000): 137–158.

Nicholson, Sharon E., David J. Nash, Brian M. Chase, Stefan W. Grab, Timothy M. Shanahan, Dirk Verschuren, Asfawossen Asrat, Anne-Marie Lézine, and Mohammed Umer, "Temperature Variability Over Africa During the last 2000 Years" *The Holocene* 23. 8 (2013): 1085–1094.

Nöldeke, T, *Sketches from Eastern History* (London: Adam and Charles Black, 1892).

Nurse, Derek and Thomas Spear, *The Swahili. Reconstructing the History and Language of an African Society, 800–1500* (Philadelphia: University of Philadelphia Press, 1985).

Owen, Roger, *The Middle East in the World Economy 1800–1914* (London: Methuen, 1981).

Pankhurst, Richard, *Economic History of Ethiopia 1800–1935* (Addis Ababa: Haile Sellassie I University Press, 1968).

Patnaik, Utsa and Manjari Dingwaney (eds.), *Chains of Servitude, Bondage and Slavery in India* (Hyderabad: Sangam Books, 1985).

Pearson, M.N. (ed.), *An Expanding World. The European Impact on World History II. Spices in the Indian Ocean World* (Gateshea: Variorum, 1996).

Pearson, Michael, *The Indian Ocean* (London: Routledge, 2003).

Pires, Tomé, *The Suma Oriental of Tomé Pires (1512–15)*, trans. A. Cortesao, 2 vols. (London: Hakluyt Society, 1944).

Platt, Virginia Bever, "The East India Company and the Madagascar Slave Trade" *William and Mary Quarterly* 26. 4 (1969): 548–577.

Ponting, Clive, *A Green History of the World* (London: Penguin, 1993).

Popovic, A., *The Revolt of African Slaves in Iraq in the 3rd/9th Century* (Princeton: Markus Wiener, 1999).

Pouwels, Randall L., "Eastern Africa and the Indian Ocean to 1800: Reviewing Relations in Historical Perspective" *International Journal of African Historical Studies* 35. 2–3 (2002): 385–425.

Prakash, Om, *Precious Metals and Commerce. The Dutch East India Company in the Indian Ocean Trade* (Aldershot, Hamps & Brookfield, Vermont: Variorum, 1994).

Prestholdt, Jeremy, *Domesticating the World: African Consumerism and the Genealogies of Consumerism* (Berkeley: University of California Press, 2008).

Quinn, William H., "A Study of Southern Oscillation-Related Climatic Activity for A.D. 622–1990 Incorporating Nile River Flood Data" in Henry F. Diaz and Vera Markgraf (eds.), *El Niño: Historical and Paleoclimatic Aspects of the Southern Oscillation* (Cambridge: Cambridge University, 1992), 119–150.

Rashidi, R., "Iraq: The African Presence in Early Iraq" in C.E.B. Davies (ed.) *Encyclopedia of the African Diaspora: Origins, Experiences, and Culture* (Santa Barbara: ABC-CLIO, 2008), 575.

Reid, Anthony (ed.), *Slavery, Bondage and Dependency in Southeast Asia* (New York: St. Martin's Press, 1983).

Southeast Asia in the Age of Commerce, 1450–1680 2 vols (New Haven: Yale University Press, 1988 and 1993).

Ricks, Thomas M., "Persian Gulf Seafaring and East Africa: Ninth-Twelfth Centuries" *African Historical Studies* 3. 2 (1970): 339–357.

Ricks, T.M., "Slave Trade: Islamic World" in P. Finkelman and J.C. Miller (eds.) *Macmillan Encyclopedia of World Slavery* vol. 2 (London: Simon & Schuster and Prentice Hall International, 1998), 833.

Robinson, Ronald and John Gallagher, *Africa and the Victorians: the Official Mind of Imperialism* (London: Macmillan, 1978).

Rockel, Stephen J., "'A Nation of Porters': The Nyamwezi and the Labour Market in Nineteenth-Century Tanzania" *The Journal of African History* 41. 2 (2000): 173–195.

Roy, Tirthankar, *India in the World Economy: From Antiquity to the Present* (Cambridge: Cambridge University Press, 2012).

Rubenson, Sven, "Some Aspects of the Survival of Ethiopian Independence in the Period of the Scramble for Africa" *University College Review* 1. 1 (1961): 8–24.

Rubenson, Sven, "Conflict and Environmental Stress in Ethiopian History: Looking for Correlations" *Journal of Ethiopian Studies* 24 (1991): 71–96.

Ruddiman, William F., "The Anthropogenic Greenhouse Era began Thousands of Years Ago" *Climate Change* 61 (2003): 261–293.

Russell J.M. and T.C. Johnson, "Little Ice Age Drought in Equatorial Africa: Intertropical Convergence Zone Migrations and El Niño–Southern Oscillation Variability" *Geology* 35.1 (2007): 21–24.

Santoro, Michael M., Fekri A. Hassan, M.M. Abdel Wahab, Randall S. Cerveny, and Robert C. Balling Jr, "An Aggregated Climate Teleconnection Index Linked to Historical Egyptian Famines of the Last Thousand Years" *The Holocene* 25. 5 (2015): 872–879.

Sauer, Carl O., *Seeds, Spades, Hearths, and Herds. The Domestication of Animals and Foodstuffs* (Cambridge: MIT Press, 1972).

Schmidt, P.R., "Early Exploitation and Settlement in the Usambara Mountains" in A.C. Hamilton and R. Bensted-Smith (eds.) *Forest Conservation in the East Usambara Mountains, Tanzania* (Gland, Switzerland: IUCN, 1989), 75–78.

Iron Technology in East Africa. Symbolism, Science, and Archeology (Bloomington: Indiana University Press, 1997).

Schottenhammer, Angela (ed.), *The Emporium of the World: Maritime Quanzhou, 1000–1400* (Leiden: Brill, 2001).

Schove, D.J., "African Droughts and the Spectrum of Time" in David Dalby, R.J. Harrison Church, and Fatima Bezzaz (eds.), *Drought in Africa* 2 (London: International African Institute, 1977), 38–53.

Selassie, Yohannes Gebre "Plague as a Possible Factor for the Decline and Collapse of the Aksimite Empire: A New Interpretation" *ITYOPIS: Northeast African Journal of Social Sciences and Humanities* 1 (2011): 36–61.

Sheriff, Abdul, *The Dhow Cultures of the Indian Ocean: Cosmopolitanism, Commerce & Islam* (London: C. Hurst, 2010).

Slaves, Spices & Ivory in Zanzibar (London: James Currey, 1987).

Sibree, James, "Industrial Progress in Madagascar" *Antananarivo Annual and Madagascar Magazine* 22 (1898): 129–136.

Silverstein, Adam J., *Islamic History: A Very Short Introduction* (Oxford: Oxford University Press, 2010).

Simpson, W. J., *A Treatise on Plague: Dealing with the Historical, Epidemiological, Clinical, Therapeutic and Preventive Aspects of the Disease* (Cambridge: Cambridge University Press, 2010).

Spinage, Clive, *African Ecology: Benchmarks and Historical Perspectives* (Berlin: Springer, 2012).

Strandes, Justus, *The Portuguese Period in East Africa* (Nairobi: Kenya Literature Bureau, 1989).

Subrahmanyam, Sanjay (ed.), *Merchants, Markets and the State in Early Modern India* (Delhi: Oxford University Press, 1990).

Sutherland, Heather, "Believing is Seeing: Perspectives on Political Power and Economic Activity in the Malay World 1700–1940" *Journal of Southeast Asian Studies* 26. 1 (1995): 133–146.

Talharni, Ghada Hashetn, "The Zanj Rebellion Reconsidered" *International Journal of African Historical Studies* 10. 3 (1977): 443–461.

The Christian Topography of Cosmas, an Egyptian Monk, trans. J.W. McCrindle (London: Hakluyt Society, 1897).

Tibebu, Teshale, "Ethiopia: The 'Anomaly' and 'Paradox' of Africa" *Journal of Black Studies* 26. 4 (1996): 414–430.

Toledano, Ehud R., *State and Society in Mid-Nineteenth-Century Egypt* (Cambridge: Cambridge University Press, 1990).

Tolmacheva, Marina A., "Towards a Definition of the Term Zanj" *Azania* 21 (1986): 105–113.

Tucker, William F., "Natural Disasters and the Peasantry in Mamlūk Egypt" *Journal of the Economic and Social History of the Orient* 24. 2 (1981): 215–224.

de Vere Allen, James, "Swahili Culture and the nature of East Coast Settlement" *International Journal of African Historical Studies* 14. 2 (1981): 306–334.

Vernet, Thomas, "Slave Trade and Slavery on the Swahili coast (1500–1750)" in Paul Lovejoy, Behnaz A. Mirzai, and Ismael M. Montana (eds.), *Slavery, Islam and Diaspora* (Trenton, NJ: Africa World Press 2009), 37–76.

Verschuren, Dirk, "Decadal and Century-Scale Climate Variability in Tropical Africa during the past 2000 Years" in R. W. Battarbee, Françoise Gasse, and Catherine E Stickley (eds) *Past Climate Variability through Europe and Africa* (Dordrecht: Kluwer 2004), 139–158.

Verschuren, Dirk, Kathleen R. Laird, and Brian F. Cumming, "Rainfall and Drought in Equatorial East Africa during the Past 1,100 Years" *Nature* 403 (2000): 410–414.

Wade, Geoff, "An Early Age of Commerce in Southeast Asia, 900–1300 CE" *Journal of Southeast Asian Studies* 40.2 (2009): 221–265.

Wade, Geoff, "Early Muslim Expansion in South-East Asia, Eighth to Fifteenth Centuries" in David O. Morgan and Anthony Reid (eds.), *The New Cambridge History of Islam vol. 3: The Eastern Islamic World Eleventh to Eighteenth Centuries* (Cambridge: Cambridge University Press, 2010), 366–408.

Wang, Xunming, Fahu Chen, Jiawu Zhang, Yi Yang, Jijun Li, Eerdun Hasi, Caixia Zhang, and Dunsheng Xia, "Climate, Desertification, and the Rise and Collapse of China's Historical Dynasties" *Human Ecology* 38 (2010): 157–172.

Warmington, E.H., *The Commerce between the Roman Empire and India* (New Delhi: Munshiram Manoharlai, 1995) – reprint of 1928 edition.

Watson, James L. (ed.), *Asian and African Systems of Slavery* (Oxford: B. Blackwell, 1980).

Wilbur, C. Martin, *Slavery in China in the former Han Dynasty, 206 B.C.–A.D. 25* (Chicago, Field Museum of Natural History Publication, 1943).

Wils, Tommy H.G., U. G. W. Sass-Klaassen, Z. Eshetu, A. Bräuning, A. Gebrekirstos, C. Couralet, I. Robertson, R. Touchan, M. Koprowski, D. Conway, K.R. Briffa, and H. Beeckman, "Towards a Reconstruction of Blue Nile Baseflow from Ethiopian Tree Rings" *The Holocene* 20. 6 (2010): 843.

Wils, T.H.G., U. G. W. Sass-Klaassen, Z. Eshetu, A. Bräuning, A. Gebrekirstos, C. Couralet, I. Robertson, R. Touchan, M. Koprowski, D. Conway, K.R. Briffa, and H. Beeckman, "Dendrochronology in the Dry Tropics: The Ethiopian Case" *Trees* (2011) DOI 10.1007/s00468-010-0521-y.

Wink, André, *Al-Hind. The Making of the Indo-Islamic World* 2 vols (Leiden: Brill, 1996 and 1997).

Wrigley, Christopher, "Speculations on the Economic Prehistory of Africa" *Journal of African History* 1. 2 (1960): 189–203.

Wright, H.T., "Early State Dynamics as a Political Experiment" *Journal of Anthropological Research* 62. 3 (2006): 305–319.

Young, Gary K., *Rome's Eastern Trade. International Commerce and Imperial Policy, 31 BC–AD 305* (London: Routledge, 2001).

Zewde, Bahru, *History of Modern Ethiopia, 1855–1974* (London: James Currey, 1991).

Index

military
  conflict, 113, 137, 143, 148, 150–151,
    160, 163–165, 185, 208, 215, 224,
    228, 240, 271
  conquest, 21, 50, 90, 103, 143, 155,
    168, 174, 208, 211, 216, 225, 229,
    242, 275
  conscription, 77, 193, 212, 220,
    221–223, 226, 227, 242, 244, 254
  technology, 203–205, 207–208, 240,
    see also armaments, weapons
mill, 205
millet, 22, 25–30, 57, 87, 120, 142, 195
mining, 122, 201, 256, 258, 278
missionaries, 105, 193, 200, 207, 221,
  225, 229
Mocha, 60, 155, 172, 173, 186,
  195, 273
Mogadishu, 110, 120, 140, 142, 169,
  170, 245, 273
Mombasa, 88, 118, 120, 131, 142, 143,
  165, 170, 171, 175
monetisation, 91, 93, 155
money, 3, 51, 55, 68, 91–93, 99, 118,
  122, 169, 195, 198, 279
  lending, 51, 91, 100, 156, 198, 221
Mongols, 105, 112, 136, 261
monsoon, 8–13, 41–43, 51–52, 60–61,
  70, 72, 91, 106–107, 118, 120,
  131, 135–137, 146, 179, *see also*
  environment, climate
Moor, 140, 265
Morea, 168
Morondava, 192
mortality, 11, 74, 78, 85, 111, 129,
  140–141, 146–151, 155–159,
  162–165, 170, 174, 185, 189, 218,
  220, 222, 227, 247–251, 261, 268,
  271, 273
mosque, 104–105, 117, 120, 131
Mozambique, 7–8, 14, 32, 40, 62–67,
  74, 81–84, 87, 115–118, 121–123,
  130–131, 141–142, 148, 163–165,
  170–173, 187, 194, 196, 231, 235,
  239, 253, 267, 269, 275, 277
  climate and environment, 14, 83, 115,
    141–142, 148, 162–163, 267
  trade, 40, 62, 64, 117–118, 121,
    130–131, 165, 196
Mrima, 132
Mubende, 121
Mughal Empire, 144, 155

Muhammad Ali (ruler of Egypt), 199,
  201–202, 218, 220, 242, 277
Muscat, 60, 141, 168, 183,
  196, 273
musk, 53, 79, 98, 109, 195
mussambazes, 170
Muteesa I (ruler of Buganda), 229
Mwanga II (ruler of Buganda), 229
Myos Hormos, 52
myrrh, 39, 57–60, 95, 97–100, 110, 141,
  186, 195

nao, 151
Napoleonic Wars, 178, 185, 194
Natal, 60, 84, 87, 141, 162–163, 238–240
Naukratis, 38
nautilus shell, 62, 88
Navarino, 204
Neolithic Revolution, 18, 22–24, 26,
  28–29, 32, 70, 256
Nepal, 146, 183
New Guinea, 13, 16, 31, 145
Nicobar Islands, 46, 94
Nile, 8, 11, 14, 22, 25–26, 34, 36–37,
  39, 50, 53, 77, 107, 138–140,
  158–159, 167, 184, 186, 209, 212,
  226, 248–249, 257
  tributaries (Blue and White Nile), 37,
    109, 112, 114, 212, 248
  Delta, 38, 47
  Valley, 14, 22, 24–26, 36, 50, 212, 262
Nishapur, 32, 33
Ntusi, 121
Nubia, 26, 37, 39, 73, 77, 108, 113, 167,
  249, 262, 265
nug, 27, 123
nutmeg, 95, 96, 97, 128, 151, 152
Nyamwezi, 189–192

oak, 43
oil, 27, 57, 130
Oman, 35, 59–60, 83, 118, 120, 171, 196,
  226, 229
Omani Sultanate, 171, 196, 229, 276
opium, 97, 98, 106, 110, 152, 156, 178, 275
Opone, 39, 47, 57
ore, 205
Oromia, 216
Oromo, 114, 138, 160, 164, 165, 216,
  217, 224, 225, 244
Ottoman Empire, 140, 167–168, 170,
  175, 212, 217, 245